The Vision of
the Prophet Isaiah

The Vision of
the Prophet Isaiah

Hope in a War-Weary World—A Commentary

A. JOSEPH EVERSON

April 20, 2019

For Art,
Joy to you!

Joe Eve

WIPF & STOCK · Eugene, Oregon

THE VISION OF THE PROPHET ISAIAH
Hope in a War-Weary World—A Commentary

Wipf & Stock
An Imprint of Wipf and Stock Publishers
199 W. 8th Ave., Suite 3
Eugene, OR 97401

www.wipfandstock.com

PAPERBACK ISBN: 978-1-5326-6748-0
HARDCOVER ISBN: 978-1-5326-6749-7
EBOOK ISBN: 978-1-5326-6750-3

Manufactured in the U.S.A.   MARCH 5, 2019

Contents

Preface

An Invitation to Walk

THE SCROLL OF ISAIAH is the first of the prophetic books. In the Christian Bible, following the lead of St. Jerome and the Latin Vulgate tradition at about 400 CE, the prophetic books were placed at the end of the Old Testament after the books of the Torah and the Writings.[1] This was done consciously to emphasize the motifs of promise and future hope in anticipation of the New Testament. But in the original Hebrew Bible, the prophetic books follow directly after the five books of the Torah (the Pentateuch). In many ways that placement helps us understand that Isaiah and the other prophetic books were primarily commentaries on the Torah and other earlier Biblical writings, offering critique and comment on how people of faith in later eras should live.

A primary thesis of this study is that we can understand the message of the Isaiah scroll in a much clearer way when we view it from the post-exilic era when it was edited and shaped as a unified collection of poetry. In that era, those who edited the scroll were clearly aware of three momentous past events: 1) the destruction of Jerusalem in 587 BCE and the subsequent era of exile and Babylonian captivity; 2) the death of Nebuchadnezzar and the fall of the Babylonian empire and 3) the rise of Cyrus and the empire of Persia that made possible the return of exiles to Jerusalem and Judah. (See the discussion in section F. "The Post-Exilic Setting"). Those events helped to give shape to the Isaiah scroll.

It was during the post-exilic era that the Isaiah scroll was set apart as canonical or sacred writing. From that era, the prophetic message comes into focus as a theological commentary on past history, and in particular,

---

1. The abbreviation CE stands for "common era;" the abbreviation BCE stands for "before the common era."

on the three-hundred-year period from the era of the prophet Isaiah in the eighth century BCE (750 to 690 BCE) to the era of the post-exilic community (539 to 400 BCE). The view in this study is in retrospect, looking back from the post-exilic era and recalling both the prophetic warnings and the words of hope first proclaimed by the prophet. The scroll honors the memory of the vision first set forth by Isaiah ben Amoz. In the latter chapters of Isaiah, the audience is addressed as "servants of the Lord." They were ordinary people who were called to live with righteousness and justice, showing particular concern for the poor, the needy, and the oppressed. Later generations of people who hear the words of this scroll are also summoned to the same tasks, and to live with courage, compassion, and hope.

Acknowledgements

THIS WORK IS DEDICATED to the Minnesota Isaiah Group, ninety congregations acting together to achieve social, economic, and racial justice, and to other similar social action groups throughout the world, who see their task as living out the vision of the prophet Isaiah.

During the summer of 1976, I had the privilege of directing the summer graduate program in Israel for St. John's University, Collegeville, Minnesota. We were a group that included fourteen Catholic sisters, four priests, my wife Susan, and our three children, Paul, Phil and Sarah. We lived together at a monastery at Ein Kerem, just outside of Jerusalem, and for six weeks we studied the scroll of Isaiah. A highlight of that summer seminar was a trip to Mt. Sinai where we stayed overnight at the historic monastery, St. Katerinia. We were up at dawn to climb the mountain and return before the afternoon heat. The journey through the Sinai wilderness was also memorable. I have been very thankful for the trust that St. John's placed in me that summer.

Now, more than forty years later, I look back on courses on Isaiah with students at Luther College in Decorah, Iowa, at United Seminary in New Brighton, Minnesota, at the St. Paul Seminary of St. Thomas University in St. Paul, and at California Lutheran University in Thousand Oaks, California, where I served on the religion department faculty for twenty-two years.

In California, I want to thank CLU President Chris Kimball, Provost Leanne Neilson, Rabbi Belle Michael, Bishops Guy Erwin and Howie Wennes, and Pastors Jeremy Kays, Steve Herder and Ken Caudill. In Minnesota, I express special thanks to Hal Dragseth, Lee Snook, Calvin Roetzel, James Limburg, Phil Eaves and Scott Tunseth. For discussions over the years with members of the Formation of Isaiah Group of the Society of Biblical Literature, I express thanks to Hyun Chul Paul Kim, Gary Stansell, Chris Franke, Marv Sweeney, Roy Melugin and Rolf Rendtorff.

As I reflect on this writing project, I am aware of how deeply indebted I am to a number of excellent teachers that I have had over the years: John Victor Halvorson at Luther Seminary, St. Paul, Minnesota; Gerhard von Rad and Claus Westerman at the University in Heidelberg, West Germany; and John Bright, James Mays and Patrick D. Miller at Union Seminary in Richmond, Virginia.

I also say a very special word of thanks to my wife, Susan Corey, for her help with this project.

A. JOSEPH EVERSON
California Lutheran University
Thousand Oaks, California
everson@callutheran.edu

Introductory Essays

ACADEMIC STUDY OF THE ISAIAH SCROLL

THROUGHOUT MOST OF THE past century, study of the book of Isaiah has been deeply influenced by the work of Theodore H. Robinson. In 1927, he described the development of prophetic literature in terms of three stages. First, there were small independent oracles collected and preserved by disciples of a prophet. Later, disciples gathered the individual oracles into collections, adding new material and arranging them into new thematic patterns. Still later these collections were reorganized and expanded into what today is commonly called the final form of the text. Much of twentieth-century research focused on Robinson's first stage, attempting to discover the words of the original prophet. Especially in chapters 1–39, scholars have attempted in various ways to discern the authentic words of the prophet. But with this approach, critical judgments must be made about what can be deemed to be authentic and what is judged to be later redactional or added material. Far too often the later redactional material comes to be understood as being of secondary importance. The principal quest has been to discover what might have been the actual message of Isaiah ben Amoz.

This approach has been very influential throughout much of the past century. The Isaiah scroll has come to be understood in terms of three distinct parts: Proto or First Isaiah, Deutero or Second Isaiah and Trito or Third Isaiah. Already in 1892, Bernhard Duhm proposed that the Isaiah scroll contained the work of writers in three distinct eras of history: First Isaiah (chapters 1–39), to be interpreted in the pre-exilic eighth-century BCE setting when the prophet Isaiah ben Amoz lived; Second Isaiah (chapters 40–55), to be interpreted against the background of the exilic era (587–539 BCE); and Third Isaiah (chapters 56–66), to be interpreted from the post-exilic era. Generations of pastors, priests, and even a number of rabbis have studied and learned to understand Isaiah in this way. This understanding remains so widespread today that new separate volumes continue to be published on each section of the scroll and seminary catalogs continue to list separate courses on First, Second, and Third Isaiah.[1]

Over the past several decades, however, a number of scholars have focused on the question of the unity of the Isaiah scroll. They have recognized that the task of discerning stages and separate authors is a highly subjective enterprise. In 1979, Brevard Childs suggested a new direction for study, contending that the Isaiah scroll should be understood as a unified canonical writing, organized as a deliberate literary and theological work. This approach has at times been referred to as "synchronic" or "canonical study."[2] The approach attempts to understand the literary structure and theological meaning of the scroll as it has been preserved. Rather than searching for the words of the original author or attempting to discern later redactions of the text, canonical study has focused on understanding the message of the overall portrait preserved in the scroll.

Historical (or "diachronic") dimensions are still very important. In this study, the diachronic dimensions of various texts are affirmed as memories. Some very specific memories are preserved in the Isaiah scroll. But they have all been preserved from the post-exilic era by a later editor and at times seem to be shaped to address people in that later time. Some of the memories are very sad, even frightening. I call them "bitter memories." But when read in context, even the memories of war are frequently framed by words of hope and encouragement. We cannot know for certain the shape of early editions of the Isaiah scroll. But we can gain a sense of how those tragic memories were remembered by later generations.[3] Hope and confidence in the promises of a gracious God undergird the entire Isaiah scroll.

---

1. See Martin Sweeney's "On the Road to Duhm" in McGinnis and Tull, *As Those Who are Taught,* 243–61. Bernhard Duhm was the first to identify and isolate four so-called servant songs in Isa 42:1–4, 49:1–7, 50:4–11 and 52:13—53:12.

2. See Childs, *Introduction to the Old Testament.* Philadelphia: Fortress, 1979.

3. See "The Book of Isaiah: A Complex Unity. Synchronic and Diachronic Reading" in Melugin and Sweeney, *New Visions of Isaiah,* 40–41. On the contrast between "sweet" and "bitter," see also Ruth 1:20–21: "Call me no longer Naomi ["pleasant or sweet"] call me Mara ["bitter"]."

Rolf Rendtorff has made the case that the present shape of the Isaiah scroll is "not the result of more or less accidental or arbitrary developments but rather that of deliberate and intentional literary and theological work."[4] This study takes that assumption with great seriousness. The Isaiah scroll is constructed and edited as a deliberate and intentional literary and theological work.

THE ISAIAH SCROLL: A TAPESTRY OF LYRIC POETRY

The Isaiah scroll presents us with a richly woven fabric of poetry. There are themes, images, and motifs that appear and then reappear in later texts. Among them are the contrasting images of deafness and hearing, blindness and sight, hardness of heart (insensitivity) and compassion, which are used to describe human people. The words may seem particularly puzzling, especially when themes of blindness and deafness are used to condemn Judah and Jerusalem. How can God condemn and judge the very people who are called into covenantal relationship?

Judah was a very small country in the ancient Near East dominated throughout most of its history by foreign empires Assyria, Babylon, and Persia. The prophet was not at all hesitant to speak words of judgment both to foreign empires and to his own people. He understood himself to be called as a herald or spokesperson for YHWH or Yahweh, the sovereign God of Israel and the creator of the world. The God of Israel is proclaimed as the sovereign ruler of all nations, large and small, whether they know it or not. The prophet announces words of judgment for rulers of great empires and for rulers of small nations, including Judah. He indicts them for acts of ruthlessness and violence or for simple lack of wisdom. At the same time, Isaiah speaks words of hope and encouragement, repeatedly encouraging people to change and to live with integrity, humility, and compassion for those in need. The poetry in Isaiah addresses both the arrogance of power and the tragic realities of those who suffer. The horrors and aftermath of war, the loss of life, and the poverty that follows from war are all themes that loom large in the background

---

4. Rendtorff, "The Book of Isaiah", in Melugin and Sweeney, 46. Rendtorff suggests a helpful way to understand the terms "synchronic" and "diachronic": He writes: "The main difference between these two approaches might be expressed by the following two questions: 1) (Synchronic) What does the text (in all its complexity) mean in its given final shape? 2) (Diachronic) In what stages did the text reach its final form?"

of Isaiah's prophetic words. Nevertheless, in the midst of those painful realities, this scroll is still very much about human hope.

In the original Hebrew scrolls, it is often very difficult to distinguish between prose and poetic writing. In some places such as Isaiah 36–39, the prose character is quite obvious. But in other passages, it is very difficult to discern. In this study, the poetry of Isaiah is centered to call particular attention to "parallelism." Parallelism may be the most striking characteristic of the Hebrew poetry. In one sense, it is very simple. Ideas are repeated or set in tandem for emphasis, to extend a thought, or to set forth a contrast. So, for example, two ideas are set forth as the poetic author of Isaiah 40:4 declares: *"Every valley shall be lifted up, and every mountain and hill be brought low!"*[5] The author of Isaiah 55:12 can link two wonderful but parallel words of hope by declaring: *"the mountains and the hills before you shall burst into song"* and *"all the trees of the field shall clap their hands."* Or to express contrast, the author of Isaiah 61:8 can set two words of the Lord in contrast: *"For I the Lord love justice, I hate robbery and wrong doing."* That is what parallelism in Hebrew poetry is all about.

MEMORIES OF THE PROPHET ISAIAH BEN AMOZ (742–687 BCE)

The Isaiah scroll is not a biography of the prophet. Instead the scroll focuses on Isaiah's vision, kept alive and expanded by successive generations of people. The opening superscription clearly states: *"The vision of Isaiah son of Amoz, which he saw concerning Judah and Jerusalem in the days of Uzziah, Jotham, Ahaz and Hezekiah, king of Judah."* Four specific times from the life of Isaiah ben Amoz receive particular attention:

The first is the era around 742 BCE when Isaiah received his call to be a prophet. Isaiah 6 is prefaced with the words *"In the year that King Uzziah died"* (742 BCE). The setting was Jerusalem where Isaiah appears to have spent his entire life. Jerusalem was the capitol of the small southern kingdom of Judah, which separated from northern Israel (sometimes called Ephraim or Samaria) at about 922 BCE, after the reign of Solomon. Isaiah's calling as a prophet is remembered by later generations in a very painful way: he was called to speak words of warning and judgment to a community that chose not to listen to his words. Later generations

---

5. Unless noted, all Biblical quotes are from the NRSV.

preserved his words of lament: *"Keep listening but do not comprehend, keep looking, but do not understand. Make the mind of this people dull, and stop their ears; and shut their eyes so they may not look with their eyes, and listen with their ears, and comprehend with their minds, and turn and be healed!"* And when the prophet asked: *"How long?"* he was told: *"Until the Lord sends everyone far away, and vast is the emptiness in the midst of the land"* (Isa 6:10–11). Like other prophets before him—Elijah, Elisha, Nathan, Amos, and Hosea—Isaiah understood his calling to be a herald or spokesman for Yahweh. As the result of crimes and greed among those around him, especially from judges, from the wealthy, and from those in positions of leadership, he saw only catastrophe coming for Judah (Isa 3:16—4:1; 5:11–13). We hear his sad words of judgment on the community of Judah expressed in the parable of the vineyard in Isaiah 5. The Lord intended that the vineyard should bear good fruit but it produces only bitter fruit. What is a vinekeeper to do with a vineyard that produces only bitter fruit?

A second cluster of memories seems to be preserved from the era about six years later. In 735–734 BCE, another era of political turmoil is recalled. It was a time when the northern kingdom of Israel joined with Syria to plot revolt against the empire Assyria (735–734 BCE). Leaders of those two countries wanted King Ahaz of Judah to join them in revolt, something Ahaz was hesitant to do. In Isaiah 7, Isaiah, joined by his son Shear-jashub (meaning "Only a remnant shall return"), goes to confront King Ahaz, pleading with him not to escalate the threat by calling on the Assyrian emperor for help. That concern is not clearly stated in Isaiah but it is quite clear in 2 Kings 16. Isaiah did not want Judah to become an occupied country. The reaction of Ahaz is seen as evidence that he is not a man of faith. He is not willing to hear or trust the word of the prophet. In Isaiah 8:3 we hear mention of Isaiah's second son whose name also conveys a word of warning: Maher-shalal-hash-baz (meaning "The spoil speeds, the prey hastens!). And in this chapter, we also hear mention of Isaiah's wife, referred to as the prophetess.

It is also from this era in history that we have the moving poetry from Isaiah concerning his hopes for an ideal "son of David." In chapters 7, 9, and 11, poetry that expresses frustrations with King Ahaz, we hear Isaiah's understanding of what God expects from one who is set apart or anointed to be a king (a "messiah"), one who will *"establish and uphold the kingdom of David with justice and righteousness . . .* (Isa 9:7).

A third cluster of memories appears to recall the era of 715–711 BCE. Hezekiah is the new king in Judah. He has been tempted by Egyptian forces to rebel against Assyria. Isaiah is remembered as strongly opposing such plans for revolt, and he walked naked as a public act of protest condemning the plan to join in revolt against Assyria (Isa 20:1–6). In chapter 28, Isaiah expresses a strong word of criticism against drunkards. Then in that word of judgment, he offers the profound word of counsel: *"This is rest; give rest to the weary!"* (Isa 28:12). Sadly, drunkards did not understand.

The fourth cluster of memories comes from the era of 701–690 BCE, also during the reign of King Hezekiah. Again, this was a time of attempted revolt against Assyria, with encouragement from Egypt. According to 2 Samuel 18:14–16, Jerusalem was surrounded in 701 BCE and Hezekiah was forced to pay a huge tribute to avoid having the city invaded and destroyed. That account seems to be supported by the Annals of Sennacherib.[6] But in Isaiah, there is a different story. In what seems to be a parallel account in Isaiah 36–39, Jerusalem experiences a miraculous deliverance. Hezekiah is remembered as a man of faith who turned to Isaiah for counsel. Most striking in the Isaiah account is that the prophet urged the king to stand firm against the Assyrians.

Scholars have offered a number of suggestions to explain the differences between the 2 Samuel account and the Isaiah memory. One explanation is that the Assyrians may have attacked Jerusalem at two different times. The Isaiah account preserves only the memory of a dramatic rescue! The Assyrian army made a sudden departure and withdrawal from Judah. The report in Isaiah 37:36–38 declares:

> Then the angel of the Lord set out and struck down one hundred
> eighty-five thousand in the camp of the Assyrians; when morning
> dawned, they were all dead bodies.

At some point in his life, Isaiah told his disciples to *"bind up the testimony"* (8:16) and to *"inscribe his words in a book"* (30:8), keeping them for a future time as a testimony. This seems to have begun the tradition of disciples seeking to address the implications of Isaiah's vision for later eras of history. We do not know their names. We sense that those disciples wanted credit to be given not to themselves but to the legacy of Isaiah ben Amoz, whose vision had inspired them. Just as the Torah was attributed to Moses, the Psalms to David, and the wisdom literature to

---

6. See the Annals of Sennacherib in Pritchard, *Ancient Near Eastern Texts*, 287–88.

Solomon, so also those disciples wanted the vision to be preserved as the legacy of Isaiah.

Isaiah's vision repeatedly involves matters of war. The horrors and consequences of war are in the background of every era during which the scroll developed. And yet, the war memories are often prefaced by the dream of peace, as in the poem in Isaiah 2:2–5. The prophet envisions that one day people might *"beat their swords into plowshares and their spears into pruning hooks"* so that nations might not learn war anymore. Isaiah's anti-war sentiment is heard clearly as he declares that *"In returning and rest, you shall be saved; in quietness and in trust shall be your strength. But you refused and said, "No, we will flee upon horses."* (Isa 30:15).

One rather shocking aspect of Isaiah's vision is that he was not a champion of national independence. Rather he was pragmatic. Above all else he was community-minded. He believed that the wisest foreign policy for Judah was to be realistic about the overwhelming power of empires. As a resident of a small country, he urged leaders to make the best possible choices in life based above all on the welfare of common people.

Isaiah contended that all energy comes from God. Whether they knew it or not, even emperors and empires were instruments of God for good or for ill. Emperors could wage war or they could make peace. In a number of places, we hear powerful words condemning "arrogance of power," especially relating to the activities of the empires of Assyria (Isa 10:5–19; 14:24–29), Babylon (Isa 13:1–22; 14:3–11; 14:22–23; 21:1–10; 47:1–15), and Egypt (Isa 19:1–15; 31:1–3). For their arrogance, nations large or small would eventually be brought low in events of judgment. In contrast a later disciple could declare that when Cyrus of Persia initiated policies to promote the wellbeing of people, that activity could be understood as evidence of God's redemptive presence at work in the world.

By the time in the post-exilic era when the Isaiah scroll was approaching its 66-chapter shape and was being set apart as sacred writing within the faith community, there was no question about Isaiah's status as a "true" prophet. In retrospect, his words of warning and his announcement of impending destruction or judgment had come to pass.[7] Those words of warning were remembered in direct connection with the destruction that came in 587 BCE. The announcement of a "day of Yahweh" for Judah had clearly come to pass. But Isaiah also spoke words

7. See Deuteronomy 8:15–22 regarding how people can discern a true or false prophet. The awesome test was to wait and see whether the prophet's words would come to pass.

of promise. And those words of promise became the foundation for the majestic poetry of hope in Isaiah 40–55 and the summons to obedient life in Isaiah 56–66. Good life, in Isaiah's vision, is evident when people live with humility and a commitment to righteousness and justice. These are human beings who can see, hear, and feel the pains and sorrows of the world.

We live in a world far different from ancient Judah. But as we read, we are challenged to ponder the implications of Isaiah's vision for our lives, for our communities, and for our world in our own time.

SEVEN THEOLOGICAL TRADITIONS IN ISAIAH

The prophet Isaiah stood in a long line of prophetic figures in ancient Israel. What is striking about prophets in ancient Israel is that they felt compelled to speak out, often at great cost, about matters of social justice. Nathan addressed King David concerning his adultery with Bathsheba and the murder of her husband, Uriah (2 Sam 11–12). Elijah confronted King Ahab and his wife Jezebel concerning their illegal theft of Naboth's vineyard (1 Kings 21). And both Amos and Hosea spoke boldly against the corruption in northern Israel in the era just before Isaiah (see especially Hos 5–6 and Amos 3–6). What all of the prophets have in common is that they draw from the rich ethical perspectives of the Torah. In Genesis, Cain is judged for killing his brother Abel; Jacob must flee from his home for deceiving his brother Esau; the brothers of Joseph must live with the knowledge that they have brought false witness and have deceived their father Jacob after selling Joseph into slavery in Egypt.

In many ways it is Moses more than anyone else who is the model for later prophets. The Ten Commandments that Moses delivered are remembered as the ethical standard for community and individual life. Moses spoke with courage to Pharaoh and addressed the injustice of the Egyptian system of slavery for the Hebrew people. Later, at about the same time when monarchy was established with Saul, David, and Solomon, prophets acquired prominence as defenders of integrity and justice. The prophets were defenders of the less privileged even as political and economic powers were being consolidated in the hands of a few.

From the vantage point of the post-exilic era, the Isaiah scroll recalls the trials of the pre-exilic era, the horrors of the exile in Babylon, the challenges of the new era that came with the rise of Cyrus of Persia, and the return of exiles to Jerusalem. Those eras provided the framework for reflecting on the presence of the Lord God among people on earth. Seven traditions seem to have influenced the vision in Isaiah in particular ways:

1. The Throne and Kingship of the Lord God

First is the undergirding conviction about the kingship of Yahweh as the creator of heaven and earth, the sovereign Lord of Israel. In the poetry of Isaiah's call vision in chapter 6, the prophet recalls being summoned to stand in the presence of God. The imagery suggests the feelings that an ordinary person might have at being summoned to stand before the throne of a great king. We hear about cherubim, seraphim, and the house being filled with smoke. Beyond this, however, there is no direct attempt to describe God. Rather we sense only feelings of holiness—majesty, awe and wonder in the presence of God.[8] Throughout the Isaiah scroll, references are made to stories of the Lord God who is the creator of all who dwell on earth, whether they acknowledge that reality or not. At the same time, the election of Israel is clearly remembered: the traditions concerning Abraham, Isaac, and Jacob and particularly, Moses and the Sinai covenant. The people are called to be servant people, living with responsibility and compassion in the world.[9]

Worldviews change and will continue to change. We have the challenging task of asking how we will speak of the Lord God in our time and place in history. But when we study Isaiah, we need to recognize that in that era, monarchy was the widely established understanding of government throughout the known world. In Israel, the king, as the Lord's representative, was to promote mercy and justice, giving particular attention to the situations of the poor, the needy, and the oppressed in the world. This understanding of divine governance and the view of God's sovereignty is set forth in a very clear way in the report of Hezekiah's prayer:

> O Lord of hosts, God of Israel,
> who are enthroned above the cherubim,
> you are God, you alone,

8. See references to "kisse" (throne) in Isaiah 6:1; 9:7; 9:7; 14:9; 14:13; 16:5; 22;23; 47:1 and 66:1.

9. See references to the throne of God in the Psalms. In Psalms 89:14, the four foundations of the throne of God are cited: righteousness and justice, steadfast love and faithfulness. See also references in Psalms 47, 93, 97, and 103.

of all the kingdoms of the earth;
You have made heaven and the earth.
(Isa 37:16)

2. The Election of Israel and the Davidic King

In keeping with the memories of Moses, Isaiah stands in full agreement
with the prophet Amos before him that Israel's calling is not to privilege
but rather to servant responsibility. Election in the Biblical context is not
preferential treatment. Rather, it involves a special sense of responsibility for just and humane life. And with Amos, that calling is defined by
righteousness (uprightness or integrity) and by commitments to social
justice (Amos 3:1-2; 9:7-10). In Isaiah, as in Amos, Hosea, Jeremiah, and
other prophetic writers, justice (*mishpat*) is defined specifically in terms
of caring for the less fortunate in society: widows, orphans, sojourners
(undocumented aliens!), the poor, the needy, and the oppressed.

In Isaiah, there is a very special focus on Jerusalem and Judah, so
much so that many will speak of "Jerusalem theology." Isaiah ben Amoz
appears to have lived most of his life within the city. Jerusalem is thus
held up as Zion, the "city of God," the model of how all communities on
earth should be.

In southern Judah, tradition held that the throne of David would
pass from father to son. The Deuteronomic historian and others, such as
the authors of the royal psalms (especially Pss 2, 72, 89, 110), declare that
divine protection would come for the king if he provided the model for
righteousness and justice among his people. But such promises were not
absolute. Already in the David and Bathsheba saga and in the accounts
of Solomon and his family, we hear that the king would not be protected
from punishment where arrogance or misconduct was present. And yet
David is remembered by later generations as a model king, not because
of his moral perfection but because, in the midst of troubles, he turned
to the Lord God with prayer, confession, and contrition (see especially Ps
51).[10] In the Isaiah scroll special mention is made of two kings in Judah.
The first was Ahaz (735-715 BCE), who is remembered as a poor king.
He seems to have been deeply involved with Canaanite religious customs,
including child sacrifice (see 2 Kgs 16). In contrast, his son Hezekiah

10. See references to David in the Isaiah scroll in 7:2; 7:13; 9:7; 16:5; 22:9; 22:22;
29:1; 37:25; 38:5, and 55:3.

(715–689 BCE) is remembered as a good king and therefore, a worthy "son of David."

Monarchy was a form of government that could provide stability and blessing for people in the ancient world. Isaiah does not question the institution of monarchy. But he understood very well the consequences that followed when kings did not practice wisdom and compassion for their people.

3. Traditions of Zion, Jerusalem, and the Jerusalem Temple

Some commentators have suggested that the Zion tradition may be the unifying theological tradition within the Isaiah scroll. The term "Zion" can refer to Jerusalem or more specifically to the temple built by Solomon at the center of the city of Jerusalem.[11] In the innermost court of the temple, a place had been made for the ark of the covenant containing the tablets of the Ten Commandments and other sacred objects. For years the ark dwelt only in a tent. But according to 1 Kings 6, Solomon was designated to build the temple as a resting place for the ark of the covenant.

In the Isaiah scroll, we hear reports of mourning and lament over the destruction of the temple and the loss of the ark. Zion, the city of David, and the temple were destroyed by the Babylonians. But in Isaiah there is also hope for the restoration of Zion. In the latter chapters of the book, the return to Zion and the rebuilding of the temple are central themes. The poetry is quite vivid: Zion is portrayed as a wife whose husband Yahweh seems to have abandoned her (Isa 49:14–18). At other times, she is described as an abandoned mother whose children are about to return home (see Isa 49:22–23). And in a most striking account, Zion is described in the midst of giving birth to a child. (Isa 65:7–11). With the return to Jerusalem and the rebuilding of the temple, a new generation of people claimed the promise that Yahweh had not left them. The poetry in Isaiah 35:10 captures the dominant theme of the Zion tradition in Isaiah:

> *And the ransomed of the Lord shall return,*
> *and come to Zion with singing;*

11. See references to Zion in the Isaiah scroll in 1:8; 1:27; 2:3; 3:16; 3:17; 4:3; 4:4; 4:5; 8:18; 10:12; 10:24; 10:32; 12:6; 14:32; 16:1; 18:7; 24:23; 28:16; 29:8; 30:19; 31:4; 31:9; 33:5; 33:14; 33:20; 34:8; 35:10; 37:22; 37:22; 37:32; 40:9; 41:27; 46:13; 49:14; 51:3; 51:11; 51:16; 52:1; 52:7; 52:8; 59.20; 60:14; 61:3; 62:1; 62:11; 64:10 and 66:8. See also, Ps 132, which declares Zion as the eternal dwelling place of God.

Everlasting joy shall be upon their heads;
they shall obtain joy and gladness
and sorrow and sighing shall flee away.

4. Creation Traditions

One of the most striking passages in Isaiah is the declaration of Yahweh found in Isaiah 55:18–19. God is the author of order in the world, not chaos:

For thus says the Lord,
who created the heavens (he is God!),
who formed the earth and made it
(he established it;
He did not create it a chaos,
he formed it to be inhabited!);
I am the Lord,
and there is no other.
I did not speak in secret,
in a land of darkness;
I did not say to the offspring of Jacob,
"Seek me in chaos";
I the Lord speak the truth,
I declare what is right.

With Jerusalem in ruins and the Davidic dynasty of kingship ended, the authors of Isaiah 40–66 turn to the memories of creation as evidence of the continuing presence of God in their lives and in the life of their community.[12] The Lord God, who created the heavens and the earth, is understood to have the power to create a new community from people who have been held captive in Babylon. Human people are not created to be slaves or indentured servants; they are created to reflect the glory of God with adequate food and shelter for living and with joy and gladness in life.

---

12. See references to God's creative activity as evidence of his ongoing care for the world in Isa 40:26; 41:20; 42:5; 43:1; 43:7; 45:7; 45:8; 45:12; 45:18; 54:16; 65:17; and 65:18.

5. Redemption Traditions

The theme of a new exodus is prominent in the Isaiah scroll and is closely connected with creation traditions. From beginning to end, the authors are convinced that if people will repent and turn from arrogant and selfish ways, God is ready to forgive and redeem them as a people.[13] That is the underlying conviction of the invitation in Isaiah 2:5: *"Come, let us walk in the way of the Lord!"* It is the hope expressed by Isaiah in chapters 7, 9, 11, and 32 when the prophet dreams of a future king who will be a model of faith and trust for all people. Most of all, it is the undergirding conviction of the author of chapters 40–55, who is convinced that a new era has appeared in a most unusual way. The Lord God redeems his people through the actions of a foreign monarch, Cyrus from Persia. This can happen even when he does not even know or acknowledge the Lord God of Israel. The Lord God, who brought people out of bondage in Egypt, is able to bring about a new exodus event in history. God does not intend that people should live in captivity.

6. Traditions about the Servant and Servants of the Lord

The servant tradition in the book of Isaiah has raised a host of questions for generations of scholars. Were the authors of the scroll thinking of a particular individual or were they speaking collectively of the remnant community that had survived the destruction of Jerusalem? And if they were speaking of an individual, was that person a royal figure such as a king, or was the servant a prophet? Kings were at times called servants in ancient Israel. Some scholars have proposed various possibilities such as David, Hezekiah, Josiah, or even the young king Jehoiachin who was exiled to Babylon in 598. On the other hand, other scholars have suggested that the authors may have been thinking of a prophetic figure such as Amos, Hosea, Isaiah ben Amoz himself, Jeremiah, or an unknown prophetic figure who lived among the exiles in Babylon. Gerhard von Rad suggested that the imagery of the servant was shaped by memories

---

13. See references to "redemption" (translated from *ga-al*) in the Isaiah scroll in 1:27; 35:9; 43:1; 44:22; 44:23; 48:20; 52:3; 59:9; 62:12; 63:4; and 63:9; see also 29:22 and 51:11 which translate *padah* also as "redemption." For a detailed study of this theme, see Everson, "Redemption and the 'New Exodus' in Isaiah." *Word and World 33* (2013) 147-56.

of Moses, who was the leader of people in exile and the leader of the first exodus, the journey out of Egypt.[14]

In a text such as Isaiah 42:1–4 it is easy to understand why many have thought that the author of this text was thinking of a particular individual:

> *Here is my servant, whom I uphold,*
> *My chosen, in whom my soul delights;*
> *I have put my spirit upon him;*
> *He will bring forth justice to the nations.*
> *He will not cry out or lift up his voice*
> *Or make it heard in the street;*
> *A bruised reed he will not break,*
> *And a dimly burning wick he will not quench;*
> *He will faithfully bring forth justice.*
> *He will not grow faint or be crushed*
> *Until he has established justice in the earth;*
> *And the coastlands wait for his teaching.*
> *(Isa 42:1–4)*

The case for interpreting the servant tradition as a particular individual grows even stronger for some in light of the passages in Isaiah 49:1–7; 50:4–11 and in particular, in light of the poetry in 52:13–53:12, where the author speaks of the servant who suffers vicariously on behalf of other people.

But at the same time, a strong case can also be made that the references to a servant really describe the community collectively as a "servant people." In fact, that view is the focus of Isaiah 41:8–10:

> *But you, Israel, my servant,*
> *Jacob, whom I have chosen,*
> *The offspring of Abraham, my friend;*
> *You whom I took from the ends of the earth,*
> *and called from its farthest corners,*

---

14. See von Rad, *Old Testament Theology, Vol II.*, 250–62. Von Rad writes: "There is, however, one strand of tradition which we must recognise as particularly important for the origin of these (servant) songs; this is that of Moses, especially as he is represented in Deuteronomy. Moses is there designated the Servant of God . . . he acts as mediator between Jahweh and Israel, he suffers, and raises his voice in complaint to Jahweh, and at last dies vicariously for the sins of his people."

saying to you,

'You are my servant,

I have chosen you and not cast you off;

Do not fear, for I am with you,

Do not be afraid for I am your God;

I will strengthen you,

I will help you,

I will uphold you with my victorious right hand.'

(Isa 41:8–10)

In the Isaiah scroll it is interesting to note the shift that happens after 54:17 when we hear not about a "servant," but rather about "servants" of the Lord.[15] It is thus possible that an author was thinking both about individuals who were servants and about the community. What seems clear is that those of us who hear or read these texts are being addressed in the same way that those in the post-exilic community were first addressed by the scroll. The author declares:

This is the heritage of the servants of the Lord,

and their vindication from me, says the Lord.

(Isa 54:17)

7. Triumph over Death

One other tradition within the Isaiah scroll deserves particular mention. This is the theme of the triumph of the forces of life over the forces of death in the world. This theological tradition was prominent in the mythology of Canaan and in other cultures that surrounded Judah and northern Israel in the ancient world.[16] Prominent in Ugaritic culture were

15. See references to servanthood in Isaiah in 14:2; 20:3 (of the prophet Isaiah); 22:20 (of Eliakim); 24:2; 36:9; 36:11; 37:5 (of the aides to King Hezekiah); 37:24; 37:35 (of the memory of King David); 41:8 (of Israel); 41:9; 42:1; 42:19; 43:10; 44:1 (of Jacob my servant); 44:2 (of Jacob); 42:19; 43:10; 44:1 (of Jacob my servant); 44:2 (of Jacob my servant); 44:21; 44:26; 45:4; 48:20; 49:3 (Israel my servant); 49:5; 49:6; 49:7; 50:10; 52:13; 53:11; 54:17. See references to servants (plural) in 54:17; 56:6; 63:17; 65:8; 65:9; 65:13; 65:14; 65:15 and 66:14.

16. The creation and redemption traditions in Isaiah were intended to counter the prevailing mythological patterns of the ancient world prevalent in ancient Canaan and in Babylon. In Isa 51:9–11, it is interesting to note the description of the work of the Lord God as creator of heaven and earth and as redeemer of Israel. It is Yahweh who

the mythic stories that attempted to explain drought, famine, and plagues as the activity of Mot, the god of death. Mot is in repeated struggles with Ba'l, the god of fertility and life, and with his sister Anat, who has power to restore life for people. In the Ugaritic mythology, Mot was understood as the cause of drought, famine, or other horrible ailments in life. Mot could swallow up life and cause death to be spread like a shroud over the earth. When a famine finally ended and fertility returned to the earth, that was the sign that the god Ba'l, the goddess Anat, or some other divine force had triumphed over Mot. In a number of places in Isaiah, it seems that an author is responding to people who held such understandings of life from their popular culture. The prophetic writer declares in the most forceful way possible that redemption and restoration of life was not the activity of Canaanite gods. Rather, redemption was the activity of Yahweh as the sovereign Lord and Creator of the world. A most powerful instance of this is heard in the text of Isaiah 25:7–8:

> And he will destroy on this mountain
> the shroud that is cast over all peoples,
> the sheet that is spread over all nations;
> he will swallow up death forever.
> Then the Lord God will wipe away the tears from all faces,
> and the disgrace of his people he will take away from all the earth,
> for the Lord has spoken.
> (Isa 25:7–8)

THE MARGINAL PERSPECTIVE IN HEBREW PROPHETIC LITERATURE

Perspective is important. In this study I suggest that it is helpful to view the Isaiah scroll from the post-exilic era when it was edited and moving toward its 66-chapter form.

It is equally important to recognize that the Isaiah scroll comes from a very small country in the ancient Near East. People who lived in ancient Judah during the three-hundred-year span from 750 BCE to 450 BCE

"cut Rahab in pieces, and who pierced the dragon" and who "dried up the sea, the waters of the great deep, who made the depths of the sea a way for the redeemed to cross over . . . "

during which the Isaiah scroll was developed and expanded knew very well what it meant to feel marginal. Empires dominated their world.

The former Catholic bishop of Recife and Olinda in Brazil, Dom Helder Camara, has described the "marginal perspective" as the feeling one has when standing on the margin of a highway, attempting to find a ride to somewhere. One may stand there alone, wishing desperately to get somewhere while cars and trucks pass by. Despite all efforts, the world simply passes by without notice. Bishop Camara reminds us that large populations of our world live with this "marginal perspective" as part of their reality of daily life.[17]

I experienced the marginal perspective myself some years ago when I was teaching in Nassau, in the Bahamas. Two incidents happened just a week apart in January 1973.

The first incident occurred during a class with a group of Benedictine sisters in a convent in Nassau. We were looking at a biblical map showing the geography of the kingdoms of northern Israel and southern Judah. We were discussing the situation of Judah after the fall of the northern kingdom and Samaria to Assyria in 722 BCE. I remember a particular moment with great clarity. An older sister, one who had been quietly studying her map, suddenly looked up with a sense of surprise and exclaimed: "Why, Judah twarn't much bigger than Nassau!" That was a revelation for her.

Nassau is a small city located on a long narrow strip of land known as New Providence Island. Along the north shore, there are broad and beautiful sand beaches; the heart of the old town stretches along a scenic old boulevard where tourists come ashore from cruise ships. To the east are the fishing district and the high bridge connecting the main island with the luxury hotels and the casino on Paradise Island. Not far away, the south shore extends for about twenty to thirty miles. In 1973, the island was still sparsely inhabited.

Nassau and New Providence Island are about the same size as ancient Judah, each with about 40 by 60 miles of inhabitable land. Yet despite its small size, ancient Judah and its capital city, Jerusalem, became the geographical center from which the Hebrew Bible and the New Testament accounts have emerged. People in ancient Judah knew that they were not the center of the world. Residents of the Bahamas also know

17. Camara, *Desert is Fertile*, 36–37,

this reality today, leading some to say that they are "the third world of the third world!" To feel that way is to understand the marginal perspective.

The second incident came a week later. I had traveled to Freeport, on Grand Bahama Island, so named because it was founded as the home of a major cement factory constructed by the U.S. Steel Corporation. That factory produced much of the concrete needed for the construction of the Kennedy Space Center and for numerous highways that dominate the east coast of the United States. In return for access to the limestone resources on the island, the U.S. Steel Corporation offered jobs and constructed modest homes for workers in the new city of Freeport. By 1973, however, the factory had grown old and there was talk of abandoning the site and relocating to another island where a new state of the art plant could be built at minimal cost. Under such conditions, labor negotiations were almost impossible for the workers at the Freeport plant.

I had come to Freeport to observe students from Luther College who were spending their January interim semester working as teaching assistants in Roman Catholic elementary schools. On a Sunday afternoon, I was invited to a host home, and I found myself with a group of men who had gathered to watch the 1973 Super Bowl. As the Miami Dolphins built up a huge lead over the Minnesota Vikings, those who had gathered seemed to lose interest in the game and the conversation turned to politics, fueled by an abundance of strong drink. One of the men grew extremely agitated as he reflected on a recent labor dispute at the cement plant. After pouring himself yet another drink, he came over to where I was sitting, pointed a threatening finger at me and said in a very intimidating voice: "You need to know that we've got problems here! And the biggest problem we've got is that damn empire out there!" Then, after a pause, he looked back at me and said: "And you know the name of that empire, don't you?"

Thinking it best not to challenge him, I simply nodded, but then I discovered that he was going to answer his own question. Without hesitating, he declared: "The name of that empire is Florida!"

I sat quietly for several moments. I was almost stunned by his answer. For most of my teaching career, I had come to understand the enormous power and influence of the United States as an empire in the world. I had even suggested some ways in which the United States was like empires from the past: Assyria, Babylon, Persia, Greece, or Rome. But I had never in my life thought of Florida as an empire!

From the perspective of the Bahamas, however, this is possible. The vast coastline, the territory, and the economic resources of Florida can seem so huge that they dwarf the limited economic realities of an offshore island country and its people. Without a great deal of agriculture or other industry, so much of the economy of the Bahamas depends directly on tourism and U.S. trade and investment.

Like the Bahamas today, Judah knew very well what it was like to live in the shadow of an empire. Judah lived with the reality that there was an empire "out there." Decisions made in a far-off capitol city (Nineveh, Babylon, or a city in Persia) could directly influence the daily life and the wellbeing of people of Judah. Foreign rulers could be arbitrary, ruthless, and unpredictable.

That reality is presupposed as a simple fact of life by the authors of the Isaiah scroll. The authors do not write from the perspective of privilege; rather, they write from a marginal perspective on the world. They call people to righteousness and justice. But the writers demonstrate again and again a pragmatic sense of realism about what is possible and what is not possible for people living in marginal situations. Those who live in a small nation must repeatedly count the cost as they make political and ethical decisions. They must deal with the questions of how best to manage the struggles of life while recognizing both the overwhelming power and the often-unexplainable whims of an empire "out there."

Many people experience the marginal perspective of life even when they live or work within an empire. There are many who suffer from illness, loss of employment, or the sudden death of a loved one. Such tragedies can bring a sense of powerlessness in the midst of life. The vision of Isaiah is focused specifically for people who have known or who presently know feelings of loss, grief, and suffering.

HAMATH

Mediterranean Sea

ARAM

Lebo

Byblos

PHOENECIA

Sidon

•Damascus

Tyre

Dan ISRAEL
     under
     Jereboam II

Kedesh

Chinereth

•Ashtaroth

Dor

•Megiddo

•Ramoth-
 gilead

Eastern Desert

Samaria

Beth-el

AMMON

Ekron

Jerusalem

•Rabbath-bene-
 ammon

Ashdod

Ashkelon•

Gath

PHILISTIA

•Lachish

Gaza•

Raphia•

Beer-sheba

MOAB

JUDAH

Kadesh-
•barnea

Brook of Egypt

Judah
under
Uzziah

EDOM

Sinai

Israel and
Judah in
Isaiah's Day

•Ezion-geber

*Gulf of
Aqaba*

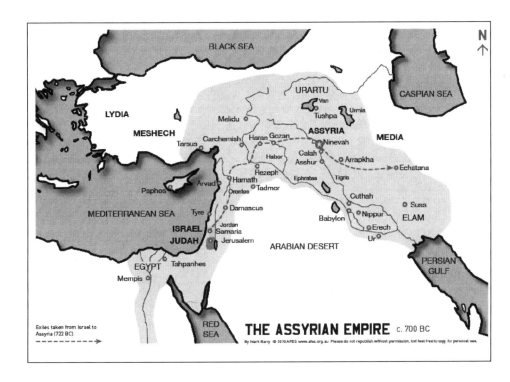

THE ASSYRIAN EMPIRE c. 700 BC

By Mark Barry © 2010 AFES www.afes.org.au Please do not republish without permission, but feel free to copy for personal use.

Exiles taken from Israel to
Assyria (722 BC)

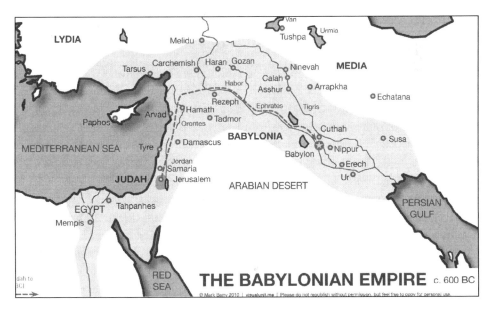

THE BABYLONIAN EMPIRE c. 600 BC

© Mark Barry 2010 | visualunit.me | Please do not republish without permission, but feel free to copy for personal use.

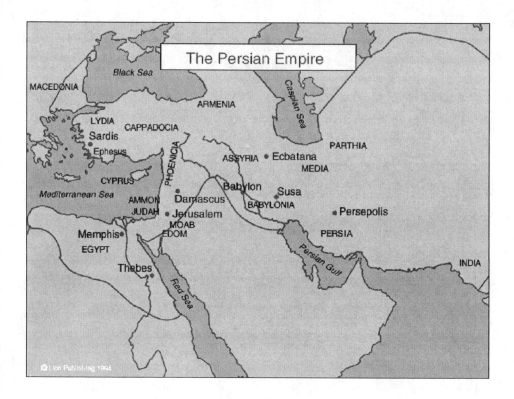

THE POST-EXILIC HISTORICAL SETTING: THREE MEMORIES THAT SHAPED THE ISAIAH SCROLL

We actually have only limited knowledge about life in Judah (Yahud) during the era when Persia dominated the world (539–333 BCE). In Isaiah 56–59, we sense that life in Judah and Jerusalem has been re-established as deportees have returned from captivity, often with great difficulties and trials. The temple appears to have been rebuilt and religious life restored. People were urged to keep Sabbath. Some foreigners had evidently become converts to Judaism, and eunuchs were to be welcomed in the community. Concern was expressed that sacrifices be offered in appropriate ways. And, in what may be a dominant theme in the latter chapters of Isaiah, an author declares: *"Maintain justice and do what is right, for soon my salvation will come, and my deliverance be revealed"* (Isa 56:1–8).

What seems clear is that the Isaiah scroll attained a place of respect among the various religious parties that developed in the post-exilic era, including the priestly classes and the followers of Ezra and Nehemiah. This led to its eventual inclusion within the collection of sacred writings and its position as the first of those prophetic writings (the Nevi'im).[18] The Isaiah scroll does not refer to any specific time in the post-exilic era. Rather, it speaks to issues that evidently were matters of faith over a long period of time.

Three momentous historic events seem to have been of particular importance in helping to shape the structure of the book of Isaiah: first, the fall of Jerusalem; second, the fall of Babylon, and third, the rise of Cyrus of Persia.

The fall of Jerusalem in 587 BCE seems clearly presupposed by the superscription in Isaiah 2:1, which introduces chapters 2–12: *"The word that Isaiah son of Amoz saw concerning Judah and Jerusalem."* That word was a strong declaration of what had happened to cause the destruction of Jerusalem and Judah. It is in that sense that the writing involves bitter memories of the pre-exilic era. Those who preserved the poetry in this opening section knew that Jerusalem had been destroyed in 587 BCE. They knew the aftermath of that horrible event of war. They knew in retrospect that Isaiah's words of warning concerning Judah and Jerusalem had come to pass.

In a similar way, the superscription in 13:1—*"The oracle concerning Babylon that Isaiah son of Amoz saw"*—introduces the second section of the scroll and calls attention to the fate of proud Babylon after the death of its mighty emperor, Nebuchadnezzar. What follows is a collection of judgment words for foreign nations and for Judah. From the post-exilic

---

18. The concluding chapters of Ezra describe a time when religious leaders in Judah felt that the integrity of their faith was in grave danger from those within the community who had married foreign women. As the religious leader in Jerusalem, Ezra had the position of authority to decide that all men who had married foreign women were to divorce them. That decree was carried out; the names of those men are actually listed in the concluding chapter, and the book of Ezra concludes with the sad report concerning the foreign women: "and they sent them away with their children" (Ezra 10:44).

It is interesting to note, however, that the author of the book of Ezra includes the report of four who dissented from the decision of Ezra. He writes: "Only Jonathan son of Asahel and Jahzeiah son of Tikvah opposed this, and Meshullam and Shabbethai the Levites supported them" (Ezra 10:15). We are left to wonder about the extent to which their dissent reflects some diversity of thought within the community. And we can wonder if the scroll of Isaiah also reflects diversity of thought apart from the world of Ezra.

perspective, people who read this scroll knew that these words of Isaiah concerning Babylon and other nations had also come to pass.

And finally, the poetry in Isaiah 40–55 presupposes the rise of Cyrus and the Persian Empire. Cyrus is mentioned by name in three texts: Isaiah 44:28, 45:1, and 45:13. In Isaiah 45:13, the author writes: "*I have aroused Cyrus in righteousness, and I will make all his paths straight; he shall build my city and set my exiles free, not for price or reward, says the Lord of hosts.*" As the Isaiah scroll was taking shape, the rebuilding tasks in Jerusalem were ongoing.

The policies of Cyrus toward captive peoples made possible a new chapter of life for those who returned to Judah. It was from that perspective that those who preserved the Isaiah scroll were doing theological reflection on past history. They understood that the words of Isaiah's vision were trustworthy. Judgment had come and earlier generations should have listened to the counsel of the prophet and the vision that he set forth.

Throughout the scroll, the authors of the Isaiah scroll use "day of the Lord" descriptive poetry. Such poetry seems to have been reserved for use with momentous events, events that could turn history in one direction or another. Isaiah warned of the fall of Jerusalem as a "day of the Lord" in 2:6–22. In Isaiah 13:1–22, a "day of the Lord" event is described for Babylon. And in Isaiah 61:1–11 and 63:1–6, "day of the Lord" poetry is used with a clear double meaning: the "day of the Lord" is a time of judgment or punishment for arrogant nations or individuals and at the same time, it is a time of liberation for trusting people of faith.

From the "post-exilic" perspective, the poetry of Isaiah 43:18–21 is particularly helpful for understanding the unity of the Isaiah scroll. There, the author contrasts the *"former things"* (memories of earlier *"bitter"* events, events that happened prior to the exile) with the *"new thing"* (the new era of hope) that came with the rise of Cyrus of Persia.

> *Do not remember the former things,*
> *Or consider the things of old,*
> *I am about to do a new thing;*
> *Now it springs forth,*
> *Do you not perceive it?*
> *I make a way in the wilderness*
> *And rivers in the desert.*
> *The wild animals will honor me,*

The jackals and the ostriches;
For I give water in the wilderness,
Rivers in the desert,
To give drink to my chosen people,
The people whom I formed for myself
So that they might declare my praise.
(Isa 43:18–21)

To understand the scope of Isaiah's vision, it is helpful to reflect on the significance of these three memories that are presupposed by the authors of Isaiah.

1. Memories of the Destruction of Jerusalem—588–587 BCE

The small book of Lamentations includes five poems that convey the enormous sense of loss experienced by those who were deported to Babylon after the destruction of Jerusalem in 587 BCE. Typical are the words of the first lament:

How lonely sits the city that once was full of people!
How like a widow she has become,
she that was great among the nations!
She weeps bitterly in the night, with tears on her cheeks;
among her lovers she has no one to comfort her . . .
(Lam 1:1–2)

And a few verses later, the poet asks:

Is it nothing to you, all you who pass by?
Look and see if there is any sorrow like my sorrow,
which was brought upon me,
which the Lord inflicted
on the day of his fierce anger.
(Lam 1:12)

Like memories of the Shoa during the era of Nazi Germany (1933–1945) that still haunt many in our modern world, so also the memories of Jerusalem's destruction haunted people long after they returned in the post-exilic era. Where was God? How could a loving God allow such tragedy? If God is active in world affairs, how did God allow this? Did God even care or notice? And did God have any specific purpose or role in the destruction of Jerusalem?

Israel first became a nation in the era between 1000 and 950 BCE under the leadership of Saul and David. Following the death of Solomon in 922 BCE, the country divided into two separate nations, Israel in the north and Judah in the south (see 1 Kgs 11–14). For almost 200 years, the two nations were able to survive despite occasional times of conflict and warfare. Then, at about 750 BCE, the Near East witnessed a dramatic change. Assyria became a dominating presence in the ancient Near East. John Bright has described the dramatic change with these moving words:

> In the third quarter of the eighth century, Israel was confronted by circumstances that altered her status decisively and permanently. Assyria took the path of empire in earnest, and the cloud long lowering on the horizon became a line storm which swept the little peoples before it like leaves. The northern state snapped before the blast and went crashing down. Though Judah managed to survive for yet a century and a half, outliving Assyria herself, she was never, save for one brief interval, to know political independence again.[19]

The prophetic writers contended that it was for acts of rebellion and short-sightedness that northern Israel was overrun by Assyria in 721 BCE and her capitol city, Samaria, destroyed. People were deported to various places throughout the Assyrian empire, never to return. It is from that era of national tragedy that references emerge concerning the "ten lost tribes of Israel." As a result of Assyrian policies of forced assimilation and intermarriage, the people of northern Israel literally disappeared among the peoples of the near east.

Judah, the southern kingdom, was able to survive by paying the required taxes or tribute to Assyria, but future generations would continue to struggle. When foreign oppression seemed excessive, leaders would struggle to find new ways to revolt. Then, in 612 BCE, a major change in world power occurred. Babylonian forces captured Nineveh, the capitol city of the Assyrian empire, and the center of world power moved south from Nineveh to Babylon, soon to be dominated by the great emperor, Nebuchadnezzar. The next twenty years were filled with war and intrigue and the tragic death of the young Judean king, Josiah. His son, Jehoiakim, struggled mightily to find some sense of balance amid the political

---

19. Bright, *History of Israel*, 267. The one exception was the era of the Maccabees between 167–73 BCE.

intrigue that involved both Egypt and Babylon. Jehoiakim actually proved to be a rather remarkable leader, giving loyalty first to the Egyptians for four years and then discovering a way to transfer his loyalty to the Babylonians when they defeated the Egyptians at the battle at Carchemish in 605 BCE. Jehoiakim remained on the throne in Jerusalem until 598 BCE, even as others among his advisors plotted new ways to revolt against Babylon. But this was the beginning of the end for Judah.

No country likes to be a vassal state for an empire! The years between 605–598 BCE were very difficult. Various attempts were made to break free from the overbearing demands from Babylon. Nationalist feelings were fueled by traditions that had been present ever since the eras of David and Solomon. Certain biblical texts declared that Yahweh had made promises of special protection for the king and for the Jerusalem temple (see especially 2 Samuel 7:1–17 and the so-called "royal psalms" such as Pss 2, 89, or 110). That nationalistic theology apparently gave encouragement to some people to plan revolt, even in times of great national peril.

Because of the ongoing sense of rebellion or unrest in Jerusalem, and most probably because the leaders withheld tribute, Babylon felt it necessary in 598 BCE to send an army to punish Jerusalem. The invading army demanded the surrender of the city. King Jehoiakim had died that year so the burden now fell on his eighteen-year-old son, Jehoiachin, who had been on the throne for only three months (see 2 Kings 24:1–20). When it became clear that the situation in the city was hopeless, a settlement was negotiated. Tribute was paid. A number of people were deported, including officials, artisans, and blacksmiths. King Jehoiachin, his mother, and a number of palace officials were also among those deported to Babylon.[20]

Still rebellion continued. Babylon installed Jehoiachin's uncle, Mattaniah, a brother of Jehoiakim, as the new king and gave him a new name, Zedekiah. But pressures to rebel against the empire still continued. Nine years later, Babylon felt compelled once again to send a new army to deal with the rebellion in Jerusalem. The year was 588 BCE. For eighteen months, the Babylonians kept a siege wall and a blockade around the city walls, cutting off all commerce and traffic in and out of her gates. Finally, the Babylonian forces made a breach in the wall. The author of 2 Kings 25:1–21 reports that by that time, famine was widespread in the city. In the dark of night, Zedekiah and a company of soldiers attempted an escape from the city but were captured in the plains of Jericho. They were

20. See 2 Kgs 24:1–7, which records the death of Jehoiakim. The brief reign of his son, Jehoiachin, and his deportation to Babylon is recorded in 2 Kgs 24:8–17.

brought to Riblah, where the emperor, Nebuchadnezzar, passed sentence on them. One by one, Zedekiah's sons were brought before him and were executed in a public place. Then, in a ceremony of ritual punishment, they put out Zedekiah's eyes. King Zedekiah would not be put to death; instead, he was to live in blindness for the rest of his life, remembering the death of his sons with his last moments of sight. Zedekiah was then bound and taken as a prisoner to Babylon. We do not hear of him again in any biblical record. He was the last king to reign in Jerusalem and in some ways, his reign marked the end of the Davidic line![21]

Jerusalem was burned and the temple was desecrated and then destroyed. The city wall was torn down and left in rubble. Those who survived must have wondered if their country had now suffered the same fate that had come for northern Israel. Would Judah also simply disappear from history forever? Was this to be the end of the tribes of Jacob? In retrospect, the author of Lamentations 1 and 3 wonders about these matters and reflects on this past tragedy as Judah's "day of the Lord."

2. Memories of the Fall of Babylon—562–539 BCE

There was a very important contrast between the earlier foreign policies of Assyria and those of Babylon regarding captive peoples. Assyria was absolutely ruthless, dispersing captive peoples to different cities, selling many as slaves and forcing intermarriage. In contrast, Babylonian authorities allowed deported peoples to live together in designated areas while in captivity. As a result, we can speak of the birth of the "ghetto" tradition. In the ghettos of Babylon, people deported from Judah could at least preserve some sense of their national and religious identity. They could maintain a sense of community, enabling them to grieve with others over the death of family members. Together they could reflect on the devastation of villages, homes, fields, and vineyards. As a result, there were some real ways in which the ghetto was a saving feature for Hebrew

---

21. In the ancient Near East, this was seen as the most cruel punishment that could be given to a king. Note, however, that because he was a king, his life was somehow deemed sacrosanct; he would be a living symbol of subservience to Babylonian authorities. The game of chess has a similar aspect in that the king is not removed from the board, only put in checkmate at the end of a game. The young king, Jehoiachin, spent the remainder of his life in Babylon; the book of 2 Kings concludes with the report that he was elevated to a place at the king of Babylon's table and given an allowance for as long as he lived (2 Kgs 25:27–30).

people in exile. Young couples could unite in marriage; new crops and orchards could be planted. But the people knew that Jerusalem and the temple were gone! The king and priests were gone! And the ark of the covenant, the resting place for the tablets of the Ten Commandments, was gone forever.[22]

Twenty-five years later, Nebuchadnezzar died. The year was 562 BCE. Nebuchadnezzar had ruled over the empire with an iron fist for forty-three years (605–562 BCE) and had achieved a reputation as a fierce military leader.[23] But by the time of his death, signs of internal corruption were apparent throughout the empire. During the seven years after his death, four different rulers attempted to govern the empire. Nebuchadnezzar's son, Amel-Marduk, ruled for only two years; he was followed by his brother-in-law, Neriglissar, apparently after a military coup. Neriglissar ruled for four years and apparently died while on a military campaign, leaving the empire for his young son, Labashi-Marduk. But he was quickly overthrown by Nabonidus, who had the support of his fellow military leaders. He would be the last recognized ruler of the great Babylonian empire.

Nabonidus (556–539) was a devotee of the moon god Sin. He spent considerable time away from his capitol city, establishing a residence in the desert town of Tema amid the hills of southern Edom. In his absence, he left the crown prince, Belshazzar, in charge of the government at Babylon. But the absence of Nabonidus caused considerable unrest among the priests and the court officials, particularly as reports of Persian military victories came from various parts of the empire.

In 539 BCE, the capitol city of Babylon came under direct siege from Cyrus and his Persian military forces. Frustrated by the absence of their king, the high priests of Babylon negotiated secretly with the Persian forces and engineered the surrender of the city. If surviving reports are correct, the priests ordered the city gates opened in the middle of the night allowing the advancing army to enter the city. The priests were hoping for a full restoration of the worship of Marduk, the sun god, who had been worshipped for generations as the high god in the pantheon of gods

22. See Jeremiah 29, where that prophet's letter to exiles in Babylon provides a moving insight into the situation in Babylon. Jeremiah counsels that they should not revolt but should "seek the welfare of the city" (Jer 29:7).

23. Sack, "Nebuchadnezzar" 1058-59. In 605 BCE, Nebuchadnezzar won a decisive victory over Egyptian forces, and then went on to conquests in Syria and Arabia before launching attacks on Jerusalem in 597 BCE and again in 588-587 BCE.

in Babylon.[24] The priests within the city of Babylon were confident that Cyrus would be tolerant. And he was. The capitol city of Babylon was not destroyed. The royal power was simply transferred away from Nabonidus to new officials representing the emperor of Persia.[25] Within weeks, the oppressive power of Babylon as an empire was gone.

3. Memories of the Rise of Cyrus of Persia

Cyrus was born in 590 BCE, probably in Farsa in the province of Fars. He became king over Persia (Iran) in 559 and waged successful military campaigns against the Medes (northern Iran) in 550 BCE that gave him control over much of the Mesopotamian valley region (Iraq). Then he conquered Lydia and Sardis (western Turkey), allowing him to control most of the Ionian areas (the Greek coastal areas) by about 547 BCE. He moved on to consolidate control over the northeast areas of the Iranian plateau (546–540 BCE) before finally focusing his efforts on bringing down the capitol city of Babylon (539 BCE).[26] Perhaps Cyrus was just a shrewd politician, gaining the favor of displaced people by allowing them to return to their homelands. But it was precisely his policy of respect for deported peoples that provided the basis for the mood of hope that is present in Isaiah 40–55.

The policies of Cyrus gave the exilic community enormous hope for a new era of history. Isaiah had declared that rulers of this world may contend that they are like God or that they may "play God" in the world for a while. But sooner or later, emperors grow old and die. Empires rise and fall! The fall of Nebuchadnezzar and his successors thus added depth of meaning to the words of Isaiah's vision that declare:

> "All people are grass . . . grass withers, the flower fades;
> but it is the Word of our God that will stand forever."

24. Sack, "Nebuchadnezzar," 971–76. Nabonidus had offended the Babylonain priests in particular by halting the annual New Year Festival and being absent from that festival for a prolonged period of time.

25. Bright, 351–55.

26. Young, "Cyrus," 1231–32. Young suggests that the career of Cyrus divides into four phases: (1) the trimphant war against Astyages and the Medes (550 BCE), (2) the campaign agaianst Lydia (5467 BCE), (3) the campaigns against the Iranian plateau (546 and 540 BCE) and the conquest of Babylon (539/539 BCE). Cyrus became known for his respect for local cultures and tolerance for diverse ethnic groups, religions, and ancient kingdoms, provided that those conquered peoples pledged loyalty to him.

(Isa 40:7–8)

Cyrus may very well have been as brutal, oppressive, or ruthless as other world emperors during his military conquests. But from the vantage point of exiles living in Babylon, his policies seemed tolerant and respectful. The hopes of the community were realized when Cyrus issued a formal edict in 539 BCE that allowed exiled captive peoples from Judah and Jerusalem to return to their homeland.[27] It is in this regard that Cyrus is remembered as a servant and agent of Yahweh. In one instance (Isa 45:1), he is even hailed as a "messiah" or liberator for the people. With Cyrus, a "day of vindication for Yahweh" comes (Isa 61:2). The arrogant are punished and the humble and contrite are raised up!

These three memories—the fall of Jerusalem, the fall of Babylon, and the rise of Cyrus—were of central importance for those who edited and shaped the 66-chapter form of the Isaiah scroll. With the generations of people in the post-exilic era who continued to live under foreign emperors from Persia, Greece, and Rome, we are invited to reflect on the opening words of the scroll: *"Come; let us walk in the light of the Lord!"* (Isa 2:5) and the challenge of the later passage: *"Incline your ear; and come to me; listen, so that you may live!"*(Isa 55:3).

A CHRONOLOGY: MEMORABLE EVENTS IN THE ISAIAH SCROLL

1000–922 BCE   Era of the "United Monarchy" kings: Saul, David, and Solomon

935–612 BCE   Era of Assyrian Empire domination in the ancient Near East.

922 BCE   The schism between northern Israel and southern Judah

750–690 BCE   Lifetime of Isaiah ben Amoz

Kings: Ahaz 735–715 BCE and Hezekiah 715–687 BCE

---

27. The edict which Cyrus issued authorizing Hebrew people to return to Judah and Jerusalem from exile is included as the last word in the Chronicler's account of Jewish history (2 Chr 36:22–23); the edict is also cited in the opening section of the book of Ezra (Ezra 1:1–4).

735–734 BCE	Syria and northern Israel attack southern Judah; Ahaz calls on Assyria for help
715–711 BCE	Southern Judah looks to Egypt to rebel against Assyria
701 BCE	Invasion of Judah and Jerusalem by Sennacherib, ruler of Assyria
612 BCE	Nineveh, capital of Assyria, falls to Nebuchadnezzar and Babylonian forces
598 BCE	Babylonian assault on Jerusalem and deportation of King Jehoiachin
587 BCE	The destruction of Jerusalem by Babylon
587–539 BCE	"The Babylonian Captivity" or "Exilic Period" (Judah and Jerusalem left in ruins)
562 BCE	Death of Nebuchadnezzar and decline of Babylon
550–539 BCE	Rise of Cyrus of Persia and the Persian Empire
450 BCE–70 CE	Era of the "Second Temple" in Jerusalem (editing and expansion of the Isaiah scroll)
336–323 BCE	Alexander the Great and the Greeks defeat the Persians
300–167 BCE	Judah under the Ptolemies and Seleucid rulers
200 BCE	Probable date of the 66-chapter Isaiah scroll from Qumran (1QIsaa)[28]

A PREVIEW: WORDS OF HOPE IN THE
SCROLL OF ISAIAH

Because the first two sections of the Isaiah scroll (chapters 2–12 and 13–35) are primarily *"bitter memories"* from earlier history, it is at times difficult to hear the primary message of hope which undergirds the entire message of this ancient scroll. Despite the painful memories of judgment, the editor of the scroll still offers encouragement with occasional words of hope. Here is a sampling of texts that set out the message of hope that runs throughout the entire Isaiah scroll:

In the introductory opening of chapter 1 (after repeated laments about the rebellion of the earlier generation), the author declares:

> *Wash yourselves; make yourselves clean; remove the evil of your doings from before my eyes; cease to do evil, learn to do good;*

28. For a more detailed chronology of historical events, see Bright, *History of Israel*, 476–84.

> *seek justice, rescue the oppressed, defend the orphan, plead for the*
> *widow.*
> *(Isa 1:16–17)*

And he continues:

> *Come now, let us argue it out, says the Lord: though your sins are*
> *like scarlet, they shall be like snow; though they are red like crim-*
> *son, they shall become like wool. If you are willing and obedient,*
> *you shall eat the good of the land.*
> *(Isa 1:18–19)*

In chapter 2, "Bitter Memories of Judah and Jerusalem: Isaiah 2–12", a vision of peace serves as an opening preface for this section of the scroll:

> *In days to come the mountain of the Lord's house shall be estab-*
> *lished as the highest of the mountains, and shall be raised above*
> *the hills; all the nations shall stream to it. Many people will come*
> *and say, 'Come, let us go up to the mountain of the Lord, to the*
> *house of the God of Jacob; that he may teach us his ways and that*
> *we may walk in his paths. For out of Zion shall go forth instruc-*
> *tion, and the word of the Lord from Jerusalem. He shall judge*
> *between the nations, and shall arbitrate for many peoples; they*
> *shall beat their swords into plowshares, and their spears into prun-*
> *ing hooks; nation shall not lift up sword against nation, neither*
> *shall they learn war anymore.*
> *(Isa 2:2–4)*

And then follows a text which captures the overall focus of the scroll:

> *O house of Jacob, come, let us walk in the light of the Lord!*
> *(Isa 2:5)*

Disillusioned with King Ahaz and the monarchy of the eighth century BCE, the prophet Isaiah is remembered envisioning a future ideal king, possibly at the birth of a new heir to the throne, one who could restore peace and security for the people:

> *. . . For a child has been born to us, a son given to us; authority*
> *rests upon his shoulders; and he is named Wonderful Counselor,*
> *Mighty God, Everlasting Father, Prince of Peace. His authority*
> *shall grow continually, and there shall be endless peace for the*
> *throne of David and his kingdom. He will establish and uphold it*

> *with justice and righteousness from this time onward and forever-*
> *more. The zeal of the Lord will do this.*
>
> *(Isa 9:6–7)*

And in this same section of the scroll, the prophet offers a classic description of what a king, a politician, or a leader in any era of history should
be like:

> *He will not judge by what his eyes see (outward appearance!), or*
> *decide by what his ears hear (hearsay!), but with righteousness*
> *(integrity!) he shall judge (fairly) for the poor, and decide with*
> *equity (fairness!) for the meek of the earth; he shall strike the*
> *earth with the rod of his mouth (with verbal skills, not with his*
> *sword!) and with the breath of his lips (his eloquence!) he shall*
> *kill the wicked. Righteousness (integrity!) shall be the belt around*
> *his waist and faithfulness (truthfulness!) the belt around his loins.*
>
> *(Isa 11:3b–5)*

Despite the sad memories that are preserved in these opening chapters,
the editors chose to close this opening section with two declarations of
praise and thanksgiving, including these words:

> *Surely God is my salvation; I will trust and will not be afraid for*
> *the Lord God is my strength and my might; he has become my*
> *salvation.*
>
> *(Isa 12:2)*

And in a second concluding word, the author adds:

> *With joy you shall draw water from the wells of salvation. And*
> *you will say in that day: Give thanks to the Lord, call on his name;*
> *make known his deeds among the nations; proclaim that his name*
> *is exalted. Sing praises to the Lord, for he has done gloriously; let*
> *this be known in all the earth. Shout aloud and sing for joy, O*
> *inhabitant of Zion, for great in the midst is the holy One of Israel.*
>
> *(Isa 12:3–6)*

In chapter 3, "Judah among the Nations: Isaiah 13–35", the author uses
a variety of poetry to recall the horrors of past wars and the devastation
which war brings to humankind. Yet in the poetry in chapters 24–27,
located in the midst of a lament about war, the author can declare:

> *And he (God) will destroy on this mountain the shroud that is*
> *cast over all peoples, the sheet that is spread over all nations; he*
> *will swallow up death forever. Then the Lord God will wipe away*

> *the tears from all faces, and the disgrace of his people he will take*
> *away from all the earth, for the Lord has spoken. It will be said on*
> *that day, Lo, this is our God; we have waited for him, so that he*
> *might save us. This is the Lord for whom we have waited; let us be*
> *glad and rejoice in his salvation. For the hand of the Lord will rest*
> *upon the mountain.*
>
> *(Isa 25:7–10)*

Amid the words of judgment on various nations in this section, an author still expresses hope with words focused on Lebanon:

> *Shall not Lebanon in a very little while become a fruitful field, and*
> *the fruitful field be regarded as a forest? On that day the deaf shall*
> *hear the words of a scroll, and out of their gloom and darkness the*
> *eyes of the blind shall see. The meek shall obtain fresh joy in the*
> *Lord, and the neediest people shall exalt in the Holy One of Israel.*
> *For the tyrant shall be no more and the scoffer shall cease to be . . .*
>
> *(Isa 29:17–21)*

Included in this section is one of the most thoughtful reflections in the scroll:

> *For thus says the Lord God, the Holy One of Israel: In return-*
> *ing and rest you shall be saved; in quietness and in trust shall be*
> *your strength. But you refused and said, "No! We will flee upon*
> *horses"—therefore you shall flee! (a condemnation of leaders so*
> *prone to rush off to war!)*
>
> *(Isa 30:15–16)*

And in chapter 35, which is the concluding section of the second part of Isaiah, there are wonderful expressions of hope, including these words:

> *Strengthen the weak hands, and make firm the feeble knees. Say*
> *to those who are of a fearful heart, "Be strong, do not fear! Here is*
> *your God. He will come to vindicate you with great power. He will*
> *come to save you."*
>
> *(Isa 35:3–4)*

In chapter 4 of this book, "Memories of King Hezekiah: Isaiah 36–39", prose material is discussed that is almost identical to the text of 2 Kings 18–20. Included are memories of King Hezekiah. In Isaiah 38:9–20, a prayer of King Hezekiah is preserved as his word of thanksgiving for recovery from illness. That prayer includes these words:

> *the Lord will save me, and we will sing to stringed instruments*

all the days of our lives, at the house of the Lord.
(Isa 38:20)

In chapter 5 of this book, "The Hopeful Memories: Isaiah 40–55," words of hope and encouragement are dominant throughout the entire section of Isaiah. The words come from the end of the Babylonian captivity era (the fifty years following the destruction of Jerusalem in 587 BCE and the deportation of many people to Babylon), the time when Cyrus of Persia had wrestled the leadership of the empire from the tyranny of Babylon (the era between 550–530 BCE). Hope was in the air! Cyrus issued a decree which allowed captive peoples to return to their homeland (see the end of 2 Chronicles and the opening chapter of the book of Ezra).

The authors of the Isaiah scroll believed that history has a way of redeeming itself. They contended that the force behind redemptive activity in history is the God of all creation. So, when they pondered past moments of goodness and liberation, they could celebrate. Some samples of the lyric poetry in Isaiah 40–55:

Comfort, O comfort my people, says your God. Speak tenderly to Jerusalem, and cry to her that she has served her term, that her penalty is paid, that she has received from the Lord's hand double for all her sins.
(Isa 40:1–2)

A voice says, "Cry out!" And I said, "What shall I cry?" All people are grass, their constancy is like the flower of the field. The grass withers, the flower fades, when the breath of the Lord blows upon it; surely the people are grass. The grass withers, the flower fades; but the Word of the Lord (words of goodness and justice!) will stand forever.
(Isa 40:6–8)

He gives power to the faint, and strengthens the powerless. Even youths will faint and be weary, and the young will fall exhausted; but those who wait for the Lord shall renew their strength, they shall mount up with eagles, they shall run and not be weary, they shall walk and not faint.
(Isa 40:29–31)

The editors of the Isaiah scroll are painfully aware of the past. And yet, in a rather amazing passage, the prophetic writer urges people to view their current situation as a "new chapter" in life:

Do not remember the former things, or consider the things of old. I am about to do a new thing; now it springs forth, do you not perceive it? I will make a way in the wilderness and rivers in the desert. The wild animals will honor me, the jackals and the ostriches; for I give water in the wilderness, rivers in the desert, to give drink to my chosen people, the people whom I formed for myself so that they might declare my praise.

(Isa 43:18–21)

The prophetic writer is much concerned about the way in which people make idols of things from the earth and then bow down to them. People, created in the image of God, are not to bow down to worship kings, money, or other things of the earth. In urging people not to trust in idols, which usually need to be propped up, the prophet declares:

Listen to me, O house of Jacob, all the remnant of the house of Israel, who have been borne by me from your birth, carried from the womb; even to old age I am he, even when you turn gray, I will carry you. I have made, and I will bear; I will carry and I will save.

(Isa 46:1–3)

In this part of the scroll, the prophetic writer describes a "servant of the Lord," identified in chapter 41 as the remnant captive community Israel (Isa 41:8, see also 41:1–5, 49:1–7, 50:4–10 and the extended portrait of the suffering that the servant endures in 52:13—53:12). Of the task of this servant, the author writes:

It is too light a thing that you should be my servant to raise up the tribes of Jacob and to restore the survivors of Israel; I will give you as a light to the nations, that my salvation may reach to the end of the earth.

(Isa 49:6)

And at the conclusion of this section of the scroll, we hear the words:

Ho, everyone who thirsts, come to the waters; and you that have no money, come, buy and eat! Come, buy wine and milk without money and price.

(Isa 55:1)

Chapter 55 concludes:

For you shall go out in joy, and be led back in peace; the mountains and the hills before you shall burst into song, and all the trees

of the field shall clap their hands. Instead of the thorn shall come
up the cypress; instead of the brier shall come up the myrtle; and
it shall be to the Lord as a memorial, for an everlasting sign that
shall not be cut off.

(Isa 55:13)

In the last major section of the scroll, discussed in chapter 6 of this book, "Living with the Vision: Isaiah 56–65," those who aspire to live with hope are addressed quite directly. We hear not just about a "servant" but rather people who are addressed as "servants of the Lord"! At the beginning of this section, the prophetic writer declares:

Maintain justice and do what is right, for soon my salvation will
come, and my deliverance be revealed. Happy is the mortal who
does this, the one who holds it fast, who keeps the Sabbath, not
profaning it, and refrains from doing any evil.

(Isa 56:1–2).

Isaiah 60–62 includes delightful poetry of hope. At the heart of these chapters is the charge to people to be like "oaks of righteousness." Servant people are sent to be helpful in the world. The prophet describes the servant:

he has sent me to bring good news to the oppressed, to bind up
the brokenhearted, to proclaim liberty to the captives, and release
to the prisoners; to proclaim the Lord's favor, and the day of vin-
dication for our God; to comfort all who mourn, to provide for
all those who mourn in Zion—to give them a garland instead of
ashes, the oil of gladness instead of mourning, the mantle of praise
instead of a faint spirit. They will be called oaks of righteousness,
the planting of the Lord to display his glory . . .

(Isa 61:1b–3).

The vision of Isaiah is a prophetic work that is serious in its critique of arrogance and evil in the world. At the same time it is a collection of poetry that calls and invites people in every era of history to a life of meaningful work in service to others and to hope, based in confidence of God's steadfast love.

The final chapter of Isaiah includes the words:

For as the new heaven and the new earth, which I will make,
shall remain before me, says the Lord; so, shall your descendants
and your name remain. From new moon to new moon, and from

sabbath to sabbath, all flesh shall come to worship before me, says
the Lord.
(Isa 66:22–23).

The Commentary

1.

An Introduction to the Vision

Isaiah 1:1–31

THE INTRODUCTORY SUPERSCRIPTION—ISAIAH 1:1

The vision of Isaiah son of Amoz,

which he saw concerning Judah and Jerusalem

in the days of Uzziah, Jotham, Ahaz and Hezekiah,

kings of Judah.

(Isa 1:1)

THE ISAIAH SCROLL WAS inspired by and named for a specific human being, Isaiah ben Amoz, who lived in Jerusalem in the era between 750 and 680 BCE. Isaiah is remembered as a man of faith, one who felt called by God to address issues related to the political, spiritual, and economic well-being of the people. He was clearly well versed in the Torah traditions. For three hundred years after his lifetime (700 to 400 BCE), Isaiah's vision was remembered, affirmed, and expanded by later generations of people.

3

The new poetry that was added to the scroll affirms the continuing relevance of Isaiah's vision for later generations of people. In the Hebrew Bible, the prophetic books (the Nevi'im) follow directly after the five books of the Pentateuch (Torah) and are intended as commentary on the Torah. In both Jewish and in Christian traditions, Isaiah is the first of the four prophetic scrolls (Isaiah, Jeremiah, Ezekiel, and the Book of the Twelve), indicating the prominence given to this scroll by later generations.[1]

THE HUMAN PREDICAMENT AND THE LORD'S COMPLAINT—ISAIAH 1:2–6

The opening poem in Isaiah, chapter 1, is a memory of God's word of judgment against the people of Judah. They have become so utterly estranged from their creator that they are no different than the residents of ancient Sodom and Gomorrah. They do not seem to know or understand what it means to be compassionate human beings! Their condition is likened to an illness which has afflicted both their heads and their hearts. They are sick from the soles of their feet to the tops of their heads.

In the opening stanza or strophe, Yahweh, who is depicted as the father of Israel and author of all creation, sets forth a legal case. Heaven and earth are summoned as witnesses. The charge is that human beings are in revolt against their maker.

> *Hear, O heavens, and listen, O earth:*
> *for the Lord has spoken:*
> *I reared children and brought them up,*
> *but they have rebelled against me.*
> *The ox knows its owner,*
> *and the donkey its master's crib;*
> *but Israel does not know,*

1. The Hebrew Bible (or Tanak) consists of three parts: the Pentateuch (Torah), the Prophetic Writings (Nevi'im) and the Writings (Ketuvim). The first letters form the word used in Hebrew tradition to refer to the sacred scriptures (TaNaK). When Jerome translated and created the Latin translation known as the Vulgate as a Christian text around the year 400 CE, he re-ordered the books of the Hebrew Bible, placing the historical books and writings ahead of the prophetic books. Some believe that the prophetic books were placed last to call attention to their prophetic character in anticipation of the New Testament writings. In the Hebrew Bible, the book of Daniel is included with the Writings, not with the Prophetic Writings.

my people do not understand.

Ah, sinful nation,
people laden with iniquity,
offspring who do evil,
children who deal corruptly,
who have forsaken the Lord,
who have despised the Holy One of Israel,
who are utterly estranged!
Why do you seek further beatings?
Why do you continue to rebel?
The whole head is sick,
and the whole heart faint.
From the sole of the foot even to the head,
there is no soundness in it,
but bruises and sores
and bleeding wounds;
they have not been drained,
or bound up,
or softened with oil.
(Isa 1:2–6)

The illness allowed human beings in an earlier era of history to justify actions that were corrupt and hurtful to others. Oxen and donkeys recognize their masters; humans refuse direction and refuse to acknowledge that they are mortal; with all of their might, they seem intent on carving out their own pathways for understanding and for dealing with the challenges of life.

ZION: LEFT LIKE A BOOTH IN A VINEYARD —ISAIAH 1:7–9

Greed combines with fear. All too often, that combination is then masked by a posture of arrogance that leads to threats, demands, warfare, and other disasters. Those who held leadership positions in Judah are remembered as being particularly guilty in their failure to take proper responsibility for the well-being of the human community. As a result, the besieged land and cities are desolate!

Your country lies desolate,
your cities are burned with fire:
in your very presence
aliens devour your land;
it is desolate, as overthrown by foreigners.
And daughter Zion is left
like a booth in a vineyard,
like a shelter in a cucumber field,
like a besieged city.
If the Lord of hosts
had not left us a few survivors,
we would have been like Sodom,
and become like Gomorrah.
(Isa 1:7–9)

In the scroll, a reader can sense that what is being presented is a panoramic view of past history and the changing fortunes of Zion.[2] Zion is the poetic name given both to Jerusalem and to the temple mount. She is remembered in her splendor; she is also remembered in ruins. The opening chapter recalls that people in the time of Isaiah were in grave danger. From the post-exilic perspective, two or three hundred years later, these memories are heightened. That community knew that a great tragedy came for Jerusalem and Judah when they were destroyed by Babylonian forces in 587 BCE. They also knew of the difficult years of exile in Babylon that extended over the following fifty years (587–539 BCE). And they also could recall the era when new hope came with the rise of Persia and the emperor, Cyrus, who allowed captive peoples to return to their homelands.

Already in this opening chapter, we hear themes that will reappear throughout the poetry of the scroll. Human people are prone to rebellious or shortsighted human conduct. Trouble and tragedies follow as a result, and yet, there are possibilities for redemption even beyond tragedy.

YOUR HANDS ARE FULL OF BLOOD—ISAIAH 1:10–15

This is a sober memory. The author remembers people who seemed to be very religious. But their day to day conduct was not pleasing to the

2. On this theme, see Seitz, *Zion's Final Destiny*. Minneapolis: Fortress, 1991.

Lord. Consequently, their sacrificial offerings were not pleasing to the Lord. Sacrifice was understood to be the primary mode of communication between humans and God. The problem was that sacrifice all too often became a shallow substitute for what was most important. Hollow sacrifice is meaningless. Human people are called above all else to be about the quest for justice, peace and upright conduct.

> *Hear the word of the Lord,*
> *you rulers of Sodom!*
> *Listen to the teaching of our God,*
> *you people of Gomorrah!*
> *What to me is the multitude of your sacrifices?*
> *says the Lord;*
> *I have had enough of burnt offerings of rams*
> *and the fat of fed beasts;*
> *I do not delight in the blood of bulls*
> *I have had enough of burnt offerings of rams*
> *and the fat of fed beasts;*
> *I do not delight in the blood of bulls,*
> *or of lambs, or of goats.*
>
> *When you come to appear before me,*
> *who asked this from your hand?*
> *Trample my courts no more;*
> *bringing offerings is futile;*
> *incense is an abomination to me.*
> *New moon and sabbath*
> *and calling of convocation—*
> *I cannot endure solemn assemblies with iniquity.*
> *Your new moons and your appointed festivals*
> *my soul hates;*
> *they have become a burden to me,*
> *I am weary of bearing them.*
> *When you stretch out your hands,*
> *I will hide my eyes from you;*
> *even though you make many prayers,*
> *I will not listen;*

your hands are full of blood.
(Isa 1:10–15)

CEASE TO DO EVIL, LEARN TO DO GOOD!
—ISAIAH 1:16-17

Here we are introduced to the fundamental summons of this prophetic scroll. The author spells out how righteousness and justice are to be measured. They are realistic commitments that those who hear this word can make.

> *Wash yourselves; make yourselves clean;*
> *remove the evil of your doings from before my eyes;*
> *cease to do evil, learn to do good;*
> *seek justice, rescue the oppressed,*
> *defend the orphan, plead for the widow.*
> *(Isa 1:16–17)*

Members of a community are to use their energy to assist those who are at the lowest end of the economic and social order within a community. Two specific groups of people are mentioned as a practical test for measuring justice: orphans and widows. Orphans are those individuals within a community who do not have the benefit of family or parental nurture, who are thus denied the attention that is their birthright during their formative years in a family structure. Widows are those who are cut off from economic means to sustain life on their own.[3]

COME, LET US ARGUE IT OUT!—ISAIAH 1:18-20

Thus far, the opening chapter reads like a court presentation. Human life allows for many choices and options, but the manner in which people choose to live makes a difference for the community as a whole. When people persist in arrogant or selfish conduct, they may prosper for a

---

3. In our day and age, "widows" may well involve men as well as women; the term speaks of those who through little fault of their own are "cut off" from economic opportunity to provide for themselves or their families; we can think of those unemployed due to layoffs, plant closings, or loss of work opportunities. In the third world today, lack of employment opportunites remains one of the major barriers for meaningful life.

while, but sooner or later, there will be consequences. That, according to Isaiah's vision, is simply the way history works!

> *Come now, let us argue it out,*
> *says the Lord:*
> *though your sins are like scarlet,*
> *they shall be like snow;*
> *though they are red like crimson,*
> *they shall become like wool.*
> *If you are willing and obedient,*
> *you shall eat the good of the land;*
> *but if you refuse and rebel,*
> *you shall be devoured by the sword;*
> *for the mouth of the Lord has spoken.*
> *(Isa 1:18–20)*

JERUSALEM IN RETROSPECT—ISAIAH 1:21-25

The poem now takes on the character of a dirge. Zion is remembered as a harlot, and Yahweh has turned against her. The memory reads like a summary of all the troubles that led to Jerusalem's destruction in 587 BCE. Isaiah had announced words of warning at times of earlier crisis; his warnings had gone unheeded long before the greater tragedy came.

> *How the faithful city*
> *has become a whore!*
> *She that was full of justice,*
> *righteousness lodged in her—*
> *but now murderers!*
> *Your silver has become dross,*
> *your wine is mixed with water.*
> *Your princes are rebels*
> *and companions of thieves.*
> *Everyone loves a bribe*
> *and runs after gifts.*
> *They do not defend the orphan,*
> *and the widow's cause*
> *does not come before them.*

> *Therefore, says the Sovereign,*
> *the Lord of hosts,*
> *the Mighty One of Israel:*
> *Ah, I will pour out my wrath*
> *on my enemies,*
> *and avenge myself on my foes!*
> *I will turn my hand against you;*
> *I will smelt away your dross as with lye*
> *and remove all your alloy.*
> *(Isa 1:21–25)*

THE RIGHTEOUS IN ZION SHALL BE REDEEMED BY JUSTICE—ISAIAH 1:26-27

Now the dirge changes to a word of hope for the righteous. The past realities of destruction and exile are remembered as a time when the nation was purified like metal cleansed by lye, or as alloy that has come through fire in a furnace. After the cleansing, the author envisions a new era when Zion will be redeemed by justice, and when those who repent will be restored by righteousness.

> *And I will restore your judges*
> *as at the first,*
> *and your counselors*
> *as at the beginning.*
> *Afterward, you shall be called*
> *the city of righteousness,*
> *the faithful city.*
> *Zion shall be redeemed by justice,*
> *and those in her who repent,*
> *by righteousness.*
> *(Isa 1:26–27)*

REBELS AND SINNERS SHALL BE DESTROYED!
—ISAIAH 1:28–31

The first chapter of Isaiah concludes with a very sober note. While the righteous are promised restoration, rebels and sinners are warned that they will leave a different legacy behind them. Later in the scroll, the righteous will be described as "oaks of righteousness" and "the pleasant planting of the Lord" (Isa 61:3). But here, rebels and sinners are warned that they will be like dead oaks or like gardens without water, serving only as fuel for the judgment fires that are certain to come for them.[4]

> But rebels and sinners
> shall be destroyed together,
> and those who forsake the Lord
> shall be consumed.
> For you shall be ashamed of the oaks
> in which you delighted;
> and you shall blush for the gardens
> that you have chosen.
> For you shall be like an oak
> whose leaf withers,
> and like a garden without water.
> The strong shall become like tinder,
> and their work like a spark;
> they and their work shall burn together,
> with no one to quench them.
> (Isa 1:28–31)

In this introductory chapter, we have seen a preview of the message of the Isaiah scroll, involving both words of warning and words of encouragement. It is striking that both in this introductory chapter 1 and in the concluding chapter 66 of the scroll, the final words are words of warning.

---

4. A number of current scholars see parallels between Isaiah 1 and Isaiah 66, suggesting that they form a "frame" around the scroll.

2.

Bitter Memories concerning Judah and Jerusalem

Isaiah 2–12

THE SUPERSCRIPTION—ISAIAH 2:1

The word that Isaiah ben Amoz saw concerning Judah and Jerusalem.

(Isa 2:1)

THE SUPERSCRIPTION FOCUSES OUR attention on the past troubles that have come for Judah and Jerusalem. A similar superscription found at the beginning of Isaiah 13 will mark the beginning of the next major section of the scroll. There the words are similar: *"The oracle concerning Babylon that Isaiah ben Amoz saw"* (Isa 13:1). Both opening sections (chapters 2–12 and 13–35) preserve bitter memories of war and destruction from the past.[1] In contrast, chapters 40–55 and chapters 56–66 preserve poetry that dates from a later era when Babylonia had lost power and when Persia under Cyrus brought a new hopeful era of history. Those

1. When I speak of "bitter memories," I am thinking specifically of the imagery of "wild or bitter grapes" (*beʾashim*) in Isa 5:4 or the use of "bitter" (*mar*) in Isa 5:20.

12

later chapters will seem like sweet memories from a very hopeful era. In the scroll, the opening two sections (chapters 2–12 and 13–35) are like a backdrop for hearing the message of comfort and encouragement that will come in chapters 40–66.

A PROLOGUE: A VISION OF PEACE AMONG NATIONS— ISAIAH 2:2–4

Bitter memories will come. But words of encouragement both open and conclude this opening section of the scroll (Isa 2:2–4 and 12:1–6). In this memorable opening poem, the prophet dreams of a day when *"nations might beat their swords into plowshares, and their spears into pruning hooks!"* Over centuries, these words have inspired people throughout the world to work for reconciliation and understanding among peoples and nations. The dream of peace is at the center of Isaiah's vision. It is not accidental that words of this text are carved on a wall just outside the United Nations headquarters in New York City. The words call upon nations to submit their grievances before a tribunal of justice rather than rushing off to war. In Isaiah's vision, justice that is fairly rendered is the reflection of the will of Yahweh, the Lord and creator of all nations.

> *In days to come*
> *the mountain of the Lord's house*
> *shall be established as the highest of the mountains,*
> *and shall be raised above the hills;*
> *all the nations shall stream to it.*
> *Many peoples shall come and say,*
> *"Come, let us go up*
> *to the mountain of the Lord,*
> *to the house of the God of Jacob;*
> *that he may teach us his ways*
> *and that we may walk in his paths."*
> *For out of Zion shall go forth instruction,*
> *and the word of the Lord from Jerusalem.*
>
> *He shall judge between the nations,*
> *and shall arbitrate for many peoples;*
> *they shall beat their swords into plowshares,*

and their spears into pruning hooks;
Nation shall not lift up sword against nation,
neither shall they learn war any more.
(Isa 2:2–4)

The author envisions a time when nations will find a way to live in peace. Wrongs will be settled through arbitration and negotiation. Jerusalem is envisioned as a place in the world from which justice and righteousness are proclaimed. People will come for insight concerning just and righteous conduct, conduct that is pleasing to Yahweh, the author and Lord of all.

The imagery in the poem suggests that the author knew about international treaties among kings and nations, especially between an emperor and small countries. In the worlds of Assyria and Babylon, small nations were obligated to submit their grievances to the greater sovereign emperor. They were charged not to revolt against the emperor and they were not to declare war on other countries. Disputes were to be submitted to the king. In the Isaiah scroll, the bold affirmation is made that it is only Yahweh who is the true sovereign ruler of nations. Nations of the world, including empires, are all to be as vassals before their sovereign Lord. They are all expected to submit their grievances for review rather than rushing off to wage war against each other. When nations make war, they "play God" and show disregard for the will of the Sovereign One. The author envisions Jerusalem as a place where nations can submit their grievances, creating an environment for reconciliation and for peaceful resolution of disputes.[2]

THE INVITATION OF THE SCROLL—ISAIAH 2:5

O house of Jacob, come, let us walk in the light of the Lord!
(Isa 2:5)

The introductory poem in Isaiah 2:1–4 is also found in Micah 4:1–3. Scholars do not know whether Isaiah borrowed the poem from Micah, whether Micah borrowed the words from Isaiah, or whether both

---

2. See in particular the research on Hittite suzerainty and parity treaties which provided background for "covenant" understandings in the Hebrew Bible. See Jeremiah Unterman, "Covenant," *Harper Collins Bible Dictionary*, Paul J. Achtemeier, ed.,208–209.

prophets drew from a common source. In Isaiah, this invitation seems added for a very specific purpose. All who hear are invited and summoned to the task of working for peace in a war-weary world.

A BITTER MEMORY: A "DAY OF THE LORD" FOR JUDAH—ISAIAH 2:6-22

Now we hear a major theme of this opening section of the Isaiah scroll. Preserved is the memory of Isaiah's announcement of judgment for Judah and Jerusalem! The sad reality was that this bold warning from the prophet was largely ignored by those who heard him and by later generations of people. Kings and their advisers made political and military decisions on the basis of other considerations. They did not heed the words of a lonely prophet. And in retrospect, their decisions proved to be disastrous for the people of their country. Repeatedly, leaders entered into military and political alliances that brought hardships and destruction for their country. It is rather shocking to note that for Isaiah, political independence was not the highest concern. As a resident of a very small country dominated by an empire, he really did not have that choice. Rather, Isaiah was quite pragmatic; his highest concern was for the health and welfare of ordinary people within the community. In particular, he expressed special concern for the welfare of the poor and the oppressed. Their wellbeing was more important than political independence or the political aspirations of particular leaders.

In this powerful "day of Yahweh" poem, we hear words condemning the arrogance and haughtiness of those who have become high and mighty among people.

The text suggests that the wealthy and powerful class within the community had little regard for the poor.

> For you have forsaken the ways of your people,
> O house of Jacob,
> Indeed, they are full of diviners form the east
> and of soothsayers like the Philistines,
> and they clasp hands with foreigners.
> Their land is filled with silver and gold,
> and there is no end to their treasures;
> their land is filled with horses,

and there is no end to their chariots.
Their land is filled with idols;
they bow down to the work of their hands,
to what their own fingers have made.
And so, people are humbled,
and everyone is brought low—
do not forgive them!
Enter into the rock,
and hide in the dust from the terror of the Lord,
and from the glory of his majesty.
The haughty eyes of people shall be brought low,
and the pride of everyone shall be humbled;
and the Lord alone will be exalted on that day.
For the Lord of hosts has a day
against all that is proud and lofty,
against all that is lifted up and high;
against all the cedars of Lebanon,
lofty and lifted up;
and against all the oaks of Bashan;
against all the high mountains,
and against all the lofty hills;
against every high tower,
and against every fortified wall;
against all the ships of Tarshish,
and against all the beautiful craft.
The haughtiness of people shall be humbled,
and the pride of everyone shall be brought low;
and the Lord alone will be exalted on that day.
The idols shall utterly pass away.

Some years ago, residents of southern California experienced the tremors of the massive Northridge earthquake. The ground literally shook! Buildings collapsed and highway bridges fell! In this poem in Isaiah, the imagery suggests that the author may have known the unsettling feelings that come with an earthquake and its aftershocks. While "day of Yahweh" poetry most often relates to war, it is possible that an earthquake memory is preserved here. The event was to be a time that would wake people up. It was a time that was intended to call people back to recognition of what

they actually are: ordinary human beings who are at their best when they
demonstrate humility and compassion toward one another.

> *Enter the caves of the rocks*
> *and the holes of the ground,*
> *from the terror of the Lord,*
> *and from the glory of his majesty,*
> *when he rises to terrify the earth.*
>
> *On that day*
> *people will throw away*
> *to the moles and to the bats*
> *their idols of silver and their idols of gold,*
> *which they have made for themselves to worship,*
> *to enter the caverns of the rocks*
> *and the clefts in the crags,*
> *from the terror of the Lord,*
> *and from the glory of his majesty,*
> *when he rises to terrify the earth.*
> *Turn away from mortals,*
> *who have only breath in their nostrils,*
> *for of what account are they?*
> *(Isa 2:6–22)*

THE SPECIFIC WARNING FOR JERUSALEM AND JUDAH—ISAIAH 3:1-15

The causes for the coming of destruction are spelled out in rather specific
terms. What most offended the prophet was the mood of rebelliousness
and arrogance among the people and their leaders. There was chaos
within the community and there was no one who could or would lead.
By their speech and by their deeds, people showed disrespect for their
creator. In a courtroom scene, the Lord is envisioned setting forth a case
against people who have *"devoured the vineyard"* and who out of greed
have taken from the poor. The Lord will bring a judgment against such
people and at the same time show empathy for the poor of the world.

> *For now the Sovereign,*

the Lord of hosts,
is taking away from Jerusalem and from Judah
support and staff—
all support of bread, and all support of water—
warrior and soldier, judge and prophet,
diviner and elder, captain of fifty and dignitary,
counselor and skillful magician
and expert enchanter.

Because people in positions of power have not been responsible, anarchy and chaos will come for the community. And the sad reality was that others in the community allowed this situation to come upon them by their own neglect and greed.

And I will make boys their princes,
and babes shall rule over them.
The people will be oppressed, everyone by another
and everyone by a neighbor;
the youth will be insolent to the elder,
and the base to the honorable.
Someone will even seize a relative,
a member of the clan, saying
"You have a cloak; you shall be our leader,
and this heap of ruins shall be under your rule."
But the other will cry out on that day, saying,
"I will not be a healer,
in my house there is neither bread nor cloak;
you shall not make me leader of the people."

It is as if the author is anticipating judgment. People can all too easily be blind, deaf and insensitive to the needs of their community. Leadership is so very important and when it is lacking or short-sighted, all in the community suffer.

For Jerusalem has stumbled and Judah has fallen,
because their speech and their deeds are against the Lord,
defying his glorious presence.
The look on their faces bear witness against them;
they proclaim their sin like Sodom,

> *they do not hide it.*
> *Woe to them!*
> *For they have brought evil on themselves.*

Here the poet distinguishes between the innocent and the guilty. And it is interesting to note the worldview of the author who thinks it strange that a time might come when "women would rule over them." Hopefully, we live in a time when people recognize that women can bring energy and talent equal to or in some cases superior to men with the tasks of leadership.

> *Tell the innocent how fortunate they are,*
> *for they shall eat the fruit of their labors.*
> *Woe to the guilty!*
> *How unfortunate they are, for what their hands*
> *have done shall be done to them.*
> *My people—*
> *children are their oppressors, and women rule over them.*

In what is remembered as an anguished plea for understanding, the prophet now asks that people might come to their senses. Note once again we may think of a court setting. Like a lawyer, "the Lord arises to argue his case."

> *O my people, your leaders mislead you,*
> *and confuse the course of your paths.*
> *The Lord rises to argue his case, he stands to judge the peoples.*
> *The Lord enters into judgment with the elders of his people;*
> *It is you who have devoured the vineyard;*
> *the spoil of the poor is in your houses.*
> *What do you mean by crushing my people,*
> *by grinding the face of the poor?*
> *says the Lord God of hosts.*
> *(Isa 3:1–15)*

JUDGMENT FOR ARROGANT WOMEN
—ISAIAH 3. 16–17

The prophet declares that haughty women are particularly offensive in the sight of Yahweh. They are condemned for their apparent self-centeredness and their lack of concern for the poor or the needy within the community.

> *The Lord said:*
> *Because the daughters of Zion are haughty*
> *and walk with outstretched necks,*
> *glancing wantonly with their eyes, mincing along as they go,*
> *tinkling with their feet;*
> *the Lord will afflict with scabs the heads of the daughters of Zion,*
> *and the Lord will lay bare their secret parts.*
> *(Isa 3:16–17)*

THE "IDOLS" OF THE ARROGANT WOMEN
—ISAIAH 3:18–26

In what appears to be an expansion of the previous announcement of judgment, the author now comments on the specific preoccupations of certain women within the community. In striking detail, we hear the prophet condemning their preoccupation with specific items of jewelry and ornamentation. We sense that he believed that such concerns distracted women from even thinking about the poor and the afflicted ones within the community.

> *In that day the Lord will take away the finery*
> *of the anklets, the headbands, and the crescents;*
> *the pendants, the bracelets, and the scarfs;*
> *the headdresses, the armlets, the sashes,*
> *the perfume boxes, and the amulets;*
> *the signet rings and nose rings;*
> *the festal robes, the mantles,*
> *the cloaks, and the handbags;*
> *the garments of gauze, the linen garments, the turbans, and the veils.*
> *Instead of perfume there will be a stench;*

and instead of a sash, a rope;
and instead of well-set hair, baldness;
and instead of a rich robe, a binding of sackcloth;
instead of beauty, shame.
Your men shall fall by the sword
and your warriors in battle.
And her gates shall lament and mourn;
ravaged, she shall sit upon the ground.
(Isa 3:18–26)

SEVEN WOMEN AND ONE MAN—ISAIAH 4:1

This text is intended to shock! The coming disaster would cause such a shortage of men that seven women would seek out a man, asking only to be called by his name—even though they would attempt to provide for themselves! We can wonder how exactly the experience of war and the loss of men in war relate to this text.

Seven women shall take hold of one man
in that day, saying,
"We will eat our own bread and wear our own clothes;
just let us be called by your name;
take away our disgrace."
(Isa 4:1)

SHADE BY DAY FROM HEAT AND SHELTER FROM STORM AND RAIN—ISAIAH 4.2-6

Now comes a pause. A word of encouragement is given. Like the opening words in Isaiah 2:1–4, the poetry now focuses on hope for the future. Those who hear the words of the Isaiah scroll are not to be discouraged by the bitter accounts of past wars and destruction. A new era will present new challenges and opportunities. Jerusalem will again one day be a place of beauty. For all who seek to walk in the light of the Lord, this new word of assurance is given. God will be present as a source of shade and a refuge in troubled times.

On that day the branch of the Lord shall be beautiful and glorious, and
the fruit of the land shall be the pride and glory of the survivors of Israel.
Whoever is left in Zion and remains in Jerusalem
will be called holy, everyone who has been recorded for life in Jerusalem,
once the Lord has washed away the filth of the daughters of Zion
and cleansed the bloodstains of Jerusalem from its midst by a spirit of
judgment and by a spirit of burning.
Then the Lord will create over the whole site of Mount Zion
and over its places of assembly a cloud by day and smoke and the shining
of a flaming fire by night. Indeed over all the glory there will be a canopy.
It will serve as a pavilion, a shade by day from the heat, and a refuge and
a shelter from the storm and rain.

(Isa 4:2–6)

THE PARABLE OF THE VINEYARD—ISAIAH 5:1-7

This is one of the most important poems in the scroll of Isaiah. In a love song, we hear of God's great hopes for his people. The covenant established at Sinai by Moses and the people clearly stands in the background. The poem breaks into two parts: a love song and a statement of the necessary work with the vineyard.

The Love Song—Isaiah 5:1–4

We are to imagine a lush vineyard, nurtured by loving and faithful care. There is a fertile hill with rocks cleared and gathered to provide a protective wall; choice vines are planted, a sturdy watchtower is built and a vat is ready for use when the fruit of the vine becomes ready in the proper season. But something has gone terribly wrong! The grapes are wild and bitter!

Let me sing for my beloved my love-song concerning his vineyard:
My beloved had a vineyard on a very fertile hill.
He dug it and cleared it of stones,
and planted it with choice vines;
he built a watchtower in the midst of it,
and hewed out a wine vat in it;

he expected it to yield grapes, but it yielded wild grapes.
And now, inhabitants of Jerusalem and people of Judah,
judge between me and my vineyard.
What more was there to do for my vineyard
that I have not done in it?
When I expected it to yield grapes, why did it yield wild grapes?
(Isa 5:1–4)

The Necessary Work—Isaiah 5:5–7

The vineyard yielded only wild, bitter grapes. The question is posed: what more was there to do? What more could a good vinekeeper have done for this vineyard? Who could explain why, given proper care, bitter fruit would appear instead of good fruit? We are left to ponder whether there was any other possible solution. But the obvious answer is then shared. The vinekeeper has no choice but to tear up the vines and start over!

In the concluding lines of the poem, the poet explicitly states that the parable is about Yahweh and the people of Judah. They are in covenant relationship and covenant people are expected to bear good fruit in the world. But that has not happened. In the final verse, the Hebrew words of the poem create two word plays. Yahweh looked for justice (*mishpat*); instead he sees violence (*mispach*); he looked for righteousness (*tsedeqah*); instead, he hears a cry of anguish (*tse'aqah*). So, the resulting announcement of judgment comes:

And now I will tell you what I will do to my vineyard.
I will remove its hedge, and it shall be devoured;
I will break down its wall, and it shall be trampled down.
I will make it a waste;
it shall not be pruned or hoed, and it shall be overgrown with briers and thorns;
I will also command the clouds that they rain no rain upon it.
For the vineyard of the Lord of hosts is the house of Israel,
and the people of Judah are his pleasant planting;
he expected justice, but saw bloodshed;
righteousness, but heard a cry!
(Isa 5:5–7)

HUMAN GREED—ISAIAH 5:8-10

Appended to the vineyard poem in Isaiah 5:1-7 are a series of poetic lines that spell out the social injustice that Isaiah saw and understood as "bitter fruit." The evidence of greed reflects the failure of the community in Judah to do justice and to practice righteousness.[3]

> *Ah, you who join house to house,*
> *who add field to field, until there is room for no one but you,*
> *and you are left to live alone in the midst of the land!*
>
> *The Lord of hosts has sworn in my hearing:*
> *Surely many houses shall be desolate,*
> *large and beautiful houses, without inhabitant.*
> *For ten acres of vineyard shall yield but one bath,*
> *and a homer of seed shall yield a mere ephah.*
> *(Isa 5:8–10)*

A WORD ABOUT DRUNKENNESS—ISAIAH 5:11-17

Drunkenness in the Isaiah scroll is a sign of escape or disregard for matters that are really important within the world.[4] We hear echoes here from the closing verses of the "day of the Lord" poem in Isaiah 2:6–22. Disasters come when matters of justice are disregarded. It is in the midst of disasters that the human family learns humility in a most dramatic and often painful way. In the midst of disaster, people quickly learn that even kings and princes are not gods. In this poem, the author declares that the Lord is "exalted by justice" and that God "shows himself holy by righteousness." The author suggests that it is when just and righteous acts are evident, from whatever source, God is exalted and his presence made known in the world.

---

3. The poem is introduced by the Hebrew term "*hoy,*" translated in the NRSV as "Ah." The term also appears in Isaiah 5:18, 20, 21, and 22 as well as in 28:1, 29:1, 15; 30.1; and 33.1. Many translators have suggested that "*hoy*" should be translated as "Woe" because it frequently introduces a word of warning. But in Isaiah 55:1, the term "*hoy*" is translated "Ho" to introduce very hopeful words: "Ho, everyone who thirsts; come to the waters." J.J.M. Roberts suggests that an appropriate translation in English is "Hey," as a term simply used to summon attention. See Roberts, *First Isaiah*, 77.

4. See also Isaiah's words concerning drunkards in chapter 28.

Ah, you who rise early in the morning
in pursuit of strong drink,
who linger in the evening to be inflamed by wine,
whose feasts consist of lyre and harp, tambourine and flute and wine,
but who do not regard the deeds of the Lord,
or see the work of his hands!

their nobles are dying of hunger, and their multitude is parched with thirst.
Therefore Sheol has enlarged its appetite
and opened its mouth beyond measure;
the nobility of Jerusalem and her multitude go down,
her throng and all who exult in her.
People are bowed down, everyone is brought low,
and the eyes of the haughty are humbled.
But the Lord of hosts is exalted by justice,
and the Holy God shows himself holy by righteousness.
Then the lambs shall graze as in their pasture,
fatlings and kids shall feed among the ruins.
(Isa 5.11–17)

A WORD FOR THOSE WISE IN THEIR OWN EYES —ISAIAH 5:18-25

We live in a world where experts are hired to put the best "spin" on particular events that happen in the world. World events seem open to many different interpretations, depending on the viewpoint or the bias of the interpreter. Some contend that negotiations with an enemy are a sign of weakness. Others contend that a willingness to negotiate with an enemy reveals inner confidence, strength, and character. Isaiah brought a very definite perspective to the realm of politics. He saw people calling evil good and calling good evil, calling light darkness and calling darkness light, calling what is sweet bitter and what is bitter, sweet. In the midst of such disarray, the prophet calls upon people to listen to the instruction of the Lord. For the prophet, that is the key for learning to walk in the light of the Lord. We have seen that "walking in the light of the Lord" really means focusing on the well-being of the community.

Ah, you who drag iniquity along with cords of falsehood,
who drag sin along with cart ropes,
who say,
"Let him make haste,
let him speed his work that we may see it;
let the plan of the Holy One of Israel
hasten to fulfillment, that we may know it!"

Now, we hear the summons *"hoy"* (Ah!) three more times to announce words of warning. In the prophet's mind, trouble or disaster will certainly be the result of falsehood, and the distortion of good and evil. Trouble will come for those who pride themselves as drunkards, who take bribes and deprive the poor of their rights.

Ah, you who call evil good and good evil,
who put darkness for light and light for darkness,
who put bitter for sweet and sweet for bitter!
Ah, you who are wise in your own eyes,
and shrewd in your own sight!
Ah, you who are heroes in drinking wine
and valiant at mixing drink,
who acquit the guilty for a bribe,
and deprive the innocent of their rights!

Now two bold declarations follow with the Hebrew expression *laken* "therefore," setting forth the inevitable consequences of such behavior.

Therefore, as the tongue of fire devours the stubble,
and as dry grass sinks down in the flame,
so their roots will become rotten, and their blossom go up like dust;
for they have rejected the instruction of the Lord of hosts,
and have despised the word of the Holy One of Israel.

Therefore, the anger of the Lord was kindled against his people,
and he stretched out his hand against them and struck them;
the mountains quaked, and their corpses were
like refuse in the streets.
For all this his anger has not turned away,

and his hand is stretched out still.

(Isa 5:18–25)

In the final line of the poem, a new theme is set forth that will be repeated in three future poems in chapter 9 and one in chapter 10 (Isa 9:8–12, 9:13–17, 9:18–21, and 10:1–4). "God's hand is stretched out!" is clearly a word of warning! The prophetic warning is that even more times of judgment are coming.

YAHWEH: THE SOVEREIGN POWER OF ALL NATIONS—ISAIAH 5:26-30

Isaiah warned that the judgment that Yahweh would bring against Judah would come through the agency of a foreign nation. Although unaware of that role, the foreign nation would serve as an instrument of judgment on behalf of the Lord. This proved to be true whether the reference was originally to Assyria or to Babylon.

The author draws from imagery relating to sacral warfare also found in other biblical writings. The prophet anticipates a military invasion. In the vision, Yahweh is seen as the commander of an invasion army. Military units from various nations will do his bidding because Yahweh is their creator. He can "whistle" for an army and they will come at his call.

He will raise a signal for a nation far away,
and whistle for a people at the ends of the earth;
Here they come, swiftly, speedily!
None of them is weary, none stumbles,
none slumbers or sleeps, not a loincloth is loose,
not a sandal-thong broken;
their arrows are sharp, all their bows bent,
their horses' hoofs seem like flint,
and their wheels like the whirlwind.
Their roaring is like a lion, like young lions they roar;
they growl and seize their prey,
they carry it off, and no one can rescue.
They will roar over it on that day, like the roaring of the sea.
And if one look to the land—
only darkness and distress;

and the light grows dark with clouds.
(Isa 5:26–30)

THE BITTER MEMORY OF ISAIAH'S COMMISSION—
ISAIAH 6:1–13

This chapter is also very important for understanding the Isaiah scroll. The text preserves the report of the very moving vision that Isaiah ben Amoz experienced. Some have contended that this was his initial "call vision" that led him to become a prophet. Others have contended that this vision account came later in his life, calling or commissioning him for a particular task.[5] In either case, we can consider the memory of Isaiah's call vision in three sections: 6:1–8, 6:9–10, and 6:11–13.

The Prophetic Call Vision—Isaiah 6:1–8

There are parallels here with other reports of biblical call visions: Moses in Exodus 3:1–17, Micaiah ben Imlah in 1 Kings 22:19–22, Jeremiah in Jeremiah 1:4–10, and Ezekiel in Ezekiel 1–3.[6] In each of those texts, a common theme is the response of the prophet: feelings of awe, humility, or inadequacy at the experience of standing in the presence of God. In Isaiah, the prophet's call comes within the context of a heavenly courtroom where Isaiah has been summoned. Regardless of how Isaiah's vision is understood, as an initial call vision or as a later commissioning experience, we sense a dramatic moment when the prophet felt he was being purified and cleansed for a particular task.

> *In the year that King Uzziah died,*
> *I saw the Lord sitting on a throne, high and lofty;*

---

5. For a summary of the debate, see Childs, *Isaiah,* 51–53.

6. Moses does not volunteer; he is given a command at Horeb in the "burning bush" narrative and he is a very reluctant volunteer (see Exod 3–4); Micaiah's vision report is similar to the report in Isaiah 6 but it is a "spirit" that volunteers for duty in response to the divine request, "Who will entice Ahab?" Micaiah simply reports what he has heard in the heavenly court (1 Kgs 22:19–23). Jeremiah does not volunteer but is commissioned "to pluck up and pull down, to destroy and to overthrow, to build and to plant" (Jer 1:10); Ezekiel is literally overpowered by his call vision that concludes with the words: "let those who will hear, hear; and let those who refuse to hear, refuse; for they are a rebellious house" (Ezek 3:27).

and the hem of his robe filled the temple.
Seraphs were in attendance above him:
each had six wings;
with two they covered their faces, and with two they covered their feet,
and with two they flew.
And one called to another and said:
"Holy, holy, holy is the Lord of hosts;
the whole earth is full of his glory."[7]
The pivots on the thresholds shook
at the voices of those who called,
and the house filled with smoke.
And I said:
"Woe is me! I am lost, for I am a man of unclean lips;
and I live among a people of unclean lips;
yet my eyes have seen the King,
the Lord of hosts!"

Then one of the seraphs flew to me,
holding a live coal that had been taken from the altar with a pair of
tongs.
The seraph touched my mouth with it and said:
"Now that this has touched your lips,
your guilt has departed and your sin is blotted out."
Then I heard the voice of the Lord saying,
"Whom shall I send, and who will go for us?"
And I said, "Here am I; send me!"
(Isa 6:1–8)

The prophet is overwhelmed at the sense that he is in the presence of God. Only after he expresses his sense of humility and feelings of unworthiness does one of the seraphim touch his mouth with a live coal and declare to him that his guilt has departed and his sin has been blotted out. Then, after the Lord God speaks, we hear the famous words remembered as the courageous response of the prophet: "Here am I, send me!" The

---

7. The concept of "glory" is very important in ancient Israel to designate the presence of the Lord, especially in conjunction with Israel's temple traditions. See further references in Isaiah 40:5, 60:1, and 66:18.

scandal, however, comes as we learn what Isaiah's calling was. Isaiah was to announce a coming time when there would be no forgiveness!

The Painful Commission for the Prophet—Isaiah 6:9–10

The words here are unambiguous. Yahweh has called Isaiah to do a strange work. People were to hear but not comprehend; they were to see but not understand. By his words, Isaiah was called to dull their minds, stop their ears, and shut their eyes so that they would not see, hear, or comprehend!

> *And he said, "Go and say to this people:*
> *'Keep listening, but do not comprehend;*
> *keep looking, but do not understand.'*
> *Make the mind of this people dull,*
> *and stop their ears, and shut their eyes,*
> *so that they may not look with their eyes and listen with their ears*
> *and comprehend with their minds, and turn and be healed."*
> *(Isa 6:9–10)*

In the rhetoric of the Isaiah scroll, the verbs clustered in verses 9 and 10 contribute in important ways to the larger canonical portrait: שמע *shema* "to hear," בין *bin* "to understand," ראה *raah* "to see," ידע *yadai* "to know," שמן *shamin* "to make fat," כבד *kavad* "to make heavy," שעע *shaah* "to shut," שוב *shuv* "to return, to repent," and רפא *rafa* "to be healed." These nine words will echo throughout the entire Isaiah scroll. In the following verses, Isaiah's call or commission is now made even stronger as a response comes to the question that he poses to the Lord.

How Long, O Lord?—Isaiah 6:11–13

The prophet asks this question of the Lord and receives a frightening answer.

> *Then I said, "How long, O Lord?"*
> *And he said:*
> *"Until cities lie waste without inhabitant, and houses without people,*
> *and the land is utterly desolate "shammah" (שממה);*
> *until the Lord sends everyone far away,*
> *and vast is the emptiness in the midst of the land.*

Even if a tenth part remain in it, it will be burned again,

like a terebinth or an oak whose stump remains standing when it is felled."

The holy seed is its stump!

(Isa 6:11–13)[8]

Only the final line holds out the possibility of some hope. Otherwise, the text declares that there was no hope and that the end would be destruction. Through his words, the prophet was strangely commanded by God to prevent repentance. This is the painful memory of Isaiah's calling that is preserved in this opening section of the scroll of Isaiah.

It is a bitter memory.

How are we to understand this text? From the perspective of his own time, this account of Isaiah's calling makes little or no sense. God did not call prophets to "make people blind and to make their hearts fat." But when we hear this text from the perspective of the post-exilic era, it comes into clear focus. From that later post-exilic setting, we can hear this text as an affirmation both of Isaiah's incredible courage and of the disappointing response that he received from the people to whom he spoke. In retrospect, the report is accurate: the people of the era in which Isaiah lived seemed to respond to his prophetic teaching only with greater blindness, deafness, and hardness of heart.[9]

With the post-exilic community, we can hear the concluding words of the text, *"The holy seed is its stump."* The past has brought destruction and exile. But those who heard this word in the post-exilic "Second Temple" era are being reminded that they are part of the "holy seed." The

---

8. The final half line is missing in the Greek LXX text. Based on the reference to "holy seed" in Ezra 9:2, some scholars have argued that the final line is a "late addition." Such suggestions imply that the final line is somehow of lesser importance. I suggest rather that the reference provides helpful insight for understanding how this text was heard in the post-exilic Second Temple era. See a summary of the debate in Childs, *Isaiah,* 58.

9. See further, "A Bitter Memory: Isaiah's Commission in Isaiah 6. 1–13" in Everson and Kim, *The Desert Will Bloom,* 57–75. The words of Isaiah 1:17–18, so consistent with the memories of the message given by other prophets in ancient Israel, seem to summarize the heart of Isaiah's proclamations: *"Cease to do evil, learn to do good; seek justice, rescue the oppressed, defend the orphan, plead for the widow."* These seem to be the very kinds of words that the prophet spoke but which brought the sad result of blindness, deafness, and hardness of heart among those whom Isaiah was called to speak.

call vision is a reminder to all future generations that when prophetic words go unheeded, frightening consequences will come sooner or later.

RESPONSIBLE LEADERSHIP—ISAIAH 7-11

Some have suggested that the poetry in these four chapters was preserved from a time when Isaiah ben Amoz was still alive. That could very well be. It is clear, however, that Isaiah ben Amoz did not actually write or collect this material himself. Chapter 7 opens with a third person biographical description of the prophet.

A common theme runs through the memories preserved in these chapters. From the opening chapter of the scroll, we have heard that Judah and Jerusalem were afflicted with a strange illness *"from the sole of the foot even to the head"* (Isa 1:6). In the call vision, we have heard the community described in terms of blindness, deafness, and hardness of heart. Now in chapters 7-11, the focus is on the illness that extends "even to the head." This seems clearly to have been a reference to corrupt or inept leadership. Leaders, and especially the king, were understood to have special responsibilities for the wellbeing of their people. When they failed in their tasks, disasters could follow for the entire nation.

Isaiah's Prophetic Sign for Ahaz—Isaiah 7:1-9

Most of what we know about the prophet Isaiah comes from chapters 7 and 8. Some of the references are fascinating. But the focus here is not really on the prophet. The focus is on King Ahaz. In Isaiah 7:1-9, we are allowed a glimpse into the small world that was ancient Judah and its capitol city, Jerusalem. Isaiah could take his son Shear-jashub and actually find and speak directly with King Ahaz, who was on an inspection tour of the water supply system.

We learn of a time when Judah was under threat of an imminent attack by combined military forces from northern Israel and their king, Pekah (referred to in the text as the "son of Remaliah"), and from Syria and their king, Rezin. King Ahaz is depicted doing exactly what a good king should be doing in a time of crisis. He is checking on the adequacy of the water supply for the city. The enemy coalition wants to remove Ahaz as the king in Judah and to install someone known as the "son of Tabeel." Ahaz understood this threat to be something very serious. Two neighboring countries were preparing to invade his country and depose him. So, who could blame him for not taking time to listen to the words of a lonely prophet and his son, even when he may have already gained a certain reputation or respect from some within the city. And we wonder what exactly it was that Isaiah wanted him to do.

> In the days of Ahaz son of Jotham son of Uzziah, king of Judah, King Rezin of Aram (Syria) and King Pekah son of Remaliah of Israel went up to attack Jerusalem, but could not mount an attack against it. When the house of David heard that Aram had allied itself with Ephraim, the heart of Ahaz and the heart of his people shook as the trees of the forest shake before the wind.
>
> Then the Lord said to Isaiah, "Go out to meet Ahaz, you and your son Shear-jashub, at the end of the conduit of the upper pool on the highway to the Fuller's Field, and say to him, Take heed, be quiet, do not fear, and do not let your heart be faint because of these two smoldering stumps of firebrands, because of the fierce anger of Rezin and Aram and the son of Remaliah. Because Aram—with Ephraim and the son of Remaliah—has plotted evil against you, saying, Let us go up against Judah and cut off Jerusalem and conquer it for ourselves and make the son of Tabeel king in it; therefore thus says the Lord God:
>> It shall not stand, and it shall not come to pass.
>> For the head of Aram is Damascus,
>> and the head of Damascus is Rezin.
>> (Within sixty-five years Ephraim will be shattered,
>> no longer a people.)
>> The head of Ephraim is Samaria,
>> and the head of Samaria is the son of Remaliah.
>> If you do not stand firm in faith,
>> you shall not stand at all.
>
> (Isa 7:1–9)

There is much that we simply do not know when we hear only this text. With later generations of people, however, we can ponder the other memories concerning Ahaz that are preserved both in 2 Kings 16 and in 2 Chronicles 28. Those texts provide possible help for understanding what was at stake in the memories preserved in Isaiah 7–8. Ahaz is depicted in both Kings and Chronicles as one who was deeply involved with Canaanite worship practices, including child sacrifice. It is reported that he "*made his son pass through fire, according to the abominable practices of the nations*" and that he participated in fertility rites "*offering sacrifice and making offerings on the high places, on the hills, and under every green tree*" (2 Kgs 16:3–4). The author of 2 Chronicles 28 adds the memory that Ahaz made cast images for the Baals and made offerings in the valley of ben Hinnom, the site of child sacrifice rites. The texts portray Ahaz as one who gave little thought to the sacred traditions affirmed by Israel's prophetic or priestly Torah traditions.

Most interesting, however, are memories that relate to the attack that came from northern Israel and Syria. That military invasion came in the era of 735–734 BCE and was remembered as the time of the "Syro-Ephraimite coalition." The author of 2 Kings 16 reports that in the midst of the crisis, Ahaz sent messengers to the Assyrian emperor, Tiglath-pileser, requesting help from the emperor to maintain his rule. This was a totally appropriate action for him to take as a vassal nation within the realm of the empire. And Tiglath-pileser was probably quite willing to intervene to defend Ahaz against Pekah and Rezin.

But that military intervention did not come without a cost. Ahaz had to strip the silver and gold from the temple to gather a special tribute for the emperor. Even worse, Judah became a country heavily-occupied by Assyrian soldiers. The author of Chronicles 28 goes to great lengths to declare that Ahaz paid a price for his disobedience and that he brought only greater chaos for Judah.

In light of these other texts, it is possible that when Isaiah spoke to Ahaz, he was primarily asking Ahaz not to overreact by calling upon the empire for help. From the perspective of a later time, the decision made by Ahaz brought a new era of greater Assyrian occupation and domination within Judah.

The Hopes for Immanuel "God with Us"
—Isaiah 7:10–17

The second poem in Isaiah 7:10–17 is clearly intended to complement the account related in 7:1–9. We hear of a second encounter between the prophet Isaiah and King Ahaz. Isaiah pleads with Ahaz to demonstrate some trust in Yahweh rather than in the realms of chance held out by the fertility cults or by the promises of the emperor. Ahaz will not listen. He is remembered as one who refused to seek a sign from the Lord or listen to the word of the prophet. In all of the portraits, Ahaz is described as an intensely religious figure; he offers sacrifices, builds altars, uses blood to consecrate holy places, and even offers his children as human sacrifices to demonstrate his religious devotion. But despite his religious activity, he is remembered primarily as one who attempted to manipulate the gods rather than trusting in the promises of the God of Abraham. The issue was not simply a matter of religious faith; Ahaz had plenty. The real issue here was how religious faith becomes evident in a person's life and the actions which follow from faith.

> Again the Lord spoke to Ahaz, saying: Ask a sign of the Lord your God; let it be deep as Sheol or high as heaven. But Ahaz said, I will not ask, and I will not put the Lord to the test. Then Isaiah said: "Hear then, O house of David! Is it too little for you to weary mortals, that you weary my God also? Therefore the Lord himself will give you a sign. Look, the young woman is with child and shall bear a son, and shall name him Immanuel. He shall eat curds and honey by the time he knows how to refuse the evil and choose the good. For before the child knows how to refuse the evil and choose the good, the land before whose two kings you are in dread will be deserted. The Lord will bring on you and on your people and on your ancestral house such days as have not come since the day that Ephraim departed from Judah—the king of Assyria."
>
> (Isa 7:10–17)

The two passages (Isa 7:1–9 and 7:10–17) are linked by the reference to the "two kings before whom you are in dread." Those references seem clearly to refer to Pekah and Rezin, the two neighboring kings who were plotting the attack on Judah. And this means that the child who is to be called by the name "Immanuel" (God with us!) evidently was a child born in that time. The text clearly states that "before the child knows how to refuse the evil and choose the good, the land before whose two kings you are in dread will be deserted." Some have speculated that this child may have been born to Isaiah and his wife, a third son in addition to Shear-jashub (mentioned in Isa 7:1–9) and Maher-shalal-hash-baz (mentioned in Isa 8:1–3). Others have argued that Immanuel was a child born within the royal family, even possibly a son of Ahaz, one who would stand in the direct line to become a future king.

The real point of the poem is that Ahaz refused to ask for a sign. For Isaiah, this was the last straw! Isaiah gave up on Ahaz as a valid "son of David" and indicated that the nation would need to look to the future and wait for a new king, one would have the commitments to justice and righteousness that Yahweh desires.[10]

A Note on the *Almah,* "Young Woman"

The Hebrew word *almah* (young woman) is used in this text and has reference to a younger woman at an age when she is able to bear children. In various Old Testament texts, the *almah* may be married or still single. We are not able to tell more from this text about the identity of this young woman.

In the Septuagint, the Greek translation of the Hebrew Bible completed around 100 BCE, translators used the Greek term *parthenos* ("virgin") to translate the Hebrew word *almah*. The word *parthenos* had a long history and a religious meaning within Greek tradition, especially relating to vestal virgins who served in various Greek temples. These were young women who had not yet had sexual intercourse. Traditions about Mary as a virgin in the New Testament (Matt 1:18–25 and Luke 1:26–56) are drawn from the Greek (Septuagint) translation of Isaiah 7:10–17 where the word *parthenos* appears.

"On that Day!" Four Additions
—Isaiah 7:18–19, 7:20, 7:21–22, and 7:23–25

Four short passages are attached to the longer poems within chapter 7. In 7:10–17, the poem concludes with the warning that Yahweh would not hesitate at a future time to punish his own people. The king of Assyria is specifically named as the instrument by which a "day" of judgment

---

10. The Hebrew word *Immanuel* means "God with us" and is clearly part of the rhetoric connected with Israel's *"messiah"* tradition. According to a Talmudic tradition (Meg. 10b), Isaiah's father, Amoz, was a brother of Amaziah, who was the king in Judah from 800–783 BCE. If correct, this would mean that Isaiah was a member of the royal family. The term *"messiah"* refers to one who was anointed and set apart to be a future king. In 2 Samuel 16, Samuel seeks out David from among the sons of Jesse and anoints him, thus designating him as a future ruler. From the time when kingship was established, religious traditions grew within Israel and Judah suggesting that God would grant special protection and guidance for a new king (see the so-called "Royal Psalms" that include Psalms 2, 72, 89, 101, 110, and 132). Amid frustrations and disappointments with reigning kings, we sense that the term came more and more to be used for thinking about a future ideal king. See further: Gitay, "The Book of Isaiah," 458–64.

will come. Echoing the themes of the "day of Yahweh" poem in Isaiah 2:6–22, we hear that the "day" that is coming that will be unprecedented in the history of this small nation, a time even more shaking than when Ephraim, northern Israel, separated from Judah (922 BCE).

The four short additions are warnings! Each begins with the introductory phrase *bayom hahu* ("On that day"). We can understand that these warnings should have been heeded. In the first warning, the Lord God will whistle and Assyrian troops will answer his call.

> *On that day*
> *The Lord will whistle for the fly*
> *that is at the sources of the streams of Egypt,*
> *and for the bee that is in the land of Assyria.*
> *And they will all come and settle in the steep ravines,*
> *and in the clefts of the rocks, and on all the thornbushes,*
> *and on all the pastures.*
> *(Isa 7:18–19)*

In the next word, the author likens God to a barber, coming with a razor! The Lord God will hire the Assyrian king and use him as a razor to shave the body hair and beards of those in Judah in preparation for their life as slaves in exile.

> *On that day*
> *The Lord will shave with a razor hired beyond the River—*
> *with the king of Assyria—*
> *the head and the hair of the feet,*
> *and it will take off the beard as well.*
> *(Isa 7:20)*

Furthermore, "on that day" the land will be so deserted that there will be sufficient room for the few who will remain with their livestock!

> *On that day*
> *one will keep alive a young cow and two sheep,*
> *and will eat curds because of the abundance of milk that they give;*
> *for everyone that is left in the land shall eat curds and honey.*
> *(Isa 7:21–22)*

And finally, echoing the vineyard parable in Isaiah 5:1–7, "on that day" lush vineyards will turn to briers and thorns. In every way that he could, the prophet was sounding a warning of impending disaster. From a later perspective, people could look back and ponder what actually happened. Jerusalem and Judah suffered through earlier days, but nothing compared to what happened in 598 and 587 BCE. Jerusalem and Judah were left as a deserted land of ruins following the destruction by Babylonian military forces! The prophetic words of Isaiah were deemed to be true because they had come to pass.

> On that day
> every place where there used to be a thousand vines,
> worth a thousand shekels of silver,
> will become briers and thorns.
> With bow and arrows one will go there,
> for all the land will be briers and thorns;
> and as for all the hills that used to be hoed with a hoe,
> you will not go there for fear of briers and thorns;
> but they will become a place where cattle are let loose
> and where sheep tread.
> (Isa 7:23–25)

Memories of the Prophet—Isaiah 8

We can almost sense that an editor placed the four concluding warnings in chapter 7 (Isa 7:18–19, 7: 20, 7: 21–22, and 7: 23–25) where they could complement the two major memories preserved in 7:1–9 and 7:10–17. Now in chapter 8, we hear a reference to Isaiah's own family and sense the way in which the prophet's calling dominated his entire life and that of his family.

Memories of Maher-Shalal-Hash-Baz—Isaiah 8:1–4

> Then the Lord said to me,
> Take a large tablet, and write on it in common characters,
> "Belonging to Maher-shalal-hash-baz."
> and have it attested for me by reliable witnesses,
> the priest Uriah and Zechariah son of Jeberechiah.
> And I went to the prophetess, and she conceived and bore a son.

Then the Lord said to me,
Name him Maher-shalal-hash-baz;
for before the child knows how to call "My father" or "My mother,"
the wealth of Damascus and the spoil of Samaria
will be carried away by the king of Assyria.
(Isa 8:1–4)

The parallels with Isaiah 7:10–17 seem obvious. The prophet is preoccupied with warning the officials and the people of Jerusalem that danger is imminent for the country. Isaiah is convinced by intellect and conscience that the Lord has spoken to him. He first records a name with trusted witnesses: the name is Maher-shalal-hash-baz ("The spoil speeds, the prey hastens!"). He then has a new child with his wife, who is called the prophetess, and he gives this symbolic name to his newborn son as a prophetic sign of impending disaster for the community![11] An enemy will come like prey who will create devastation and leave with the spoils of war.

As in the previous "sign" passage (Isa 7:10–17), Isaiah declares that before this new child is old enough to call his father or mother by name, Syria (named here by its capitol city, Damascus) and northern Israel (Samaria) will be destroyed![12]

An Impending Assyrian Flood—Isaiah 8:5–7

The "former things" have been the subject throughout these early chapters. Isaiah is remembered again for his warning that the Assyrians would come as an "instrument of Yahweh," not for liberation but as judgment on nations of the area, including northern Israel, Syria, and Judah.[13] Again

---

11. Some scholars have contended that Isaiah had three children: Shear-jashub, Immanuel, and Maher-shalal-hash-baz. Each had a symbolic name of warning or promise for the people.

12. When we attempt to understand this passage from the eighth-century era of Isaiah, there are major problems. One could argue that Ahaz was doing exactly what he had to do in a time of national emergency. He called upon his Assyrian overlords to defend his kingdom against invading forces from northern Israel and Syria. Had Ahaz joined northern Israel and Syria in revolt, Judah and the people of Jerusalem would certainly have met with the same retaliation that came for those two countries. In retrospect from the post-exilic era, Ahaz was remembered as bringing a time of greater domination by Assyria.

13. It is interesting to ponder the "water" imagery present in this poem, suggesting the contrast between Yahweh and the gods of Assyria. A contrast is made between the

we hear "day of the Lord" rhetoric: Assyria will come like a "river at flood time" sweeping over the land and leaving devastation in its wake. Like people responding to an earthquake (Isa 2:9–11), people here are envisioned as being overwhelmed as in the midst of a flood when Assyria enters their land.

> The Lord spoke to me again:
> Because this people has refused
> the waters of Shiloah that flow gently,
> and melt in fear before Rezin and the son of Remaliah;
> therefore, the Lord is bringing up against it
> the mighty flood waters of the River,
> the king of Assyria and all his glory;
> it will rise above all its channels
> and overflow its banks;
> it will sweep on into Judah as a flood, and, pouring over,
> it will reach up to the neck;
> and its outspread wings will fill the breadth of your land,
> O Immanuel.
>
> Band together, you peoples, and be dismayed;
> listen, all you far countries;
> gird yourselves and be dismayed;
> gird yourselves and be dismayed!
> Take counsel together, but it shall be brought to naught;
> speak a word, but it will not stand,
> for God is with us ("Immanuel").
> (Isa 8:5–7)

The two references to Immanuel ("God with us!") are puzzling, recalling the words of Isaiah 7:1–9 and 7:10–17. The second reference in the final line may well be a word of hope. The Hebrew conjunctive "but" can just as well be read "and." If so, then this concluding word may be a word of encouragement: "Take counsel, speak a word (and) such things will not

---

quiet and gentle stream of the "waters of Shiloh," the aqueduct which flowed within Jerusalem from the Gihon spring on the east side of the city, and "the mighty flood waters of the River"—meaning the legendary Tigris and Euphrates rivers of Assyria and later Babylon. The latter river systems, while mighty and strong, were not to be preferred.

happen! Speak a word (and) it will not stand, for God is with us (*Immanuel*)! The people were to remember that God wanted to be present among them.

The Lord: A Strong Sanctuary—Isaiah 8:11–15

Prophets in ancient Israel were often viewed as "loners."[14] Elijah and Elisha, Amos and Hosea, Jeremiah and Ezekiel all are remembered as being quite solitary figures. They marched to a different drum than those who were part of the guilds of prophets, groups evidently financed by various kings. In this passage, we sense a loneliness of spirit and the reliance that the prophet placed on Yahweh as the Lord of hosts. In his life, words, and deeds, Isaiah sought to be a voice for Yahweh.

> *For the Lord spoke thus to me*
> *while his hand was strong upon me,*
> *and warned me not to walk in the way of this people, saying:*
> *Do not call conspiracy all that this people calls conspiracy,*
> *and do not fear what it fears, or be in dread.*
> *But the Lord of hosts,*
> *him you shall regard as holy;*
> *let him be your fear, and let him be your dread.*
> *He will become a sanctuary, a stone one strikes against;*
> *for both houses of Israel he will become a rock one stumbles over—*
> *a trap and a snare for the inhabitants of Jerusalem.*
> *And many among them shall stumble;*
> *they shall fall and be broken;*
> *they shall be snared and taken.*
> *(Isa 8:11–15)*

14. One prominent reference to the "court prophets" is found in 1 Kings 22:6 (where four hundred give their assent to a decision of Jehoshaphat to go to war); the king is hesitant and still wants to hear a word from the "loner" prophet who is Micaiah ben Imlah. See the fascinating account in 1 Kings 22:1–28, where most of the characteristics of the so-called "classical" (writing) prophets are already present.

Frustration: Bind Up the Testimony—Isaiah 8:16–22

This is a very telling moment and memory within the Isaiah scroll. We learn here that Isaiah clearly had a group of disciples or associates around him. We learn that at a particular time, certain of Isaiah's words were committed to writing! We cannot be sure but it would seem likely that the words that were sealed were announcements of impending judgment for the nation. And we sense here that Isaiah felt extreme frustration because his counsel went unheeded by officials and the king.

The text suggests that a scroll was completed and secured with a wax seal as a witness for a future time or generation. The prophet tells his followers that they will simply need to "wait on the Lord" who is evidently "hiding his face" from the house of Jacob.

> Bind up the testimony, seal the teaching among my disciples.
> I will wait for the Lord,
> who is hiding his face from the house of Jacob,
> and I will hope in him.
> See, I and the children whom the Lord has given me
> are signs and portents in Israel from the Lord of hosts,
> who dwells on Mount Zion.
>
> Now if people say to you, "Consult the ghosts
> and the familiar spirits that chirp and mutter;
> should not a people consult their gods,
> the dead on behalf of the living, for teaching and for instruction?"
> surely, those who speak like this will have no dawn!"
> They will pass through the land,
> greatly distressed and hungry;
> when they are hungry, they will be enraged
> and will curse their king and their gods.
> They will turn their faces upward, or they will look to the earth,
> but will see only distress and darkness, the gloom of anguish;
> and they will be thrust into thick darkness.
> (Isa 8:16–22)

Isaiah is remembered as being equally frustrated by people who sought guidance by consulting the dead as he was by reckless rulers. For Isaiah,

Yahweh's words about integrity and justice were more reliable counsel than the examination of entrails of animals, ghosts or spirits of the dead.

Hopes for an Ideal Future King—Isaiah 9:1–7

It is important to remember that in ancient Israel, monarchy was the only form of effective government that people knew. When people recalled the earlier era of judges, it was with very mixed feelings. That was an era of tribal rivalries and close calls with potential chaos. Kingship had been adopted in the time of Saul because centralized leadership seemed to provide far greater security for the tribes as they experienced military threats and assaults from neighboring countries. Over the years there were some good and many poor rulers. Prophets had to summon great courage when they dared to speak words of criticism about reigning kings. But that is exactly what Isaiah did. Throughout chapters 7–8, we have heard the frustrations that Isaiah felt about King Ahaz.

Now, in chapter 9, the prophet dreams of the future. Isaiah envisions a leader of character, one who will have convictions born of faith and commitments to justice and righteousness. Isaiah's hopeful spirit seems focused here around the birth of a child. This is lyric poetry at its finest. At the birth of a child, people are given the opportunity to hope that good things may come in a future generation.

> *But there will be no gloom for those who were in anguish.*
> *In the former time he brought into contempt*
> *the land of Zebulun and the land of Naphtali,*
> *but in the latter time he will make glorious the way of the sea,*
> *the land beyond the Jordan, Galilee of the nations.*
>
> *The people who walked in darkness have seen a great light;*
> *those who lived in a land of deep darkness—*
> *on them light has shined.*
> *You have multiplied the nation, you have increased its joy;*
> *they rejoice before you as with joy at the harvest,*
> *as people exult when dividing plunder.*
>
> *For the yoke of their burden, and the bar across their shoulders,*
> *the rod of their oppressor,*
> *you have broken as on the day of Midian.*

For all the boots of the trampling warriors
and all the garments rolled in blood
shall be burned as fuel for the fire.

For a child has been born for us, a son given to us;
authority rests upon his shoulders;
and he is named Wonderful Counselor,
Mighty God, Everlasting Father, Prince of Peace.
His authority shall grow continually, and there shall be endless peace
for the throne of David and his kingdom.
He will establish and uphold it with justice and with righteousness
from this time onward and for evermore.
The zeal of the Lord of hosts will do this.
(Isa 9:1–7)

One image in the poem is frightening. The prophet draws from imagery of war in his own era and alludes to the joy that victorious people experienced when dividing the spoils of war. We wonder if the joyous celebration of captured booty also involved the common practice of taking foreign slaves and concubines.

The poem also echoes themes from the vision of peace set out in 2:2–4. The dream is that one day garments of war might be burned and destroyed, that a time might come when wars would cease and the need for weapons of war might end.

Particularly moving is the array of titles envisioned for the new ideal king:

Wonderful Counselor, Mighty God, Everlasting Father, Prince of Peace! In the tapestry of poetry which makes up the Isaiah scroll, the memory of an ideal king is preserved, even when there was no longer any king in the post-exilic era. In the latter chapters of the scroll, we will hear rhetoric concerning "servants of the Lord." In a certain sense, we see here already how the scroll preserves a dynamic between the "one" who is a role model for others and the "many" who are called to serve. In their own ways, the "king" and the "servants of the Lord" share in the responsibility for the welfare of the community, drawing on the instruction and the promises of God. The vision of an ideal future king is intended to inspire joy and confidence about the future.[15]

Yahweh's Hand Stretched Out
—Isaiah 9:8–12, 9: 13–17, 9: 18–21; 10:1–4

Returning to the theme of judgment, four poems appear to be appended to the vision of a coming ideal king. Each concludes with the warning that "Yahweh's hand is stretched out." With each poem, we sense that this phrase is intended to convey a sense of warning.

The Bricks Are Fallen—Isaiah 9:8–12

In the first poem, the fall of the northern kingdom in 721 BCE is remembered as a lesson for people in southern Judah; the prophet wonders whether leaders in Judah have learned anything from the fall of Ephraim, another name for the northern kingdom of Israel.

> The Lord sent a word against Jacob, and it fell on Israel;
> and all the people knew it—
> Ephraim and the inhabitants of Samaria—
> but in pride and arrogance of heart they said:
> "The bricks are fallen, but we will build with dressed stones;
> the sycamores have been cut down, but we will put cedars in their place."
> So the Lord raised adversaries against them,
> and stirred up their enemies,
> the Arameans on the east and the Philistines on the west,

---

15. We use the term "typology" to speak of an established tradition which is used again by people in a later time in history. In our contemporary culture, we have traditions involving certain expectations and hopes for an "ideal type" for a U.S. president, supreme court judge or other officials. When the authors of the New Testament gospels, Matthew, Mark, Luke, and John, as well as the apostle Paul and other writers use imagery from Israel's messiah and servant traditions to describe and interpret the work of Jesus, they are not proclaiming literal futuristic fulfillment of ancient prophecies; rather they are declaring that Jesus is the embodiment of all that the ancient tradition anticipated. In this sense, they can declare that Jesus "fulfills the prophecy" of Isaiah. We will see that the same pattern of an established "typology" or pattern of behavior is evident with the servant tradition later in the scroll. The evangelist Mark seems most clearly to combine "messiah" and "servant" traditions when describing and interpreting the life and work of Jesus.

and they devoured Israel with open mouth.
For all this his anger has not turned away;
his hand is stretched out still.
(Isa 9:8–12)

Left in Confusion—Isaiah 9:13–17

The second poem focuses on the corruption within northern Israel, involving elders, dignitaries, and false prophets. The poetry focuses on the responsibility of leaders within a society. As a result of poor leadership, an entire community became corrupt. And when leaders failed in their responsibilities, the unthinkable happened: God did not even have pity on their young people, orphans, or widows:

> *The people did not turn to him who struck them,*
> *or seek the Lord of hosts.*
> *So the Lord cut off from Israel head and tail,*
> *palm branch and reed in one day—*
> *elders and dignitaries are the head,*
> *and prophets who teach lies are the tail;*
> *for those who led this people led them astray,*
> *and those who were led by them were left in confusion.*
>
> *That is why the Lord did not have pity on their young people,*
> *or compassion on their orphans and widows;*
> *for everyone was godless and an evildoer,*
> *and every mouth spoke folly.*
> *For all this his anger has not turned away;*
> *his hand is stretched out still.*
> *(Isa 9:13–17)*

Wickedness Burned Like a Fire—Isaiah 9:18–21

In a third poem, the poet speaks eloquently of tribal warfare that caused dissension and wickedness "burning like a fire" throughout the northern territories as Manasseh and Ephraim devoured each other and as northern Israel turned on Judah.

For wickedness burned like a fire, consuming briers and thorns;
it kindled the thickets of the forest,
and they swirled upward in a column of smoke.
Through the wrath of the Lord of hosts
the land was burned,
and the people became like fuel for the fire;
no one spared another.
They gorged on the right, but still were hungry,
and they devoured on the left, but were not satisfied;
they devoured the flesh of their own kindred;
Manasseh devoured Ephraim, and Ephraim Manasseh,
and together they were against Judah.
For all of this his anger has not turned away;
his hand is stretched out still!
(Isa 9:18–21)

The Needy, the Poor, Widows, and the Orphans—Isaiah 10:1–4

Chapter 10 of Isaiah opens with a poem that addresses the very heart of Isaiah's vision. One could argue that this is an indictment primarily directed against judges or others who have responsibility for laws in a land: decrees and statutes, welfare laws, social security matters, and housing provisions. Here we see how Isaiah's vision focuses on the well-being of the poor, the needy, and widows. The author is concerned for those who do not have access to adequate resources to sustain their lives, and for those who are not provided for by adults within a community. Yahweh knows their situation! Yahweh sees the patterns of greed and selfish conduct in the world. Those patterns become most visible when viewed from the perspective of needy people. To ignore their plight is to offend Yahweh. To listen and to do all that is possible to assure that orphans, widows, and the needy of the world are treated fairly is the calling of servants of the Lord. As in the previous three texts, this poem also ends with the warning: "his hand is stretched out still!"

Ah, you who make iniquitous decrees,
who write oppressive statutes,
to turn aside the needy from justice
and to rob the poor of my people of their right,

that widows may be your spoil,
and that you may make the orphans your prey!
What will you do on the day of punishment,
in the calamity that will come from far away?
To whom will you flee for help, and where will you leave your wealth,
so as not to crouch among the prisoners or fall among the slain?
For all of this his anger has not turned away;
his hand is stretched out still!
(Isa 10:1–4)

Assyria, the Arrogant Empire!—Isaiah 10:5–11

Now we hear the definitive portrait of how the prophet understood world empires. The prophet is thinking first and foremost about the situation of his own small country, Judah. Because he saw short-sighted and arrogant conduct within the leadership of his own country, he is certain that retaliation or punishment would come from the empire. He declares that what is happening in the world is not an accident. It is not just Assyria; it is Yahweh who is bringing judgment against his own people. Assyria will be the instrument used to carry out that judgment.

At the same time, the prophet is well aware of the excessive violence so typical of military forces. Here the poet depicts the "arrogance of power" that seems to be a hallmark of empires. We hear a voice from Assyria boasting about cities that have been destroyed, military victories that should be a warning for Jerusalem. Like Assyria, empires through the centuries seem again and again to believe that somehow, they are God's gift to the world and that "might makes right."

Ah, Assyria, the rod of my anger—
the club in their hands is my fury!
Against a godless nation I send him,
and against the people of my wrath, I command him,
to take spoil and seize plunder,
and to tread them down like the mire of the streets.

But this is not what he intends, nor does he have this in mind;
but it is in his heart to destroy, and to cut off nations not a few.

For he says:
'Are not my commanders all kings?
Is not Calno like Carchemish?
Is not Hamath like Arpad?
Is not Samaria like Damascus?
As my hand has reached to the kingdoms of the idols
whose images were greater than those of Jerusalem and Samaria,
shall I not do to Jerusalem and her idols
what I have done to Samaria and her images?
(Isa 10:5–11)

Judgment for the Arrogant Empire—Isaiah 10:12–19

Isaiah now expands on his theological interpretation of Yahweh and the empires. Assyria may be used as an instrument to accomplish the work of Yahweh in bringing punishment and judgment on Judah. But that does not mean that Assyria understands the world in that way.

The Arrogance of Power—Isaiah 10:12–14

Secure in her military strength, Assyria feels "like a bull;" she is able to bring down nations. Her arrogance is depicted as "one who gathers eggs" from nests with no one able to object as she "gathers to herself the wealth of peoples." For her own brutality and arrogance, Assyria will bring judgment upon herself in due course.

When the Lord has finished all his work on Mount Zion and on
Jerusalem,
he will punish the arrogant boasting of the king of Assyria and his
haughty pride.
For he says:
"By the strength of my hand I have done it, and by my wisdom,
for I have understanding;
I have removed the boundaries of peoples, and have plundered their
treasures;
like a bull I have brought down those who sat on thrones.
My hand has found, like a nest, the wealth of the peoples;

and as one gathers eggs that have been forsaken,
so I have gathered all the earth;
and there was none that moved a wing, or opened its mouth,
or chirped."
(Isa 10:12–14)

Two Rhetorical Questions—Isaiah 10:15–19

Two rhetorical questions focus the issue at the end of the poem. When a woodsman goes to the forest to cut down a tree, should the ax be in charge or the woodsman? Or when a carpenter uses his saw to create a building, should the saw be in charge instead of the carpenter? Isaiah understands that empires and their rulers can be used as instruments for good or for evil in the hand of their creator. They have freedom and a responsibility to decide how they will use power. But rulers are expected to use power wisely in keeping with the will of their creator. However they use their power, they still remain instruments of the Lord and will one day be held accountable for their actions.

Shall the ax vaunt itself over the one who wields it,
or the saw magnify itself against the one who handles it?
As if a rod should raise the one who lifts it up,
or as if a staff should lift the one who is not wood!

Therefore, the Sovereign, the Lord of hosts,
will send wasting sickness among his stout warriors,
and under his glory a burning will be kindled,
like the burning of fire.

The light of Israel will become a fire, and his Holy One a flame;
and it will burn and devour his thorns and briers in one day.
The glory of his forest and his fruitful land
the Lord will destroy, both soul and body,
and it will be as when an invalid wastes away.
The remnant of the trees of his forest will be so few
that a child can write them down.
(Isa 10:15–19)

Assurance for the Faithful Remnant—Isaiah 10:20–23

This poem may also date from the era of Isaiah. But within the scope of the completed scroll, the message takes on an enduring meaning for people of faith in every age. Servants of the Lord are called upon to reflect carefully about the source of their trust and hope in life. The promises of the Holy One of Israel are more reliable than the promises of kings or empires.

> *On that day*
> *the remnant of Israel and the survivors of the house of Jacob*
> *will no more lean on the one who struck them,*
> *but will lean on the Lord,*
> *the Holy One of Israel, in truth.*
> *A remnant will return, the remnant of Jacob,*
> *to the mighty God.*
>
> *For though your people Israel were like the sand on the sea,*
> *only a remnant of them will return.*
> *Destruction is decreed, overflowing with righteousness.*
> *For the Lord God of hosts will make a full end,*
> *as decreed, in all the earth.*
> *(Isa 10:20–23)*

In retrospect, the post-exilic community knew that many crises had come for people both in northern Israel and in Judah. Northern Israel disappeared as a nation. A full end also came for Judah with the fall of Jerusalem to the Babylonians. Even when the "destruction from God" (*shod meshaddai*) had been decreed and had come, the faithful remnant was called upon to continue to trust in the Lord and to learn from past history.

Do not fear the Empire—Isaiah 10:24–27

The issue in this poem is timeless. The focus is not on Assyria. Nor is it on Babylon or Egypt. The focus is on faith. Even in the era of Persia, people of faith were to be cautious and avoid bending too quickly to the whims of an empire. Sooner or later, the arrogant conduct of nations would bring its own consequences.

Faith brings a different perspective. Faithful people are called to live in such a manner that the entire human family may prosper. Justice and fairness become evident in actions that assist those in greatest economic and social need within a society.

> *Therefore thus says the Lord God of hosts:*
> *O my people, who live in Zion,*
> *do not be afraid of the Assyrians*
> *when they beat you with a rod*
> *and lift up their staff against you*
> *as the Egyptians did.*
> *For in a very little while*
> *my indignation will come to an end,*
> *and my anger will be directed to their destruction.*
>
> *The Lord of hosts will wield a whip against them,*
> *as when he struck Midian at the rock of Oreb;*
> *his staff will be over the sea,*
> *and he will lift it, as he did in Egypt.*
> *On that day his burden will be removed from your shoulder,*
> *and his yoke will be destroyed from your neck.*
> *(Isa 10:24–27)*

The Path of An Enemy Invasion Route—Isaiah 10:28–32

This is one of the most striking poems in the scroll of Isaiah. The imagery is crisp and specific. The route from the northern border heading south through the hill country of Samaria was evidently well-known from earlier eras when enemy military forces had invaded Judah from the north. Specific towns are mentioned, including Michmash, where the baggage train of war wagons, so essential to any invading army, had halted in preparation for an attack. The account is intended to engender terror at the prospect of an imminent assault from an enemy force moving within their land.

> *He has gone up from Rimnon, he has come to Aiath;*
> *he has passed through Migron,*
> *at Michmash he stores his baggage;*

they have crossed over the pass,
at Geba they lodge for the night:
Ramah trembles, Gibeah of Saul has fled.

Cry aloud, O daughter Gallim! Listen, O Laishah!
Answer her, O Anathoth! Madmenah is in flight,
the inhabitants of Gebim flee for safety.
This very day he will halt at Nob
he will shake his fist at the mount of daughter Zion,
the hill of Jerusalem.
(Isa 10:28–32)

The most frightening aspect of this poem is to recall that Yahweh, in his role as the divine warrior, is understood to be leading the assault on Jerusalem. Isaiah believed that leaders were bringing catastrophe on their own country. Yahweh was bringing judgment on his own people for their poor judgment and lack of wisdom.

The Power of the Sovereign Lord of History—Isaiah 10:33–34

The poem echoes the themes set out in Isaiah 2:6–22. Like great trees that are cut down, so shall the "high and lofty" ones be brought low! Arrogance will bring its own bitter fruit. Yahweh intends that human people, wherever they live and work, should seek to be part of the human family, demonstrating humility and compassion in their daily activity. Those involved with international affairs have special responsibilities in this regard.

Look, the Sovereign, the Lord of hosts,
will lop the boughs with terrifying power;
the tallest trees will be cut down,
and the lofty will be brought low.
He will hack down the thickets of the forest with an ax,
and Lebanon with its majestic trees will fall.
(Isa 10:33–34)

A Vision of Ideal Leadership—Isaiah 11:1–5

The poem speaks of the qualities that an ideal leader should possess. We are invited to think about all those who hold positions of responsible leadership: presidents of countries, senators, governors, mayors, as well as local leaders of schools, churches, synagogues, mosques, or other community groups. More than any other passage in the Isaiah scroll, this poem conveys a portrait of how ideal leadership was envisioned. The virtues of wisdom, good counsel, strength, and knowledge are coupled here with a commitment to listening. A sense of fairness and discernment of issues is implied. Most of all, the ideal leader is to have a sense of personal integrity and the ability to identify with those most in need within a community. The hope expressed here was for a future king of Judah. But the passage is also a classic vision of good leadership in any age within any form of government.

> *A shoot shall come out from the stump of Jesse,*
> *and a branch shall grow out of his roots.*
> *The spirit of the Lord shall rest on him,*
> *the spirit of wisdom and understanding,*
> *the spirit of counsel and might,*
> *the spirit of knowledge and the fear of the Lord.*
> *His delight shall be in the fear of the Lord.*
> *He shall not judge by what his eyes see,*
> *or decide by what his ears hear;*
> *but with righteousness he shall judge the poor,*
> *and decide with equity for the meek of the earth;*
> *he shall strike the earth with the rod of his mouth,*
> *and with the breath of his lips he shall kill the wicked.*
>
> *Righteousness shall be the belt around his waist,*
> *and faithfulness the belt around his loins.*
> *(Isa 11:1–5)*

Peace extending to the Animal World—Isaiah 11:6–9

Good leadership has the possibility of bringing peace for a community in such a way that it can extend even to nature and to the animal world, even overcoming the strife evident among animals. The poet envisions a future time when a small child might be able to play over the dwelling place of a poisonous snake without fear. Such is the dream envisioned by the quest for the "knowledge of the Lord!"

> *The wolf shall live with the lamb,*
> *the leopard shall lie down with the kid,*
> *the calf and the lion and the fatling together,*
> *and a little child shall lead them.*
> *The cow and the bear shall graze,*
> *their young shall lie down together;*
> *and the lion shall eat straw like the ox.*
> *The nursing child shall play over the hole of the asp,*
> *and the weaned child shall put its hand on the adder's den.*
> *They will not hurt or destroy on all of my holy mountain;*
> *for the earth will be full of the knowledge of the Lord*
> *as the waters cover the sea.*
> *(Isa 11:6–9)*

Again, Concern for the Remnant Community—Isaiah 11:10–16

The chapter concludes with a reminder of the exodus from Egypt. It was Yahweh who provided strength for Moses and strength for the people to leave Egypt in an earlier era of history. That memory can inspire new courage. Yahweh is still the source of power behind the events of world history. In this poetry, there is, however, almost a sense of powerlessness concerning the future. Envisioned is an era when things will be reversed: Yahweh will lead a restored nation and a new David figure (the "root of Jesse") will bring restoration to the land. Neighboring countries will be conquered as in the old times of the conquest. It is interesting to note the reference to "the four corners of the world," reflecting the world view of this time in history, stretching from southern Egypt and Ethiopia, to Elam and Assyria on the east, to Hamath in the northern region of Syria, and to the northwestern islands of Phoenician islands in the north. As in Isaiah 2:1–4, peace among peoples throughout the known world is envisioned with the restoration of Zion and a king from the Davidic family.

The author envisions that in that future time, enmity between northern
Israel (Ephraim) and southern Judah may be overcome as well.[16]

> On that day, the root of Jesse shall stand as a signal to the peoples; the
> nations shall inquire of him, and his dwelling shall be glorious.
> On that day, the Lord will extend his hand yet a second time
> to recover the remnant that is left of his people,
> from Assyria, from Egypt, from Pathos, from Ethiopia,
> from Elam, from Shinar, from Hamath, and from the coastlands of the sea.
> He will raise a signal for the nations,
> and will assemble the outcasts of Israel,
> and gather the dispersed of Judah
> from the four corners of the earth.
> The jealousy of Ephraim shall depart,
> the hostility of Judah shall be cut off;
> Ephraim shall not be jealous of Judah,
> and Judah shall not be hostile toward Ephraim.
> But they shall swoop down on the backs of the Philistines in the west,
> together they shall plunder the people of the east.
>
> They shall put forth their hand against Edom and Moab,
> and the Ammonites shall obey them.
> And the Lord will utterly destroy the tongue of the sea of Egypt;
> and will wave his hand over the River with his scorching wind;
> and will split it into seven channels,
> and make a way to cross on foot;
> so there shall be a highway from Assyria
> for the remnant that is left of his people,
> as there was for Israel when they came up
> from the land of Egypt.
> (Isa 11:10–16)

16. Viewed in isolation, the poetry in Isaiah 11:11–16 seems harsh and nationalistic. It is important to remember that throughout the early chapters of Isaiah, future
peace is envisioned as that attained by a strong king, who can maintain order and
well being for his people through military strength. The New Testament writings will
challenge this basic assumption about power, as will the poetry about the "servant of
the Lord" (see chapters 5–6).

TWO CONCLUDING DOXOLOGIES
—ISAIAH 12:1-2 AND 3-6

The opening section of Isaiah (chapters 2–12) began with a preface that envisioned future peace. Now with two short hymns of praise, the first section of the Isaiah scroll concludes. Memories of Isaiah's "bitter words of judgment" have been preserved. And those words of judgment have come to pass in history. Judah and Jerusalem were left devastated by destruction, but a remnant community has survived. Along with the bitter memories, words of hope and encouragement have also been preserved. Isaiah is remembered both for his words of judgment and for his words of encouragement and hope. People of faith are to learn from history, to celebrate life, and to find energy for new tasks in life that are upright and just. That is what a life of hope is all about. The bitter memories preserved here are not to cause despair; they are preserved to encourage serious reflection on the past and the discernment of wisdom for life in a new era.

God is My Salvation—Isaiah 12:1-2

> *You will say in that day:*
> *I will give thanks to you, O Lord,*
> *for though you were angry with me,*
> *your anger turned away, and you comforted me.*
> *Surely God is my salvation;*
> *I will trust, and will not be afraid,*
> *for the Lord God is my strength and my might;*
> *he has become my salvation.*
> *(Isa 12:1–2)*

The Wells of Salvation—Isaiah 12:3-6

> *With joy you will draw water from the wells of salvation.*
> *And you will say in that day:*
> *Give thanks to the Lord, call on his name;*
> *make known his deeds among the nations;*
> *proclaim that his name is exalted.*

Sing praises to the Lord, for he has done gloriously;
let this be known in all the earth.
Shout aloud and sing for joy, O royal Zion,
for great in your midst is the Holy One of Israel.
(Isa 12:3–6)

3.

Bitter Memories of Judah among the Nations

Isaiah 13–35

INTRODUCTION

THE POETRY IN THE second large section of the scroll broadens the perspective of Isaiah's vision, strengthening the claim that Yahweh is Lord not just over Israel and Judah but also over all nations. The section begins with words of judgment both for Babylon and Assyria (Isa 13–14). Throughout the opening group of poems (Isa 13–23), words of judgment recall times of warfare that have come for various nations. But this is not simply a collection of oracles addressed to foreign nations; in Isaiah 22, a memory of warfare within Judah is also preserved. The poetry in Isaiah 24–27 has a distinctive character; there the poems have a particular sense of unity and seem to be placed at the center of this second section of the scroll to highlight the life and death struggles that are so central in Isaiah's vision.[1] Then, chapters 28–33 recall struggles that Isaiah endured, especially during a time when Egypt was involved with Judah in political

---

1. Often in commentaries, Isaiah 24–27 are referred to as a "little apocalypse." There is debate about what exactly that term means; here it is enough to say that in retrospect, the poetry deals with memories of death and suffering that come with the horrors of war.

intrigue. Isaiah 34–35 conclude the second section with a moving poem that recalls the pain of war and then announces rescue and new life for faithful people.

NATIONS UNDER JUDGMENT—ISAIAH 13-23

The Superscription—Isaiah 13:1

> *The oracle concerning Babylon that Isaiah ben Amoz saw.*
>
> *(Isa 13:1)*

All evidence suggests that Isaiah was active as a prophet in Judah during the years between 742–687 BCE. During that time, Assyria was the dominant world empire. Assyria remained in power until the destruction of its capitol city, Nineveh, by Babylon in the year 612 BCE. This happened more than seventy years after the death of Isaiah. The superscription in Isaiah 13:1 confirms that Isaiah's vision continued to have meaning and power long after the death of the prophet. People understood that Isaiah's vision had implications for Babylon as well as for Assyria. Isaiah 10 proclaimed a word for arrogant Assyria. Now a similar word announcing judgment comes for the arrogant empire, Babylon.

As world empires go, Babylon did not dominate the world for a very long period of time, only for 73 years from 612 to 539 BCE. After the death of Nebuchadnezzar in 562 BCE, the empire declined in power quite rapidly until it fell to Cyrus and Persia in 539 BCE.

An Army Assembling for Battle—Isaiah 13:2-9

The poetry in Isaiah 13–14 provides a perspective for understanding the entire second section of the scroll.[2] In chapter 13 we hear military

---

2. Nine poems in chapters 13–23 are introduced with the Hebrew word or formula *massa* ("oracle" or "burden," see Isa 13:1; 15:1; 17:1; 19:1; 21:1; 21:11; 21:13; 22:1; 23:1). Scholars have not agreed on the basic meaning of this term because it is used in different ways in different texts. Brevard Childs writes: "In its present literary setting, the oracles are directed primarily to Israel and designed to explain events in the world of affairs as an act of Yahweh. Thus, as has been frequently pointed out, these oracles are concerning the nations and not necessarily against them." See Childs, *Isaiah*, 113–14.

commands typical of "day of Yahweh" poetry.[3] The poet suggests the sounds of an army gathering on a hill in a muster for battle! The mountains ring with the tumult of a mighty military force. But this is no ordinary army. As we learn the identity of the divine warrior who will lead this force in battle, we know from the outset that the outcome is already certain. Yahweh, ruler of the heavenly hosts (Yahweh Sabaoth!), has summoned forces from a distant land and from the end of the heavens. No one can withstand such an array of power!

> On a bare hill raise a signal, cry aloud to them;
> wave the hand for them to enter the gates of the nobles.
> I myself have commanded my consecrated ones,
> have summoned my warriors, my proudly exulting ones,
> to execute my anger.
>
> Listen, a tumult on the mountains as of a great multitude!
> Listen, an uproar of kingdoms, of nations gathering together!
> The Lord of hosts is mustering an army for battle.
> They come from a distant land, from the end of the heavens,
> the Lord and the weapons of his indignation,
> to destroy the whole earth.
> Wail, for the day of the Lord is near;
> it will come like destruction from the Almighty ("shod meShaddai")!
>
> Therefore, all hands will be feeble,
> and every human heart will melt,
> and they will be dismayed.
> Pangs and agony will seize them;
> they will be in anguish like a woman in labor.
> They will look aghast at one another;
> their faces will be aflame.
> See, the day of the Lord comes,
> cruel, with wrath and fierce anger,
> to make the earth a desolation,
> and to destroy its sinners from it.
> (Isa 13:2–9)

3. See the discussion of "day of Yahweh" in chapter 2 above and in Isa 22, 34, 61, and 63.

Celestial Dimensions of a "Day of the Lord" Event
—Isaiah 13:10–16

The poet draws from reports of the horrors of war. He suggests that those horrors extend even into heavenly places. He knows that in war, human beings are capable of committing terrible atrocities. Innocent people, including women and children, are slaughtered without mercy. Infants are killed, houses plundered, young and old women are raped by wanton foot-soldiers. Memories of war clearly haunt the author.

The poet declares that the event is a "day of Yahweh." There is no word of any grace or mercy here. Instead, the vision is of total destruction.

> For the stars of the heavens and their constellations
> will not give their light;
> the sun will be dark at its rising,
> and the moon will not shed its light.
> I will punish the world for its evil,
> and the wicked for their iniquity;
> I will put an end to the pride of the arrogant,
> and lay low the insolence of tyrants.
>
> I will make mortals more rare than fine gold,
> and humans than the gold of Ophir.
> Therefore I will make the heavens tremble,
> and the earth will be shaken out of its place,
> at the wrath of the Lord of hosts
> in the day of his fierce anger.
>
> Like a hunted gazelle,
> or like sheep with no one to gather them,
> all will turn to their own people,
> and all will flee to their own lands.
> Whoever is found will be thrust through,
> and whoever is caught will fall by the sword.
> Their infants will be dashed to pieces
> before their eyes;
> their houses will be plundered,

and their wives ravished.

(Isa 13:10–16)

This "Day of Yahweh" is for Babylon—Isaiah 13:17–19

Some have suggested that the poetry in Isaiah 13:2–9 and 13:10–16 may have originally been a poem directed against Assyria. In the description, there is no specific reference to any particular nation. But now in 13:17–19, a clarification is provided. The poem is to be heard as a word directed against Babylon.

Jerusalem and Judah had their "day of Yahweh" in 587 BCE at the hands of Babylon. Memories of destruction and exile over the years from 587–539 BCE were bitter! But now, it is "Babylon, the glory of kingdoms, the splendor of the Chaldeans," that is to be like Sodom and Gomorrah.

> *See, I am stirring up the Medes against them,*
> *who have no regard for silver*
> *and do not delight in gold.*
> *Their bows will slaughter the young men;*
> *they will have no mercy on the fruit of the womb;*
> *their eyes will not pity children.*
> *And Babylon, the glory of kingdoms,*
> *the splendor and pride of the Chaldeans,*
> *will be like Sodom and Gomorrah when God overthrew them.*
> *(Isa 13:17–19)*

Those who read or heard this text in the post-exilic era knew that Babylon's "day of the Lord" had also come.[4]

The Devastation (Herem) of a "Day of Yahweh"—Isaiah 13:20–22

A profound sense of sadness is present in the concluding portion of the poem. It is almost as though the poet has personally walked through the remains of a city that has been totally destroyed. All that remain are rubble, ruins, and weeds which have become the haunts of wild animals.

---

4. For a summary of the activity of Nebuchadnezzar and the end of the Babylonian empire, see Watts, *Isaiah 1–33*, 223–42; Blenkinsopp, *Isaiah 1–39*, 271-82.

In the aftermath of war, buildings that once had been beautiful palaces or pleasant dwelling places were left in total ruin. Utter destruction (*herem*) was envisioned by the poet as the worst imaginable punishment for a city, people, or nation.[5]

> *It will never be inhabited or lived in for all generations;*
> *Arabs will not pitch their tents there,*
> *shepherds will not make their flocks lie down there.*
> *But wild animals will lie down there,*
> *and its houses will be full of howling creatures;*
> *there ostriches will live,*
> *and there goat-demons will dance.*
>
> *Hyenas will cry in its towers,*
> *and jackals in the pleasant palaces;*
> *its time is close at hand, and its days will not be prolonged.*
> *(Isa 13:20–22)*

A Word of Reassurance—Isaiah 14:1–2

After such a strong announcement of judgment for Babylon, a word of reassurance for Judah is added. Within this word, the imagery is shocking. The poet speaks of dramatic reversal of fortunes. One day, the situation will change! One day, foreign people will be brought to Jerusalem, and then they will learn what it is like to be servants or slaves.

> *But the Lord will have compassion on Jacob*
> *and will again choose Israel,*
> *and will set them in their own land;*
> *and aliens will join them*
> *and attach themselves to the house of Jacob.*
> *And the nations will take them and bring them to their place,*
> *and the house of Israel will possess the nations*

5. In the fall of 1960, I walked through block after block of bombed-out buildings in Mannheim, Germany. Fifteen years after World War II had ended, the rubble from bombing raids still remained. Where apartments and industry had once flourished, there were only skeletal remains of large brick buildings. The photos from 9/11 in New York in 2001 were frightening but in Mannheim, similar destruction went on for block after block.

as male and female slaves in the Lord's land;
they will take captive those who were their captors,
and rule over those who oppressed them.
(Isa 14:1–2)

The writer speaks of taking slaves. The references remind us again that this poetry comes from a situation where people were feeling rage, frustration, and anger. The perspective comes from a culture in the distant past. Slavery was a reality of life in that world. Unless we have lived in similar situations of severe oppression in the world, we may not be able to grasp the bitterness that the author is expressing in this text. Clearly the author is writing from a marginal situation in the world.[6] The dream is that one day there will be a reversal of roles. Instead of seeing family members treated with brutality or taken as slaves to a foreign country, there will be a time when that situation will be reversed. One day it will be the foreigners who will serve those in the community of the faithful; captors will be taken captive; oppressors will be ruled by the oppressed.

A Taunt Song for the Proud Tyrant: The King of Babylon —Isaiah 14:3–11

There are times when life seems filled with pain. It is difficult enough when pain results from bodily illness or injury. When pain has been inflicted by a tyrant empire that acts as if it owns the world, the pain can be excruciating. A taunt song provides an outlet for expressing pent-up feelings and the frustrations of rage. Such rhetoric allows people in marginal situations to rejoice when an arrogant leader or nation is brought low. In this taunt song, the author envisions a time when Babylon will experience some of the pain that the captive people of Judah have known during their "Babylonian captivity" days.

When the Lord has given you rest from your pain and turmoil and the
hard service with which you were made to serve, you will take up this
taunt against the king of Babylon:
How the oppressor has ceased!
How his insolence has ceased!
The Lord has broken the staff of the wicked,
the scepter of rulers,

6. See the discussion in the introduction on "the marginal perspective."

that struck down the peoples in wrath with unceasing blows,

that ruled the nations in anger with unrelenting persecution.

The whole earth is at rest and quiet;

they break forth into singing.

The cypresses exult over you, the cedars of Lebanon, saying:

"Since you were laid low, no one comes to cut us down."

Sheol beneath is stirred up to meet you when you come;

it rouses the shades to greet you,

all who were leaders of the earth;

it raises from their thrones

all who were kings of the nations.

All of them will speak and say to you:

"You too have become as weak as we!

You have become like us!"

Your pomp is brought down to Sheol,

and the sound of your harps;

maggots are the bed beneath you,

and worms are your covering.

(Isa 14:3–11)

Like the Fall of the Daystar!—Isaiah 14:12–17

The taunt song now alludes to mythological sagas probably well-known to the audience. The imagery is similar to patterns of thought seen in Greek or Babylonian mythology. During the past century, archaeologists have recovered fascinating records from Ugarit, an ancient city in northern Syria. Tablets recovered from the ruins of a library in that ancient city provide interesting parallels for understanding this text. Among the tablets discovered at Ugarit is the account of the god Helel, the morning star. Helel comes to the sacred mountain of the north, Mt. Saphon, where she sets out a challenge to the high God, El, resulting in a cosmic battle. After a struggle, Helel is thrown down to Sheol from a heavenly place.[7] In

---

7. Scholars in past centuries saw connections here with Greek mythology concerning Venus. Others saw connections with the Babylonian-Assyrian myth of Ishtar's descent into the underworld. But far closer parallels can be found in Canaanite mythology, especially since the discovery of the Ugaritic texts. See further, Childs, *Isaiah*, 126–27.

this poem, Assyria, like Helel, is thrown down from her high place. It is Yahweh, not El, who brings down a nation that has acted with arrogance.

> How are you fallen from heaven,
> O Day Star, son of Dawn!
> How are you cut down to the ground,
> you who laid the nations low!
> You said in your heart,
> "I will ascend to heaven;
> I will raise my throne above the stars of God;
> I will sit on the mount of assembly on the heights of Zaphon;
> I will ascend to the tops of the clouds,
> I will make myself like the Most High."
> But you are brought down to Sheol, to the depths of the Pit.
> Those who see you will stare at you, and ponder over you:
> "Is this the man who made the earth tremble,
> who shook kingdoms,
> who made the world like a desert and overthrew its cities,
> who would not let his prisoners go home?"
> (Isa 14:12–17)

No Great Memories for this Tyrant—Isaiah 14:18–21

What legacy does a leader leave behind when he or she dies? A leader who rules by coercion and brute force may manage to stay in place for a time. But that leader will not be remembered with any great affection by those who have suffered during his lifetime. Rather, people will rejoice at his death. Here the poet is celebrating the death of a tyrant.

> All the kings of the nations lie in glory,
> each in his own tomb;
> but you are cast out, away from your grave,
> like loathsome carrion, clothed with the dead,
> those pierced by the sword,
> who go down to the stones of the Pit,
> like a corpse, trampled underfoot.
> You will not be joined with them in burial,
> because you have destroyed your land,

you have killed your people.
May the descendants of evildoers nevermore be named!
Prepare slaughter for his sons
because of the guilt of their father.
Let them never rise to possess the earth
or cover the face of the world with cities.
(Isa 14:18–21)

Babylon Cut Off!—Isaiah 14:22–23

The taunt now concludes with a clear announcement that Yahweh will
assure the downfall of Babylon. Such is the fate for arrogant and self-
centered empires of the world!

I will rise up against them, says the Lord of hosts,
and will cut off from Babylon name and remnant,
offspring and posterity,
says the Lord.
And I will make it a possession of the hedgehog,
and pools of water,
and I will sweep it with the broom of destruction,
says the Lord of hosts.
(Isa 14:22–23)

A Memory of Assyrian Arrogance—Isaiah 14:24–27

A memory of judgment announced for Assyria is preserved here. The
poem concludes with the warning heard in earlier announcements of
judgment: "His hand is still stretched out!" (See Isa 5:25; 9:12; 9:17; 9:21;
10:4.)

The Lord of hosts has sworn:
As I have designed, so shall it be;
and as I have planned, so shall it come to pass:
I will break the Assyrian in my land,
and on my mountains trample him under foot;
his yoke shall be removed from them,

and his burden from their shoulders.

This is the plan that is planned concerning the whole earth;
and this is the hand that is stretched out
over all the nations.
For the Lord of hosts has planned, and who will annul it?
His hand is stretched out, and who will turn it back?
(Isa 14:24–27)

Judgment for the Philistines (The Gaza Strip)—Isaiah 14:28–32

Now come a number of poems that announce judgment for other neighboring nations. Humane behavior was expected of all people and all kings. The first poem was addressed to a territory that had been at odds with Judah throughout recorded history; in biblical times, it was the home of Goliath and the Philistines. Today it is known as the Gaza strip.

In the year that King Ahaz died this oracle came:
Do not rejoice, all you Philistines,
that the rod that struck you is broken,
for from the root of the snake will come forth an adder,
and its fruit will be a flying fiery serpent.
The firstborn of the poor will graze,
and the needy lie down in safety;
but I will make your root die of famine.
and your remnant, I will kill.

Wail, O gate; cry, O city;
melt in fear, O Philistia, all of you!
For smoke comes out of the north,
and there is no straggler in its ranks.
What will one answer
the messengers of the nations?
"The Lord has founded Zion,
and the needy among his people
will find refuge in her."
(Isa 14:28–32)

An Oracle concerning Moab—Isaiah 15:1–9

Moab, located just east of the Dead Sea (modern-day southern Jordan), is remembered with her cities in ruin. The author evidently knew the country well; a number of cities and villages are mentioned: Ar, Kir, Dibon, Nebo, Medeba, Heshbon, Elealeh, Jahaz, Zoar, Egalth-shelishiyah, Lihith, Horonaim, Nimron, Eglaim, Beer-elim, and Dibon. All lie in ruins! Moab's fall is remembered as the result of excessive pride and insolence (see Isa 16:1–7). In a poignant way, the poet expresses deep empathy and sorrow for both the land and the people of Moab.

> An oracle concerning Moab.
> Because Ar is laid waste in a night, Moab is undone;
> because Kir is laid waste in a night, Moab is undone.
> Dibon has gone up to the temple, to the high places to weep;
> over Nebo and over Medeba Moab wails.
> On every head is baldness, every beard is shorn;
> in the streets they bind on sackcloth;
> on the housetops and in the squares
> everyone wails and melts in tears.
> Heshbon and Elealeh cry out,
> their voices are heard as far as Jahaz;
> therefore the loins of Moab quiver;
> his soul trembles.
> My heart cries out for Moab;
> his fugitives flee to Zoar,
> to Egalth-shelishiyah.
> For at the ascent of Luhith they go up weeping;
> on the road to Horonaim they raise a cry of destruction;
> the waters of Nimrim are a desolation;
> the grass is withered, the new growth fails,
> the verdure is no more.
>
> Therefore the abundance they have gained
> and what they have laid up they carry away
> over the Wadi of the Willows.
> For a cry has gone around the land of Moab;
> the wailing reaches to Eglaim,

the wailing reaches to Beer-elim.
For the waters of Dibon are full of blood;
yet I will bring upon Dibon even more—
a lion for those of Moab who escape,
for the remnant of the land.
(Isa 15:1–9)

Send Lambs to Poor Moab—Isaiah 16:1–14

In a time in the world where we agonize over the plight of human families and tribes in Somalia, Afghanistan, and Iraq, it is moving to hear an
ancient prophetic writer express empathy and sorrow at the horrors of
war that have come for neighboring Moab. Just as moving, perhaps, is the
word of encouragement given to leaders in Jerusalem to provide aid and
comfort for exiles from Moab who have made it to the border with Judah.
"Let the outcasts of Moab settle among you; be a refuge to them from the
destroyer!" sets out a prophetic word for the ages.

Send lambs to the ruler of the land,
from Sela, by way of the desert,
to the mount of daughter Zion.
Like fluttering birds,
like scattered nestlings,
so are the daughters of Moab
at the fords of the Arnon.

"Give counsel, grant justice;
make your shade like night at the height of noon;
hide the outcasts, do not betray the fugitive;
let the outcasts of Moab settle among you;
be a refuge to them from the destroyer."

When the oppressor is no more and destruction has ceased,
and marauders have vanished from the land,
then a throne shall be established in steadfast love
in the tent of David,

and on it shall sit in faithfulness
a ruler who seeks justice and is swift to do what is right.

In the concluding section, the poet declares that Moab's problem was excessive arrogance. It was excessive pride and insolence that led to trouble.

We have heard of the pride of Moab—how proud he is!—
of his arrogance, his pride, and his insolence;
his boasts are false.
Therefore let Moab wail, let everyone wail for Moab.
Mourn, utterly stricken, for the raisin cakes of Kir-hareseth.

For the fields of Heshbon languish, and the vines of Sibmah,
whose clusters once made drunk the lords of the nations,
reached to Jazer and strayed to the desert;
their shoots once spread abroad and crossed over the sea.
Therefore I weep with the weeping of Jazer
for the vines of Sibmah;
I drench you with my tears, O Heshbon and Elealeh;
for the shout over your fruit harvest
and your grain harvest has ceased.

Joy and gladness are taken away from the fruitful field;
and in the vineyards no songs are sung,
no shouts are raised;
no treader treads out wine in the presses;
the vintage-shout is hushed.
Therefore my heart throbs like a harp for Moab,
and my very soul for Kir-heres.
When Moab presents himself, when he wearies himself upon the high place, when he comes to his sanctuary to pray, he will not prevail.
This was the word that the Lord spoke concerning Moab in the past. But now the Lord says, In three years, like the years of a hired worker, the glory of Moab will be brought into contempt, in spite of all its great multitude; and those who survive will be very few and feeble.

(Isa 16:1–14)

An Oracle Concerning Damascus—Isaiah 17:1–6

Here a sad memory of Damascus and Syria is preserved. Isaiah warns about dangerous alliances that northern Israel had made with Syria. We know that the alliance resulted in tragedy for both Damascus and the northern kingdom of Israel. The imagery is particularly striking. The destruction is depicted with images of a field gleaned of grain, an olive tree that has been beaten, or a fruit tree where only two, three, or possibly four or five berries remain. Such is the devastation of war in every age.

> *An oracle concerning Damascus.*
> *See, Damascus will cease to be a city,*
> *and will become a heap of ruins.*
> *Her towns will be deserted forever;*
> *they will be places for flocks, which lie down*
> *and no one will make them afraid.*
> *The fortress will disappear from Ephraim,*
> *and the kingdom from Damascus;*
> *and the remnant of Aram will be*
> *like the glory of the children of Israel,*
> *says the Lord of hosts.*
>
> *On that day,*
> *the glory of Jacob will be brought low,*
> *and the fat of his flesh will grow lean.*
> *And it shall be as when reapers gather standing grain*
> *and their arms harvest the ears,*
> *and as when one gleans the ears of grain*
> *in the Valley of Rephaim.*
> *Gleanings will be left in it,*
> *as when an olive tree is beaten—*
> *two or three berries in the top of the highest bough,*
> *four or five on the branches of a fruit tree,*
> *says the Lord God of Israel.*
> *(Isa 17:1–6)*

Look to your Creator—Isaiah 17:7–11

People in every age seem prone to believe that they can solve all problems with their own human resources. In Psalm 100, the psalmist declares, *"Know this; it is the Lord who is God. He has made us; we have not made ourselves; we are his; the sheep of his pasture"* (Ps 100:3). The psalmist is reminding people that they are mortal beings, bounded by birth and death.

In the poem before us, the author also reminds people of their mortality, urging them to rejoice in the God of their salvation, the one who is like a rock of refuge.

> *On that day people will regard their Maker, and their eyes will look to the Holy One of Israel; they will not have regard for the altars, the*
> *work of their hands, and they will not look to what their own fingers have made, either the sacred poles or the altars of incense.*
> *On that day, their strong cities will be like the deserted places of the Hivites and the Amorites, which they deserted because of the children of Israel, and there will be desolation.*
> *For you have forgotten the God of your salvation,*
> *and have not remembered the Rock of your refuge;*
> *therefore, though you plant pleasant plants*
> *and set out slips of an alien god,*
> *though you make them grow*
> *on the day you that plant them,*
> *and make them blossom in the morning that you sow;*
> *yet the harvest will flee away*
> *in a day of grief and incurable pain.*
> *(Isa 17:7–11)*

Judgment on Arrogant Nations—Isaiah 17:12–14

This poetry correlates with Psalm 1. Both the psalm and this Isaiah passage set out a contrast between good and evil people. In Psalm 1, righteous people are likened to healthy trees, planted by streams of water, that prosper and yield good fruit. The wicked, on the other hand, are likened to chaff. They have no lasting substance but are subject to the winds of the world that can blow them in all directions! (See Ps 1:3–4.) Here chaff imagery is also used. For a time, arrogant nations or leaders may appear to be as powerful as a storm on the sea or the rushing waters of a mighty river. But before God, they are like chaff.

> *Ah, the thunder of many peoples,*
> *they thunder like the thundering of the sea!*
> *Ah, the roar of nations,*
> *they roar like the roaring of mighty waters!*
> *The nations roar like the roaring of many waters,*
> *but he will rebuke them,*
> *and they will flee far away,*
> *chased like chaff on the mountains before the wind*
> *and whirling dust before the storm.*
> *At evening time, lo, terror!*
> *Before morning, they are no more.*
> *This is the fate of those who despoil us,*
> *and the lot of those who plunder us.*
> *(Isa 17:12–14)*

An Oracle concerning Ethiopia—Isaiah 18:1–7

The memory preserved here may very well come from the military crisis that arose soon after the revolt by the coastal city state of Ashdod against Assyria at about 714 BCE. Egypt and Ethiopia apparently gave support for that effort. From references in this text and in Isaiah 19–20, we sense that the leaders in Judah were invited (or coerced) into joining a revolt against the empire. The text sets out the striking portrait of tall Ethiopian ambassadors arriving in Jerusalem. It is not difficult to understand the patriotic feelings and the aspirations of leaders in small countries or city states that wanted to break free from the tyranny of an empire such as Assyria. Nationalism was then and is still today a powerful force that binds people to their homelands. Isaiah was strongly opposed to the plans for rebellion, believing that they would bring only disastrous results for the country and the region. He declared that such rebellion would result in disaster like the brutal pruning of vines before the time of harvest. But Isaiah's words of warning went unheeded and disaster came! In 711 BCE, Sargon II of Assyria sent a military force against Ashdod, conquered the city, replaced its king and imposed even greater financial tribute on the

people. Memories of that era may well have prompted the preservation of
this word for Ethiopia and Egypt.

> Ah, land of whirring wings beyond the rivers of Ethiopia,
> sending ambassadors by the Nile in vessels of papyrus on the waters!
> Go, you swift messengers,
> to a nation tall and smooth,
> to a people feared near and far,
> a nation mighty and conquering,
> whose land the rivers divide.
> All you inhabitants of the world,
> you who live on the earth,
> when a signal is raised on the mountains, look!
> When a trumpet is blown, listen!
> For thus the Lord said to me:
> I will quietly look from my dwelling
> like clear heat in sunshine,
> like a cloud of dew in the heat of harvest.
> For before the harvest,
> when the blossom is over
> and the flower becomes a ripening grape,
> he will cut off the shoots with pruning hooks,
> and the spreading branches he will hew away.
>
> They shall all be left
> to the birds of prey of the mountains
> and to the animals of the earth.
> And the birds of prey will summer on them,
> and all the animals of the earth will winter on them.
>
> At that time gifts will be brought to the Lord of hosts from a people tall
> and smooth, from a people feared near and far, a nation mighty and
> conquering, whose land the rivers divide, to Mount Zion, the place of the
> name of the Lord of hosts.
>
> (Isa 18:1–7)

An Oracle Concerning Egypt—Isaiah 19:1–15

Yahweh is the sovereign Lord also of the pharaoh in Egypt, even when the pharaoh does not know that. The pharaoh in Egypt has the same responsibilities that other world leaders have; when he sets forth plots and plans that will cause suffering and death for people, he and his country will eventually pay a price. The pharaoh is responsible for his own actions. Civil war is understood as a failure of the ruler to be sensitive to various groups within his country. In prophetic perspective, civil war in such situations reflects the judgment of God on a ruler who is lacking in wisdom.

> *An oracle concerning Egypt.*
> *See, the Lord is riding on a swift cloud and comes to Egypt;*
> *the idols of Egypt will tremble at his presence,*
> *and the heart of the Egyptians will melt within them.*
>
> *I will stir up Egyptians against Egyptians,*
> *and they will fight, one against the other,*
> *neighbor against neighbor,*
> *city against city, kingdom against kingdom;*
> *the spirit of the Egyptians within them will be emptied out,*
> *and I will confound their plans;*
> *they will consult the idols*
> *and the spirits of the dead and the ghosts*
> *and the familiar spirits;*
> *I will deliver the Egyptians into the hand of a hard master;*
> *a fierce king will rule over them,*
> *says the Sovereign, the Lord of hosts.*

In Egypt, much of life was oriented around the waters of the Nile river. As creator, Yahweh ultimately has control also over those waters. No greater punishment could be imagined for Egypt than to have the waters of the Nile dry up. Such is the punishment envisioned for Pharoah and Egypt for their misdeeds.

> *The waters of the Nile will be dried up,*
> *and the river will be parched and dry;*
> *its canals will become foul,*

and the branches of Egypt's Nile
will diminish and dry up,
reeds and rushes will rot away.
There will be bare places by the Nile,
on the brink of the Nile;
and all that is sown by the Nile will dry up,
be driven away, and be no more.
Those who fish will mourn;
all who cast hooks in the Nile will lament,
and those who spread nets on the water will languish.
The workers in flax will be in despair,
and the carders and those at the loom will grow pale.
Its weavers will be dismayed,
and all who work for wages will be grieved.

Particular scorn is now expressed for learned counselors from the Egyptian city of Tanis, referred to twice as "the princes of Zoan," advisors who evidently gave encouragement for their dangerous war policies.

The princes of Zoan are utterly foolish;
the wise counselors of Pharaoh give stupid counsel.
How can you say to Pharaoh,
"I am one of the sages, a descendant of ancient kings"?

Where now are your sages?
Let them tell you and make known
what the Lord of hosts has planned against Egypt.
The princes of Zoan have become fools,
and the princes of Memphis are deluded;
those who are the cornerstones of its tribes
have led Egypt astray.

The Lord has poured into them a spirit of confusion;
and they have made Egypt stagger in all its doings
as a drunkard staggers around in vomit.
Neither head nor tail, palm branch or reed,
will be able to do anything for Egypt.
(Isa 19:1–15)

Five Sayings regarding Egypt
—Isaiah 19:16–17, 19:18, 19:19–22, 19:23, and 19:24.

Here we sense the historical (or diachronic) dimensions of the Isaiah scroll. It would appear that over a period of time, these five short poetic words were added to this chapter focused on Egypt. Each has the introductory phrase "On that day." We can sense in these additions how closely the affairs of Judah were tied to the affairs of neighboring countries, especially Egypt. In the Hebrew text, all are set forth as prose accounts.

Judgment for Egypt—Isaiah 19:16–17

One day, roles will be reversed; it will be Egypt that will be in fear and dread before Judah. They will be in terror before the plan of Yahweh.

> On that day the Egyptians will be like women, and tremble with fear before the hand that the Lord of hosts raises against them. And the land of Judah will become a terror to the Egyptians; everyone to whom it is mentioned will fear because of the plan that the Lord of hosts is planning against them.
>
> (Isa 19:16–17)

One Day, Greater Understanding!—Isaiah 19:18

The mood changes from judgment to hope. The reference to the "language of Canaan" probably refers to Hebrew people living in Egypt. We know that after the destruction of Jerusalem in 587 BCE, some residents of Judah were deported to Egypt, including the prophet Jeremiah. According to Jeremiah 44:1, there were Hebrew settlements at Migdol, Tahpanhes, Memphis, and the area of Pathros. The city of the sun in this passage seems to refer to Heliopolis, the city of Re, the Egyptian sun-god. Even there, Yahweh will be known.

> On that day there will be five cities in the land of Egypt that speak the language of Canaan and swear allegiance to the Lord of hosts. One of these will be called the City of the Sun.
>
> (Isa 19:18)

Worship of Yahweh in Egypt—Isaiah 19:19–22

The poet envisions a day when worship of Yahweh will also be a reality in Egypt. As Moses once delivered Hebrew people from bondage in Egypt, the author here envisions that one like Moses will come to Egypt to defend and deliver them.

> On that day there will be an altar to the Lord in the center of the
> land of Egypt, and a pillar to the Lord at its border. It will be a sign
> and a witness to the Lord of hosts in the land of Egypt; when they
> cry to the Lord because of oppressors, he will send them a savior,
> and will defend and deliver them. The Lord will make himself
> known to the Egyptians; and the Egyptians will know the Lord
> on that day, and worship with sacrifice and burnt offering, and
> they will make vows to the Lord and perform them. The Lord will
> strike Egypt, striking and healing; they will return to the Lord, and
> he will listen to their supplications and heal them. (Isa 19:19–22)

A Highway from Egypt to Assyria—Isaiah 19:23

The theme is hopeful. In Isaiah 11:10–16, the poetry includes the description of a highway crossing from Assyria as a way home for refugees. That highway was to be like the pathway that had allowed people to come up out of the land of Egypt. In Isaiah 40, a highway is described that will allow people to cross from captivity in Babylon through the wilderness to their homes in Judah. Here the poet seems to believe that peace can be enhanced by the building of a highway stretching from Egypt to Assyria. He even dreams of a time when those diverse worlds can worship together.

> On that day there will be a highway from Egypt to Assyria,
> and the Assyrians will come into Egypt, and the Egyptian into Assyria,
> and the Egyptians will worship with the Assyrians.
> (Isa 19:23)

Blessings for Egypt, Assyria and Israel—Isaiah 19:24

This is a remarkable passage. Egypt and Assyria were among the chief oppressors of Judah. Still, the poet envisions a time of future blessing that will include both of those nations along with Israel.

> *On that day Israel will be the third with Egypt and Assyria,*
> *a blessing in the midst of the earth, whom the Lord of hosts has blessed,*
> *saying, "Blesssed be Egypt my people, and Assyria the work of my hands,*
> *and Israel my heritage."*
> *(Isa 19:24)*

The Memory of Isaiah's Prophetic Protest—Isaiah 20:1–6

This prose account recalls a time during the era when Ashdod, Egypt, and Ethiopia initiated a rebellion against Assyria (714–711 BCE). Isaiah is remembered here for his protest actions (sometimes called a "sign-act") against the policies of his own government. Over a three-year period, Isaiah demonstrated by walking naked and barefoot through the streets of Jerusalem. His message would have been clearly understood. He was warning that if the leaders decided to join in rebellion against Assyria, they would bring slavery and deportation for their people! In what appears to be a prose account, a memory is preserved of the bold war protest undertaken by Isaiah.

> *In the year that the commander-in-chief, who was sent by King Sargon of Assyria, came to Ashdod and fought against it and took it—at that time the Lord had spoken to Isaiah son of Amoz, saying, "Go, and loose the sackcloth from your loins and take your sandals off your feet," and he had done so, walking naked and barefoot. Then the Lord said, "Just as my servant Isaiah has walked naked and barefoot for three years as a sign and a portent against Egypt and Ethiopia, so shall the king of Assyria lead away the Egyptians as captives and the Ethiopians as exiles, both the young and the old, naked and barefoot, with buttocks uncovered, to the shame of Egypt. And they shall be dismayed and confounded because of Ethiopia their hope and of Egypt their boast. In that day the inhabitants of this coastland will say, 'See, this is what happened*

to those in whom we hoped and to whom we fled for help and de-
liverance from the king of Assyria! And we, how shall we escape?'"

(Isa 20:1–6)

The Oracle Concerning the Wilderness of the Sea
—Isaiah 21:1–10

War in any age is a horrifying experience. It is like unleashing chaos because no one can clearly predict where warfare will lead. War brings out
the worst in the human community as warriors get caught up in patterns
of revenge and retaliation. All too often, the original causes of a conflict
are forgotten as new battles rage and innocent people are caught in the
turmoil of life and death struggles.

This poem laments war. The title is cryptic and is not readily related
to any one particular nation or event. A vision of whirlwinds in the Judean desert suggests the blinding chaos of war. The author is filled with
anxiety and trembles at the prospect of what may come.

> *The oracle concerning the wilderness of the sea.*
> *As whirlwinds in the Negeb sweep on,*
> *it comes from the desert,*
> *from a terrible land.*
> *A stern vision is told to me;*
> *the betrayer betrays,*
> *and the destroyer destroys.*
> *Go up, O Elam, lay siege, O Media;*
> *all the sighing she has caused*
> *I bring to an end.*
> *Therefore my loins are filled with anguish;*
> *pangs have seized me,*
> *like the pangs of a woman in labor;*
> *I am bowed down so that I cannot hear,*
> *I am dismayed so that I cannot see.*
> *My mind reels, horror has appalled me;*
> *the twilight I longed for*
> *has been turned for me into trembling.*
> *They prepare the table, they spread the rugs,*

BITTER MEMORIES OF JUDAH AMONG THE NATIONS   83

they eat, they drink.
Rise up, commanders, oil the shield!

The command is now given to post a lookout to listen and to observe with diligence. The reference to Babylon may well be used here as a symbolic name for any nation or people that has known war. In the final lines, we sense a feeling of pathos as the prophet literally weeps for the people and for what is coming. He expresses sorrow for "my threshed and winnowed one." The poetry speaks of people who have seen life destroyed in the sad jaws of war.

> *For thus the Lord said to me:*
> *"Go, post a lookout, let him announce what he sees.*
> *When he sees riders, horsemen in pairs,*
> *riders on donkeys, riders on camels,*
> *let him listen diligently, very diligently."*
> *Then the watcher called out:*
> *"Upon a watchtower I stand, O Lord,*
> *continually by day, and at my post*
> *I am stationed throughout the night.*
> *Look, there they come, riders, horsemen in pairs!"*
> *Then he responded, "Fallen, fallen is Babylon;*
> *and all the images of her gods*
> *lie shattered on the ground."*
> *O my threshed and winnowed one,*
> *what I have heard from the Lord of hosts,*
> *the God of Israel,*
> *I announce to you.*
> *(Isa 21:1–10)*

The Oracle concerning Dumah—Isaiah 21:11–12

It is nighttime. Watchmen are on guard on a city wall. As sentinels, the guards are charged to watch and listen for reports. The poem recalls a time when there was no news to report. The night air, however, is filled with fear and anxiety. The issue is obviously the fear of an impending battle.[8]

> *The oracle concerning Dumah.*
> *One is calling to me from Seir,*
> *"Sentinel, what of the night?*
> *Sentinel, what of the night?"*
> *The sentinel says: "Morning comes, and also the night.*
> *If you will inquire, inquire; come back again."*
> *(Isa 21:11–12)*

The Oracle Concerning the Desert Plain—Isaiah 21:13–16

Against the backdrop of the vast wasteland of the Arabian desert, the poet urges a caravan of Dedanites to show hospitality to refugees who are fleeing from warfare. "Bring water to the thirsty!" is the plea of the author. We can feel an overwhelming sense of sadness about war. The oracle is a "weighty matter" for Yahweh. The glory of Kedar will be destroyed and her warriors dead. There is no glory in war!

> *The oracle concerning the desert plain.*
> *In the scrub of the desert plain you will lodge,*
> *O caravans of Dedanites.*
> *Bring water to the thirsty, meet the fugitive with bread,*
> *O inhabitants of the land of Tema.*
> *For they have fled from the swords,*
> *from the drawn sword,*
> *from the bent bow, and from the stress of battle.*
> *For thus the Lord said to me: Within a year,*
> *according to the years of a hired worker,*
> *all the glory of Kedar will come to an end;*
> *and the remaining bows of Kedar's warriors will be few;*
> *for the Lord, the God of Israel, has spoken.*
> *(Isa 21:13–16)*

---

8. See Ezekiel 3:16–21, where the imagery of a "faithful watchman" is used to describe the prophet's calling, even in the midst of imminent danger to the community and when people do not want to hear a warning.

The Memory of a Close Call for Judah—Isaiah 22:1–14

In Isaiah 22, the focus is again directly on the people of Judah. The countryside and Jerusalem have suffered a terrible invasion by a foreign country. The siege seems to have ended and the poem is written as a response to those events. This is a very important text within the Isaiah scroll. At the end of the poem, a warning is sounded because the people and their leaders evidently have not learned anything from this "close call" with disaster. The message remains clear for future generations of people and nations.

Commentators have debated the historical situation that may have prompted this poem. It is altogether possible that the poem was written as a response to the invasion of Judah by Sennacherib in 701 BCE. But from the perspective of the post-exilic community, the memory of the fall of Jerusalem in 587 BCE puts this poetry into an even more dramatic light. The prophet's warning at the end of this poem has now come to pass! Isaiah's words and his counsel should have been heeded. The key for understanding this poem is to recognize that the author is interpreting a past event. A "day of the Lord" event has happened! Jerusalem has come through a close call with disaster! And the real tragedy about that event is that the people in Jerusalem did not learn from the devastation that had come to their country. Their failure to understand and their frivolous reactions guaranteed that more tragic "days" would come in the future!

The poem breaks clearly into four parts; three are in poetic form and verses 22:8b–11 are apparently in prose. All four sections of the poem describe an event that had already happened in and around Jerusalem.

Let Me Weep Bitter Tears—Isaiah 22:1–4

People are celebrating after a narrow escape from the attack on their city. The prophet is in despair. In the midst of the celebration, he asks how people can celebrate when such widespread tragedy has come? He laments: "Do not try to comfort me for the destruction of my people!"

> *The oracle concerning the valley of vision.*
> *What do you mean that you have gone up,*
> *all of you, to the housetops,*
> *you that are full of shoutings,*
> *tumultuous city, exultant town?*

Your slain are not slain by the sword,

nor are they dead in battle.

Your rulers have all fled together;

they were captured without the use of a bow.

All of you who were found were captured,

though they had fled far away.

Therefore, I said: Look away from me,

let me weep bitter tears;

do not try to comfort me

for the destruction of my beloved people.

(Isa 22:1–4)

He has taken away the covering of Judah—Isaiah 22:5–8a

The prophet now offers an interpretation of the military attack that has
come.

The attack on Judah and Jerusalem was a "day of the Lord," an event
of war which involved battering down of walls and military combat. It
was a moment of judgment for the nation. Valleys had been filled with
chariots and there were many casualties throughout Judah, resulting in
the loss of villages, soldiers, and treasured goods. The poet declares: "He
has taken away the covering of Judah!"

For the Lord God of hosts has had a day

of tumult and trampling and confusion

in the valley of vision,

a battering down of walls and a cry for help to the mountains.[9]

Elam bore the quiver with chariots and cavalry,

and Kir uncovered the shield.

Your choice valleys were full of chariots,

and the cavalry took their stand at the gates.

He has taken away the covering of Judah.

(Isa 22:5–8a)

9. In this section, the NRSV translates: "For the Lord God of hosts has a day of
tumult and trampling and confusion . . ." I have translated the verse as a reference to a
past event: "For the Lord God of hosts has had a day of tumult, and trampling and confusion . . . in keeping with the past references in the three other sections of this poem.

You did not look to him who did it!—Isaiah 22:8b–11

The prophet continues his words of condemnation. Leaders were think-ing only of military preparations for the defense of the city, strengthening the city wall and attending to the water supply. But in all of that planning, they demonstrated little regard for their own heritage of faith! In other words, the leaders failed to consider the cost in human life when they initiated their plans for rebellion.[10]

> On that day you looked for the weapons of the House of the Forest,
> and you saw that there were many breaches in the city of David,
> and you collected the waters of the lower pool. You counted the
> houses of Jerusalem, and you broke down the houses to fortify the
> wall. You made a reservoir between the two walls for the water of
> the old pool. But you did not look to him who did it, or have regard
> for him who planned it long ago.
>
> (Isa 22:8b–11)

Eat, drink and be merry!—Isaiah 22:12–14

The prophet suggests that in the aftermath of a tragedy, there should be serious reflection on what has just happened within the nation. He suggests that weeping and mourning would have been an appropriate response, along with serious reflection on the causes for the tragedy that had come for the country and its people. Instead, all he sees around him are frivolous responses of a community celebrating escape after a close call with disaster. People are preoccupied with slaughtering and feasting on oxen, sheep, and wine. Their mood is described with the words: "Let us eat and drink for tomorrow we die!"

> In that day the Lord God of hosts
> called to weeping and mourning,
> to baldness and putting on sackcloth;
> but instead there was joy and festivity,
> killing oxen and slaughtering sheep,
> eating meat and drinking wine.
> "Let us eat and drink, for tomorrow we die."

10. The "House of the Forest" refers to the armory in the royal palace in Jerusalem that was built by King Solomon (1 Kgs 7:2 and 10:17).

The Lord of hosts has revealed himself in my ears:
Surely this iniquity will not be forgiven you until you die,
says the Lord God of hosts.
(Isa 22:12–14)

We must listen carefully to the message of this poem. It is a timeless word about the importance of learning from history. When a nation fails to learn from past mistakes, that failure has a way of guaranteeing that new times of judgment will come again. Because people in Judah did not learn from history, the prophet declared that a new "day of the Lord" would come![11]

A "Day of the Lord" for the Steward, Shebna—Isaiah 22:15–19

This oracle is unique in the Isaiah scroll; it is a word of judgment directed against an individual, Shebna. We can only wonder about the situation that prompted Isaiah's intense anger toward Shebna, an official who evidently had some prominence within the royal court in Jerusalem. The word of judgment seems purposely placed in this location, just after the dramatic words of warning sounded in Isaiah 22:1–14. There, inhabitants of Judah are warned about irresponsible conduct and its consequences. Now, Shebna is condemned for his arrogance, evident in part by his project to carve out a majestic tomb for himself. In this prose account, Isaiah declares that Shebna will have a "day of the Lord" experience. For his lack of humility, Yahweh will hurl him from his post and he will die in disgrace.

Thus says the Lord God of hosts:
Come, go to the steward, to Shebna, who is master of the
household, and say to him: What right do you have here? Who are
your relatives here, that you have cut out a tomb here for yourself,
cutting a tomb on the height, and carving a habitation for yourself
in the rock?
The Lord is about to hurl you away violently, my fellow. He
will seize firm hold on you, whirl you round and round, and throw
you like a ball into a wide land; there you shall die and there your

---

11. Amid all of the discussions and reactions to the 9/11 tragedy, it is interesting to ponder how little attention has been given to the question: why did those who attacked the World Trade Center and the Pentagon feel so much hostility for the United States? Israel's prophetic tradition suggests that this is a painful question that requires ongoing serious reflection.

splendid chariots shall lie, O you disgrace to your master's house! I will thrust you from your office, and you will be pulled down from your post. (Isa 22:15–19)

Concerning Eliakim ben Hilkiah—Isaiah 22:20–25

Shebna is to be replaced. A new steward, Eliakim, is to receive Shebna's robe and sash, signs that he will now be entrusted with the responsibilities for the keys and other valuable items in the palace. We can only ponder the situation that prompted the writing of this oracle. Eliakim evidently held office for only a brief period of time. But the final lines indicate that Eliakim, like Shebna, also fell from power. The lesson seems to be that positions of authority can often lead people to arrogance and arrogance brings trouble. Like nations, individuals can also rise and fall!

On that day I will call my servant Eliakim son of Hilkiah, and will clothe him with your robe and bind your sash on him. I will commit your authority to his hand, and he shall be a father to the inhabitants of Jerusalem and to the house of Judah. I will place on his shoulder the key of the house of David; he shall open, and no one shall shut; he shall shut, and no one shall open. I will fasten him like a peg in a secure place, and he will become a throne of honor to his ancestral house. And they will hang on him the whole weight of his ancestral house, the offspring and issue, every small vessel, from the cups to all the flagons.

On that day, says the Lord of hosts, the peg that was fastened in a secure place will give way; it will be cut down and fall, and the load that was on it will perish, for the Lord has spoken.

(Isa 22:20–25)

An Oracle Concerning Tyre—Isaiah 23:1–18

The last of the "prophetic oracles" (*massa*) in this section of the scroll relates to Tyre and Sidon, the coastal cities of Phoenicia (Lebanon), and to Cyprus, all known for their sailors and international trade. Like trading cities throughout history, these cities survived by transporting goods for a fee from various nations.

The oracle concerning Tyre.

Wail, O ships of Tarshish, for your fortress is destroyed.
When they came in from Cyprus they learned of it.
Be still, O inhabitants of the coast, O merchants of Sidon,
your messengers crossed over the sea and were on the mighty waters;
your revenue was the grain of Shihor, the harvest of the Nile;
you were the merchant of the nations.
Be ashamed, O Sidon, for the sea has spoken,
the fortress of the sea, saying: "I have neither labored nor given birth,
I have neither reared young men nor brought up young women."
When the report comes to Egypt,
they will be in anguish over the report about Tyre.
Cross over to Tarshish—wail, O inhabitants of the coast!
Is this your exultant city whose origin is from days of old,
whose feet carried her to settle far away?

Dishonest activities have evidently become commonplace for Tyre. The author poses the question about who has planned the destruction that will come for Tyre and then answers it in dramatic fashion: The Lord of hosts has planned it!

Who has planned this against Tyre,
the bestower of crowns,
whose merchants were princes,
whose traders were the honored of the earth?
The Lord of hosts has planned it—to defile the pride of all glory,
to shame all the honored of the earth.
Cross over to your own land, O ships of Tarshish;
this is a harbor no more.
He has stretched out his hand over the sea,
he has shaken the kingdoms;
the Lord has given command concerning Canaan
to destroy its fortresses.
He said: You will exult no longer,
O oppressed virgin daughter Sidon;
rise, cross over to Cyprus—even there you will have no rest.
Look at the land of the Chaldeans!
This is the people;
it was not Assyria.

They destined Tyre for wild animals.
They erected their siege towers,
they tore down her palaces,
they made her a ruin.

The prophetic writer uses "prostitute" imagery to speak of Tyre. As a trading city, she will perform whatever services a nation requires, often without considering the consequences or the moral issues that are involved. The author anticipates destruction for her beautiful harbor; Tyre is to experience what other nations have already experienced: the horror of an invasion!

Wail, O ships of Tarshish
for your fortress is destroyed.
From that day Tyre will be forgotten for seventy years,
the lifetime of one king.
At the end of seventy years,
it will happen to Tyre as in the song about the prostitute:
Take a harp, go about the city,
you forgotten prostitute!
Make sweet melody,
sing many songs,
that you may be remembered.
     At the end of seventy years, the Lord will visit Tyre, and she
will return to her trade, and will prostitute herself with all the
kingdoms of the world on the face of the earth. Her merchandise
and her wages will be dedicated to the Lord: her profits will not be
stored or hoarded, but her merchandise will supply abundant food
and fine clothing for those who live in the presence of the Lord.
(Isa 23:1–18)

Tyre and Sidon are to learn that even those who simply carry cargoes for others will not escape judgment.

MATTERS OF LIFE AND DEATH—ISAIAH 24-27

Some commentators have suggested that these chapters were originally a separate collection of poems and that together they are to be understood as predicting a future eschatological era. But given their location within the scroll, it seems clear that they are intended as the centerpiece for "bitter memories" about the past, the collection that began in Isaiah 13 with the announcement of a "day of the Lord" for Babylon. The poetry addresses matters of death and life, war and peace, and chaos and order in the world. Using mythic imagery, the poetry reflects on the frailty of the earth and the horrors that war brings for both the guilty and for the innocent. These chapters continue to offer theological reflection on themes preserved throughout Isaiah 1–12 and 13–23.

A Vision of Coming Destruction—Isaiah 24:1–23

In Isaiah's vision, God is present in all that happens in the world. At one moment, the poet can speak of the horrors of war committed by ruthless people and declare that people themselves are responsible for their actions. In the next moment, the poet can declare that what is happening is in fact part of God's plan for punishing evil or for dealing with forces in the world that seem to be aligned with death.[12] The poetic rhetoric is descriptive of what the poet has observed in the world. Whether they know it or not, people are the instruments of God's presence in the world, for good or for evil. Human freedom and human responsibility are affirmed. But in good or in evil actions, God can still be discerned as present in the world.

Imminent Judgment for the Earth—Isaiah 24:1–3

The author begins this poem declaring that judgment that is coming upon the earth as the result of reckless human conduct.

> Now the Lord is about to lay waste the earth and make it desolate,
> and he will twist its surface and scatter its inhabitants.
> And it shall be,
> as with the people, so with the priest;

---

12. A number of commentators see Isaiah 24–27 as a late addition to the Isaiah scroll, reflecting dualistic thinking typical of late apocalyptic thought. I disagree with the late dating and contend that the themes seen in these chapters all have roots in ancient Near Eastern mythology known to the community during the pre-exilic and exilic eras. It is striking that these chapters are located in the center of the second section of Isaiah (Isa 13–35) which focuses on Judah, struggling with questions of war and peace among the nations and amid the tumult of war waged among empires and nations, both large and small.

as with the slave, so with his master;
as with the maid, so with her mistress;
as with the buyer, so with the seller;
as with the lender, so with the borrower;
as with the creditor, so with the debtor.
The earth shall be utterly laid waste and utterly despoiled;
for the Lord has spoken this word.
(Isa 24:1–3)

Drought and Decay—Isaiah 24:4–6

When nations are at war, the earth is neglected or run over. It is as though the earth suffers along with people in the midst of war.

The earth dries up and withers, the world languishes and withers;
the heavens languish together with the earth.
The earth lies polluted under its inhabitants;
for they have transgressed laws,
violated the statutes,
broken the everlasting covenant.
Therefore a curse devours the earth,
and its inhabitants suffer for their guilt;
therefore the inhabitants of the earth dwindled,
and few people are left.
(Isa 24:4–6)

Joy Disappears in the City—Isaiah 24:7–13

When vines dry up, wine disappears. Celebrations cease. Joy disappears from the community. The destruction that is described is so severe that survivors will be like the few remaining gleanings from an olive tree after a harvest.

The wine dries up, the vine languishes,
all the merry-hearted sigh.
The mirth of the timbrels is stilled,
the noise of the jubilant has ceased,

> *the mirth of the lyre is stilled.*
> *No longer do they drink wine with singing;*
> *strong drink is bitter to those who drink it.*
> *The city of chaos is broken down,*
> *every house is shut up so that no one can enter.*
> *There is an outcry in the streets for lack of wine;*
> *all joy has reached its eventide;*
> *the gladness of the earth is banished.*
> *Desolation is left in the city,*
> *the gates are battered into ruins.*
> *For thus it shall be on the earth*
> *and among the nations,*
> *as when an olive tree is beaten,*
> *as at the gleaning when the grape harvest is ended.*
> (Isa 24:7–13)

Celebration Among the Nations—Isaiah 24:14–16

People in distant countries may rejoice and celebrate over the fall of an enemy country. In the midst of victory, they may even express words of praise to God. But understood in the context of other poetry in this section, such praise may be only momentary responses amid the horrors and sadness of war.

> *They lift up their voices, they sing for joy;*
> *they shout from the west over the majesty of the Lord.*
> *Therefore in the east give glory to the Lord;*
> *in the coastlands of the sea*
> *glorify the name of the Lord, the God of Israel.*
> *From the ends of the earth we hear songs of praise,*
> *of glory to the Righteous One.*
> *But I say, I pine away,*
> *I pine away. Woe is me!*
> *For the treacherous deal treacherously,*
> *the treacherous deal very treacherously.*
> (Isa 24:14–16)

More Days of Judgment and Pain—Isaiah 24:17–23

The prophetic writer is in distress. The violence that seems to be so prevalent in the world makes future judgment appear as a future certainty.

> *Terror and the pit, and the snare*
> *are upon you, O inhabitant of the earth!*
> *Whoever flees at the sound of the terror*
> *shall fall into the pit;*
> *and whoever climbs out of the pit*
> *shall be caught in the snare.*
> *For the windows of heaven are opened,*
> *and the foundations of the earth tremble.*
> *The earth is utterly broken,*
> *the earth is torn asunder,*
> *the earth is violently shaken.*
> *The earth staggers like a drunkard,*
> *it sways like a hut;*
> *its transgression lies heavy upon it,*
> *and it falls, and will not rise again.*
>
> *On that day the Lord will punish the host of heaven in heaven,*
> *and on earth, the kings of the earth.*
> *They will be gathered together*
> *like prisoners in a pit;*
> *they will be shut up in a prison,*
> *and after many days*
> *they will be punished.*
>
> *Then the moon will be abashed,*
> *and the sun ashamed;*
> *for the Lord of hosts will reign*
> *on Mount Zion and in Jerusalem,*
> *and before his elders*
> *he will manifest his glory.*
> *(Isa 24:17–23)*

In this poem, military solutions seem again to be the immediate response of nations when they experience threats to their sovereignty. If this is true for small countries, it is even more so for empires. Empires have so much to protect. When their power is threatened, they retaliate in part because they typically have superior numbers of soldiers and superior quantities of weapons at their disposal. But more than that, empires have always been prone to see their power as essential for sustaining order in the world. The author laments the endless cycle of violence that seems to continue unabated in every generation of human history.

Thanksgiving for Deliverance—Isaiah 25:1–5

How can the prophet praise God when cities lie in ruin? When Jerusalem was destroyed, the common view of most people in the world would have been that the gods of Babylon had defeated the god of Judah. And when Babylon fell, people understood that the gods of Babylon were defeated by the gods of Persia. The Isaiah tradition disputes that understanding of the world. Yahweh has spoken words of judgment against his own people, Israel and Judah. Yahweh's sovereignty is not tied to the fortunes of Judah or Jerusalem. Rather, when nations fall, a deep truth about the world becomes evident. Nations and emperors are not gods! In such moments, Yahweh, the creator of heaven and earth, is proclaimed as the reliable source of life. It is Yahweh who is the source of truthfulness that lasts, not the pharaohs or the emperors of the world. Yahweh's word can trusted from generation to generation. The author declares that Yahweh is a refuge for the poor and the needy; a shelter from the rainstorm and a shade from the heat.

> O Lord, you are my God;
> I will exalt you, I will praise your name;
> for you have done wonderful things,
> plans formed of old, faithful and sure.
> For you have made the city a heap,
> the fortified city a ruin;
> the palace of aliens is a city no more,
> and it will never be rebuilt.
>
> Therefore strong peoples will glorify you;

cities of ruthless nations will fear you.
For you have been a refuge to the poor,
a refuge to the needy in their distress,
a shelter from the rainstorm
and a shade from the heat.
When the blast of the ruthless was like a winter rainstorm,
the noise of aliens like heat in a dry place,
you subdued the heat with the shade of clouds;
the song of the ruthless was stilled.
(Isa 25:1–5)

The Defeat of Death—Isaiah 25:6–10a

Prominent in the mythology of Canaan was the imagery of a banquet on a "mountain of the north," the dwelling place of the gods. Among the gods gathered there, the most frightening was Mot, the god of death. Mot was always hungry, looking for all that he could devour to satisfy his hunger. When droughts occurred, it meant that Mot was consuming all available water. When famine or plague came, it meant that Mot was consuming life. Mot asked for the sacrifice of a first-born child from every home. When that sacrifice was offered, people could hope to have other healthy children and be free from the needs of Mot. Sometimes that way of thinking seemed to be confirmed when parents had numerous children and they lived; at other times, amid times of illness and death, it seemed that Mot needed to devour more children from the human family. Mot's presence is at times depicted with the imagery of a shroud or dark veil hanging over the earth. In one scene from the epic story from Ugarit, we hear of Ba'l, the god of fertility and life, entering into combat with Mot. In the battle, Ba'l loses. He is defeated by Mot, who simply opens his mouth and swallows Ba'l. What this means for the earth is an extended period of severe drought. The forces of death have defeated the forces of life and vitality. In one account, after a time of extensive drought and famine, Ba'l's sister, the goddess Anat, cannot stand it any longer and she enters into battle with Mot. With the righteous rage of a sister, she defeats Mot and brings an end to the severe famine that has come upon the earth. As the rains return, Anat slices Mot into pieces and spreads him like dung on the land! Ba'l is rescued. The land is restored and crops can grow. Sadly, in a later season of life, Mot once again reappears.[13]

This poem in Isaiah seems to draw from that world of mythic thought. But now it is neither Ba'l nor Anat who comes to destroy death. It is Yahweh, the sovereign Lord of heaven and earth. That is the hope offered to those who trust in his promises. It is a warning for all who align with forces of death in the world.[14]

> *On this mountain*
> *the Lord of hosts will make for all peoples*
> *a feast of rich food,*
> *a feast of well-aged wines,*
> *of rich food filled with marrow,*
> *of well-aged wines strained clear.*
> *And he will destroy on this mountain*
> *the shroud that is cast over all peoples,*
> *the sheet that is spread over all nations;*
> *he will swallow up death forever.*
> *Then the Lord God will wipe away the tears from all faces,*
> *and the disgrace of his people*
> *he will take away from all the earth,*
> *for the Lord has spoken.*
> *It will be said on that day,*
> *Lo, this is our God;*
> *we have waited for him,*
> *so that he might save us.*
> *This is the Lord for whom we have waited;*
> *let us be glad and rejoice in his salvation.*
> *For the hand of the Lord will rest on this mountain.*
> *(Isa. 25:6–10a)*

13. See Parker, *Ugaritic Narrative Poetry*, 87–180.

14. The apostle Paul quotes from this text in 1 Corinthians 15:54 when he writes: *"When this perishable body puts on imperishability, and this mortal body puts on immortality, then the saying that is written will be fulfilled: 'Death has been swallowed up in victory.' Where, O death, is your victory? Where, O death, is your sting?"*

Judgment for Moab—Isaiah 25:10b–12

Behind this text stands a long history of animosity and bitterness toward Moab. Moab will be brought down in disgrace. Her high fortifications will not help her.

Her excessive pride will bring its own consequences: when judgment has been decreed, punishment will come!

> *The Moabites shall be trodden down in their place*
> *as straw is trodden down in a dung-pit.*
> *Though they spread out their hands in the midst of it,*
> *as swimmers spread out their hands to swim,*
> *their pride will be laid low despite the struggle of their hands.*
> *The high fortifications of his walls will be brought down,*
> *laid low, cast to the ground,*
> *even to the dust.*
> *(Isa 25:10b–12)*

Judah's Song of Victory—Isaiah 26:1–6

In contrast to Moab, Judah is here envisioned as a righteous nation. The message of reassurance is given: all who trust in the Lord can hope for peace. For them, Yahweh is like an everlasting rock!

> *On that day this song will be sung in the land of Judah:*
> *We have a strong city;*
> *he sets up victory like walls and bulwarks.*
> *Open the gates,*
> *so that the righteous nation that keeps faith*
> *may enter in.*
> *Those of steadfast mind*
> *you keep in peace—*
> *in peace because they trust in you.*
>
> *Trust in the Lord forever,*
> *for in the Lord God*
> *you have an everlasting rock.*
> *For he has brought low the inhabitants of the height;*

the lofty city he lays low.
He lays it low to the ground,
casts it to the dust.
The foot tramples it,
the feet of the poor,
the steps of the needy.
(Isa 26:1–6)

A Community Lament—Isaiah 26:7–21

In these verses a mood of lament is heard involving serious reflection on war and at the same time, a prayer for peace. Again and again, armed conflict appears to have been the response of nations when confronted by conflict. The Lord of Israel ordains peace as his will for people. As conflicts swirl and devour, the prophet can only counsel that the righteous hide themselves until the pains of war may pass.

The way of the righteous is level;
O Just One, you make smooth
the path of the righteous.
In the path of your judgments,
O Lord, we wait for you;
your name and your renown
are the soul's desire.
My soul yearns for you in the night,
my spirit within me earnestly seeks you.
For when your judgments are in the earth,
the inhabitants of the world learn righteousness.

In this poem, we sense the loneliness that a person of faith can feel when evil seems to triumph and when there seems to be no clear answers to prayer. The poet suggests that when the wicked triumph, they learn nothing about upright conduct. Rather, they seem to be encouraged for their perverse deeds. Still, the author declares that trust in the Lord of life is the trustworthy guide for life.

If favor is shown to the wicked,
they do not learn righteousness;

in the land of uprightness they deal perversely
and do not see the majesty of the Lord.
O Lord, your hand is lifted up,
but they do not see it.
Let them see your zeal for your people,
and be ashamed.
Let the fire for your adversaries consume them.
O Lord, you will ordain peace for us,
for indeed, all that we have done,
you have done for us.

O Lord our God,
other lords besides you have ruled over us,
but we acknowledge your name alone.
The dead do not live;
shades do not rise—
because you have punished and destroyed them,
and wiped out all memory of them.
But you have increased the nation, O Lord,
you have increased the nation;
you are glorified;
you have enlarged all the borders of the land.
O Lord, in distress they sought you,
they poured out a prayer
when your chastening was on them.

Expectations and hopes for the future had been very high in the past. But as with the sadness of a woman who has experienced a failed pregnancy, hopes have been dashed! Here a lament is spoken and the counsel is given: "Hide yourself for a while until the wrath passes!"

Like a woman with child,
who writhes and cries out in her pangs
when she is near her time,
so were we because of you, O Lord;
we were with child, we writhed,
but we gave birth only to wind.
We have won no victories on earth,

and no one is born to inhabit the world.
Your dead shall live, their corpses shall rise.
O dwellers in the dust, awake and sing for joy!
For your dew is a radiant dew,
and the earth will give birth
to those long dead.

Come, my people, enter your chambers,
and shut your doors behind you;
hide yourselves for a little while
until the wrath is past.
For the Lord comes out from his place
to punish the inhabitants of the earth
for their iniquity;
the earth will disclose
the blood shed on it,
and will no longer cover its slain.
(Isa 26:7–21)

Leviathan Punished—Isaiah 27:1

In a number of places throughout the Bible we hear about the conflict between God and the power of chaos. In the ancient near east, Tiamat (or Rahab) was understood to be the great sea monster, the source of chaos whose activity can be seen when a storm rages on the sea. Leviathan is another name for this power of chaos.

From Ugarit, we know of an account in which Ba'l, the god of fertility and life, does battle with the god of the sea, the chaos-monster Yamm. In a climactic battle, Ba'l defeats Yamm and restores order over chaos in the world.[15] In Isaiah 51:9–11, we hear a similar allusion to Yahweh's triumph over the chaos-dragon, Rahab. The author declares in that passage that the God of Israel is stronger than the forces of chaos in the world. In this passage, the chaos-monster, Leviathan, is described as a serpent or dragon. Yahweh goes into battle and defeats Leviathan.

On that day the Lord with his cruel and great and strong sword

---

15. See further Psalm 74:12–17; Psalm 104:1–9; and Job 41:1–11.

will punish Leviathan the fleeing serpent, Leviathan the twisting serpent,
and he will kill the dragon that is in the sea.
(Isa 27:1)

Assurances of the Redemption of Israel—Isaiah 27:2–6

The parable of the vineyard in Isaiah 5:1–7 is now recast as an allegory. As in chapter 5, Yahweh is portrayed as a vine-keeper. The garden is properly tended and watered; the anticipation is that it will produce good and abundant fruit. If it does not, God will declare war on the thorns and briers. This poem is not a bitter memory, however. It is a portrait of what can be, expressing a word of hope for the future. The garden will be a place where God's peace is evident. Jacob is not to be a wasteland. Rather, the land is to be a fruitful vineyard whose blossoms bring joy to the world. This passage was certainly heard as a word of encouragement for the post-exilic community.

> *On that day:*
> *A pleasant vineyard, sing about it!*
> *I, the Lord, am its keeper; every moment I water it.*
> *I guard it night and day so that no one can harm it;*
> *I have no wrath.*
> *If it gives me thorns and briers, I will march to battle against it,*
> *I will burn it up.*
> *Or else let it cling to me for protection,*
> *let it make peace with me, let it make peace with me.*
>
> *In days to come*
> *Jacob shall take root, Israel shall blossom*
> *and put forth the shoots,*
> *and fill the whole world with fruit.*
> *(Isa 27:2–6)*

One More Bitter Memory—Isaiah 27:7–11

Quite abruptly, the mood changes. A rhetorical question frames the question: is there any difference between the judgment on Judah and the judgment that comes for other nations? For the righteous remnant within Judah, past guilt will be forgiven. But it is a different story for those who still have no understanding or compassion. For them, they are like other nations and there is no forgiveness.[16]

> Has he struck them down
> as he struck down those who struck them?
> Or have they been killed as their killers were killed?
> By expulsion, by exile you struggled against them;
> with his fierce blast he removed them in the day of the east wind.
> Therefore by this the guilt of Jacob will be expiated,
> and this will be the full fruit of the removal of his sin:
> when he makes all the stones of the altar
> like chalkstones crushed to pieces,
> no sacred poles or incense altars will remain standing.

A fortified city, after it has been destroyed, is a very sad place. It is a place of desolation and despair. There cattle will graze and amid the ruins, people will search for firewood.

> For the fortified city is solitary,
> a habitation deserted and forsaken, like the wilderness;
> the calves graze there, there they lie down,
> and strip its branches.
> When its boughs are dry, they are broken;
> women come and make a fire of them.
> For this is a people without understanding;
> therefore he that made them will not have compassion on them,
> he that formed them will show them no favor.
> (Isa 27:7–11)

16. I agree with Brevard Childs when he writes about this text: "The punishment served to atone for the guilt of Jacob, but Israel's full cleansing would occur only when it responded by removing the remaining signs of pagan worship" (Childs, *Isaiah*, 198). But I disagree with him when he goes on to declare: "In contrast, the punishment of the nations is completely lacking in a pedagogical intent." There are a number of texts in the Isaiah scroll that convey God's empathy and concern also for other nations. Like Judah, they are also to learn from the horrors of war and destruction.

A Trumpet will Sound!—Isaiah 27:12–13

Throughout Isaiah, we have noted a number of places where momentous events are interpreted with "day of Yahweh" imagery. Here the author envisions the sound of a trumpet summoning forces for a battle. Yahweh will punish ruthless oppressors from Babylon to Egypt. When this happens, those who have been taken captive from Israel and Judah, whether exiled in Assyria, Babylon or in Egypt, will return to worship at the temple mount in Jerusalem.

> On that day the Lord will thresh from the channel of the Euphrates to the Wadi of Egypt, and you will be gathered one by one, O people of Israel. And on that day a great trumpet will be blown, and those who were lost in the land of Assyria and those who were driven out to the land of Egypt will come and worship the Lord on the holy mountain at Jerusalem.
>
> (Isa 27:12–13)

WORDS OF WARNING—ISAIAH 28–35

In this section of the scroll there is a prevailing sense of sadness. The poetry recalls moments from the lifetime of Isaiah and the era of Assyrian rule. The overall arrangement is theological rather than chronological. As in earlier poetry in Isaiah 13–23, the author declares that it is the lack of compassionate or responsible leadership that leads to the devastations of war.[17]

The Folly of Drunkards—Isaiah 28:1–6

The poem recalls a time before the destruction of the northern kingdom in 722 BCE. Misguided leaders of northern Israel (Ephraim) are described as drunkards who are not able to see or act in a thoughtful manner. A storm is predicted. Like a hailstorm, the prophet envisions an enemy army striking suddenly across the land. Ephraim will be left as a trampled garland or ripe fig. In the last lines of the poem, the author assures the remnant of his people that Yahweh will be for them a garland of glory and a diadem of beauty for the remnant of his people.

17. See further Blenkinsopp, Isaiah 1–39, 380–84.

> *Ah, the proud garland of the drunkards of Ephraim,*
> *and the fading flower of its glorious beauty,*
> *which is on the head of those bloated with rich food,*
> *of those overcome with wine!*
> *See, the Lord has one who is mighty and strong;*
> *like a storm of hail, a destroying tempest,*
> *like a storm of mighty, overflowing waters;*
> *with his hand he will hurl them down to the earth.*
> *Trampled under foot will be*
> *the proud garland of the drunkards of Ephraim.*
> *And the fading flower of its glorious beauty,*
> *which is on the head of those bloated with rich food,*
> *will be like a first-ripe fig before the summer;*
> *whoever sees it, eats it up as soon as it comes to hand.*

The poem concludes with a word of encouragement to those who serve as judges or who have political responsibilities within a community. Those who have any kind of responsibility for others are urged to maintain a spirit of justice and strength.

> *In that day*
> *the Lord of hosts will be a garland of glory,*
> *and a diadem of beauty, to the remnant of his people;*
> *and a spirit of justice to the one who sits in judgment,*
> *and strength to those who turn back the battle at the gate.*
> *(Isa 28:1–6)*

God's Response to Drunken Priests and Prophets—Isaiah 28:7–10

This is one of the most memorable poems in the entire Bible. In one sense, it is even quite humorous—the Lord God will imitate the speech of a drunkard! The author has expressed God's frustration with people who appear to be intoxicated when they have special responsibilities for others in the community. Here specifically the focus is on priests and prophets who have responsibility for giving wise and reliable counsel. Like drunkards, they seem to be in disarray, unable to deliver wise counsel to others. In their confusion, they stagger like those who are under the influence of strong drink. Consequently, their recommendations sound like gibberish as they utter words that make no sense. In Hebrew, the text sounds like sav *lasav, sav lasav, kav lakav, kav lakav, z'ir sam, z'ir sam!* Translators have attempted to convey the Hebrew with the words: "precept upon precept, line upon line, here a little, there a little!" Whatever these words may mean in English, they also convey the sense that given their condition, the prophet or priest has little to offer by way of help.

> *These also reel with wine and stagger with strong drink;*
> *the priest and the prophet reel with strong drink,*
> *they are confused with wine,*
> *they stagger with strong drink;*
> *they err in vision, they stumble in giving judgment.*
> *All tables are covered with filthy vomit;*
> *no place is clean.*
> *"Whom will he teach knowledge,*
> *and to whom will he explain the message?*
> *Those who are weaned from milk,*
> *those taken from the breast?*
> *for it is precept upon precept [sav lasav],*
> *precept upon precept [sav lasav],*
> *line upon line [kav lakav],*
> *line upon line [kav lakav],*
> *here a little [zi-er sham],*
> *there a little [zi-er sham]."*
> *(Isa 28:7–10)*

Isaiah's Counsel: Give Rest to the Weary!—Isaiah 28:11–13

Two remarkable features now come in this poem. The first is a fundamental theme that is at the very heart of Isaiah's vision. If people are looking for *minukah* ("rest"), they are to find it by giving rest to the weary. Sadly, those described in this text who were supposed to help seem to be in no condition to offer counsel.

The second remarkable feature in this poem comes with the response that the Lord God gives to the drunkards. Yahweh will respond to them with the same words uttered by the priests and the prophets: *sav lasav, sav lasav, kav lakav, kav lakav, z'ir sam, z'r sam!* God can speak gibberish like one who is intoxicated just as well as they can!

> *Truly, with stammering lip and with alien tongue*
> *he will speak to this people,*
> *to whom he has said,*
> *"This is rest; give rest to the weary;*
> *and this is repose";*
> *yet they would not hear.*
> *Therefore the word of the Lord will be to them,*
> *"Precept upon precept [sav lasav],*
> *precept upon precept [sav lasav],*
> *line upon line [kav lakav],*
> *line upon line [kav lakav],*
> *here a little [zi-er sham],*
> *there a little [zi-er sham];"*
> *in order that they may go,*
> *and fall backward, and be broken,*
> *and snared, and taken.*
> *(Isa 28:11–13)*

An Alliance with Egypt Remembered—Isaiah 28:14–22

Justice was to be the line and righteousness the plummet for measuring the integrity of the community of the house of David. Lies and falsehood brought nothing but trouble and destruction. The prophet charges that leaders in the past made a covenant with death, whether that meant an alliance with a foreign country such as Egypt or with the gods of Canaan. In the post-exilic era after the destruction of Jerusalem, the era of the exile and the time of restoration under Cyrus of Persia, the reference to a new "cornerstone being laid in Zion" takes on considerable significance. In the opening chapter of the scroll, the promise was made: *"I will restore your judges as at the first, and your counselors as at the beginning. Afterward you shall be called the city of righteousness, the faithful city. Zion shall be redeemed by justice, and those in her who repent, by righteousness . . ."* (Isa 1:26–27). Now those words are reaffirmed. Righteousness and justice

are to be the guides and the cornerstone by which successive generations
of the community can live.

> *Therefore hear the word of the Lord,*
> *you scoffers who rule this people in Jerusalem.*
> *Because you have said,*
> *"We have made a covenant with death,*
> *and with Sheol we have an agreement;*
> *when the overwhelming scourge passes through*
> *it will not come to us; for we have made lies our refuge,*
> *and in falsehood we have taken shelter";*
> *therefore thus says the Lord God,*
> *See, I am laying in Zion a foundation stone,*
> *a tested stone, a precious cornerstone, a sure foundation:*
> *"One who trusts will not panic."*

It is almost shocking to hear the ancient poet refer to the tools of a carpenter that are still in wide usage today. A line gives evidence of correct
horizontal accuracy; a plummet allows for discernment of vertical accuracy. Even allowing for advances in technology, those fundamentals
remain: like a line and a plummet, justice and righteousness are trustworthy tests for an honest society.

> *And I will make justice the line,*
> *and righteousness the plummet;*
> *hail will sweep away the refuge of lies,*
> *and waters will overwhelm the shelter.*
> *Then your covenant with death will be annulled,*
> *and your agreement with Sheol will not stand;*
> *when the overwhelming scourge passes through*
> *you will be beaten down by it.*
> *As often as it passes through, it will take you;*
> *for morning by morning it will pass through,*
> *by day and by night;*
> *and it will be sheer terror to understand the message.*
> *For the bed is too short to stretch oneself on it,*
> *and the covering too narrow to wrap oneself in it.*

> *For the Lord will rise up as on Mount Perazim,*

he will rage as in the valley of Gibeon
to do his deed—strange is his deed!—
and to work his work—alien is his work!
Now therefore do not scoff,
or your bonds will be made stronger;
for I have heard a decree of destruction
from the Lord God of hosts upon the whole land.
(Isa 28:14–22)

Words on Wise Farming—Isaiah 28:23–29

The world of agriculture requires knowledge of the earth and discernment concerning matters of seedtime and harvest. A good farmer is a person who is wise in such matters. The ground must be carefully prepared and seeds sown in proper places and at the proper depth. Dill must be handled very carefully. It is not to be threshed with a threshing sledge. The same is true for cumin and wheat.[18] Grains must be threshed but they should not be pulverized. Yahweh, who is Lord of all creation, is not just the source of all that grows; Yahweh is also the source of wisdom for those who care for the earth. The poem continues a theme from the previous passages that deplore drunkards. Just as leaders need to discern righteousness and justice for governing a community, so farmers also need to discover wisdom for their work. Wisdom is a gift that comes from the Lord.[19]

Listen, and hear my voice;
Pay attention, and hear my speech.
Do those who plow for sowing plow continually?
Do they continually open and harrow their ground?
When they have leveled its surface,
do they not scatter dill, sow cummin,
and plant wheat in rows and barley in its proper place,
and spelt as the border?

18. Cumin (spelled cummin in the NRSV) is an herb whose seeds were added as a spice for bread. See Deut 14:22–23 and Matt 23:23.

19. On agricultural images in Isaiah, see further "Persistent Vegetative States: People as Plants and Plants as People in Isaiah" by Patricia Tull in Everson and Kim, *The Desert Will Bloom*, 17–34.

For they are well instructed;

their God teaches them.

Dill is not threshed with a threshing sledge,

nor is a cart wheel rolled over cummin;

but dill is beaten out with a stick, and cummin with a rod.

Grain is crushed for bread, but one does not thresh it forever;

one drives the cart wheel and horses over it,

but does not pulverize it.

This also comes from the Lord of hosts;

he is wonderful in counsel, and excellent in wisdom.

(Isa 28:23–29)

Siege and Deliverance for Jerusalem—Isaiah 29:1–8

Again, a bitter memory concerning Jerusalem is recalled. Judah was not able to comprehend the will and intention of Yahweh in the era before the destruction of Jerusalem.[20] War brings sorrowful realities; in war there are no victors! When the effort is made to discern the presence of Yahweh in history, the first thing to note is that the task is extremely complex and often puzzling. Still, faith clings to the conviction that God is the source of truth, wisdom, and peace.

Ah, Ariel, Ariel,

the city where David encamped!

Add year to year; let the festivals run their round.

Yet I will distress Ariel,

and there shall be moaning and lamentation,

and Jerusalem shall be to me like an Ariel.

And like David I will encamp against you;

I will besiege you with towers

and raise siegeworks against you.

Nations may think that they have triumphed over Jerusalem (Ariel) but all too soon they discover that earthly power lasts only for a brief moment in time. Then leaders and nations pass into history like chaff or as a dream in the night.

20. The term "Ariel" is used here as a descriptive term for Jerusalem. It may also refer to a feature of the altar hearth in the temple (Ezek 43:15–16).

Then deep from the earth you shall speak,
from low in the dust your words shall come;
your voice shall come from the ground
like the voice of a ghost,
and your speech shall whisper out of the dust.
But the multitude of your foes shall be like small dust,
and the multitude of tyrants like flying chaff.
And in an instant, suddenly,
you will be visited by the Lord of hosts
with thunder and earthquake and great noise,
with whirlwind and tempest,
and the flame of a devouring fire.
And the multitude of all the nations
that fight against Ariel,
all that fight against her and her stronghold,
and who distress her, shall be like a dream,
a vision of the night.

Just as when a hungry person dreams of eating
and wakes up still hungry,
or a thirsty person dreams of drinking
and wakes up faint, still thirsty,
so shall the multitude of all the nations be
that fight against Mount Zion.
(Isa 29:1–8)

The Blindness of Judah—Isaiah 29:9–16

All things come from Yahweh. Yahweh is the source of energy and creativity, whether that energy is used for good or for ill purposes in the world. And yet, the prophet declares that individuals and communities make their own decisions and are responsible for the way that they use their God-given energy or creativity. This is the strange paradox about prophetic speech. We hear echoes in this text from the call vision in Isaiah 6 and from the words of warnings to drunkards in Isaiah 28. Once again, the author uses imagery of blindness and drunkenness to describe people who are selfish or who simply lack wisdom.

> *Stupefy yourselves and be in a stupor,*
> *blind yourselves and be blind!*
> *Be drunk, but not from wine;*
> *stagger, but not from strong drink!*
> *For the Lord has poured out upon you a spirit of deep sleep;*
> *he has closed your eyes, you prophets,*
> *and covered your heads, you seers.*
>
> *The vision of all this has become for you like the words of a sealed document. If it is given to those who can read, with the command, "Read this," they say, "We cannot, for it is sealed." And if it is given to those who cannot read, saying "Read this," they say, "We cannot read."*
>
> *The Lord said:*
> *Because these people draw near with their mouths*
> *and honor me with their lips,*
> *while their hearts are far from me,*
> *and their worship of me is a human commandment*
> *learned by rote;*
> *so I will again do amazing things with this people,*
> *shocking and amazing.*
> *The wisdom of their wise shall perish,*
> *and the discernment of the discerning shall be hidden.*

In the concluding lines of this poem, we hear the frustration felt by the prophetic writer when his words seem to bring only greater confusion and distortion. Humans have a strange need to be like a potter; they want to treat their Creator as clay.

> *Ha! You who hide a plan too deep for the Lord,*
> *whose deeds are in the dark,*
> *And who say, "Who sees us? Who knows us?"*
> *You turn things upside down!*
> *Shall the potter be regarded as the clay?*
> *Shall the thing made say of its maker,*
> *"He did not make me";*
> *or the thing formed say of the one who formed it,*

"He has no understanding"?
(Isa 29:9–16)

Hope for the Future—Isaiah 29:17–24

Isaiah is remembered both for his words of judgment and his words of
hope. Amid the bitter memories, there have been repeated words of encouragement. The meek and the needy are to be comforted. The tyrant
and the scoffer are to be brought low. Here a word of hope is spoken for
those who are blind and deaf.

> *Shall not Lebanon in a very little while*
> *become a fruitful field,*
> *and the fruitful field be regarded as a forest?*
> *On that day the deaf shall hear the words of a scroll,*
> *and out of their gloom and darkness*
> *the eyes of the blind shall see.*
> *The meek shall obtain fresh joy in the Lord,*
> *and the neediest people shall exult in the Holy One of Israel.*
>
> *For the tyrant shall be no more,*
> *and the scoffer shall cease to be;*
> *all those alert to do evil shall be cut off—*
> *those who cause a person to lose a lawsuit,*
> *who set a trap for the arbiter in the gate,*
> *and without grounds deny justice*
> *to the one in the right.*

Help will come from the Lord, the Holy One of Israel, the Lord who redeemed Abraham, the Holy One of Jacob, the God of Israel!

> *Therefore thus says the Lord,*
> *who redeemed Abraham, concerning the house of Jacob:*
> *No longer shall Jacob be ashamed,*
> *no longer shall his face grow pale.*
> *For when he sees his children,*
> *the work of my hands, in his midst,*
> *they will sanctify my name;*

> *they will sanctify the Holy One of Jacob,*
> *and will stand in awe of the God of Israel.*
> *And those who err in spirit will come to understanding,*
> *and those who grumble will accept instruction.*
> *(Isa 29:17–24)*

The Futility of Reliance on Egypt—Isaiah 30:1–5

Political leaders in Judah forgot to ask for the counsel of Yahweh. What this means is that they forgot to keep their focus on the well-being of the people, especially on those within the community who were most in need. When rulers entered into secret relationships or treaty relationships with Egypt, they very likely believed that their actions would bring prestige or greater freedom, allowing them to break free from oppressive Assyrian rule. Isaiah is pragmatic. He urges leaders to count the cost! He contends that joining in an alliance with Egypt against the wishes of Assyria will in reality become a matter of shame, humiliation, and disgrace.

> *Oh, rebellious children,*
> *says the Lord,*
> *who carry out a plan, but not mine;*
> *who make an alliance, but against my will, adding sin to sin;*
> *who set out to go down to Egypt without asking for my counsel,*
> *to take refuge in the protection of Pharaoh,*
> *and to seek shelter in the shadow of Egypt;*
> *Therefore the protection of Pharaoh*
> *shall become your shame,*
> *and the shelter in the shadow of Egypt your humiliation.*
> *For though his officials are at Zoan*
> *and his envoys reach Hanes,*
> *everyone comes to shame through a people that cannot profit them,*
> *that brings neither help nor profit, but shame and disgrace.*
> *(Isa 30:1–5)*

A Further Word against an Alliance with Egypt—Isaiah 30:6–7

The scene is from the wilderness area in the southern part of Judah, the home of lions, vipers, and other desert creatures. A caravan of donkeys and camels moves through that desolate terrain bringing treasures to Egypt. The prophet warns that the assistance from Egypt in exchange for gifts will do nothing to enhance the welfare of the people in Judah. Rather, dealing with Egypt will usher in a time of greater chaos. Egypt is like a time bomb; she is *"Rahab who sits still."* Soon, she will be seen for what Rahab really is: the sea monster who brings chaos and sorrow to the world!

> *An oracle concerning the animals of the Negeb.*
> *Through a land of trouble and distress,*
> *of lioness and roaring lion, of viper and flying serpent,*
> *they carry their riches on the back of donkeys,*
> *and their treasures on the humps of camels,*
> *to a people that cannot profit them.*
> *For Egypt's help is worthless and empty,*
> *therefore I have called her,*
> *"Rahab who sits still."*
> *(Isa 30:6–7)*

Seal a Word for a Future Time—Isaiah 30:8–14

In frustration because his words of counsel went unheeded, Isaiah is remembered summoning a scribe to write down the testimony he had given. His words are to be sealed as a witness for future generations. We have heard a similar sad report in Isaiah 8:16, where the prophet told a scribe to *"bind up the testimony."*

> *Go now, write it before them on a tablet,*
> *and inscribe it in a book,*
> *so that it may be for the time to come*
> *as a witness forever.*
> *For they are a rebellious people,*
> *faithless children,*
> *children who will not hear the instruction of the Lord;*

> Who say to the seers,
> "Do not see";
> and to the prophets,
> "Do not prophesy to us what is right;
> speak to us smooth things, prophesy illusions,
> leave the way, turn aside from the path,
> let us hear no more about the Holy One of Israel."

We do not know the specific details of the crisis that led Judah to form an alliance with Egypt. What is clear from this text is that Isaiah was deeply concerned with the policies of the king and court officials. What seems equally clear is that his counsel was not heard or appreciated.

The actions of political leaders are likened here to a high wall of a house *"bulging out, and about to collapse."* The deceitful activities of certain leaders will bring that wall crashing down. The coming disaster will be like watching a potter's vessel as it is smashed so ruthlessly that not even a shard for dipping water will be left.

> Therefore thus says the Holy One of Israel:
> Because you reject this word,
> and put your trust in oppression and deceit,
> and rely on them;
> therefore this iniquity shall become for you
> like a break in a high wall,
> bulging out, and about to collapse,
> whose crash comes suddenly, in an instant;
> its breaking is like that of a potter's vessel
> that is smashed so ruthlessly
> that among its fragments not a sherd is found
> for taking fire from the hearth,
> or dipping water out of the cistern.
> (Isa 30:8–14)

Isaiah deplores the actions of his government as short-sighted and dangerous. The national policies were disastrous because they violated the treaty stipulations set forth for them by Assyria. As unjust as those stipulations (heavy taxes or tribute) may have been, the prophet contended that the devastations that would follow in retaliation from the empire will be worse. This is the political realism found in prophetic theology. The welfare of the community, especially the condition of the poor and the needy, is more important than political independence!

In Returning and Rest You will find Salvation—Isaiah 30:15–17

This is another classic text within the Isaiah scroll. Isaiah is remembered lamenting that when confronted by a national crisis, government leaders quickly chose to respond with military solutions. Leaders of Judah put their trust in mounted cavalry. Isaiah urges people of faith to pause for a time to reflect on their heritage of faith before rushing off to war. Strength will not be found in military solutions but in quiet reflection, trust, and clear thinking.[21]

> For thus says the Lord God, the Holy One of Israel:
> In returning and rest you shall be saved;
> In quietness and in trust shall be your strength.
> But you refused and said,
> "No! We will flee upon horses"—
> therefore you shall flee!
> and
> "We will ride upon swift steeds"—
> therefore your pursuers shall be swift!
> A thousand shall flee at the threat of one,
> at the threat of five you shall flee,
> until you are left like a flagstaff
> on the top of a mountain,
> like a signal on a hill.
> (Isa 30:15–17)

21. I first wrote these words on the day after President George W. Bush ordered a surge of additional armed forces for the war zone in Baghdad as an answer to the situation of chaos in Iraq. Like President Lyndon Johnson in an earlier era, President Bush was convinced that chaos could be resolved by sending greater numbers of soldiers. I wrote then: "Whatever happens in Iraq, history will remember that at the outset, the United States rushed to a military solution at a time when no weapons of mass destruction were actually present in Iraq."

The Promise to Zion—Isaiah 30:18–26

How did Isaiah know "the way"? How could he be so confident that he knew what it meant to "walk in the light of the Lord"? People in his own era certainly must have wondered. Later generations preserved these words of warning precisely because the events of judgment came to pass. His reading of history proved to be correct. The prophet warned of the danger of worshipping idols made of silver and gold. Such objects do not bring justice or peace.

> *Therefore the Lord waits to be gracious to you;*
> *therefore he will rise up to show mercy to you.*
> *For the Lord is a God of justice;*
> *blessed are all those who wait for him.*

And now the prophetic writer continues in a prose account:

> *Truly, O people in Zion, inhabitants of Jerusalem, you shall weep no more. He will surely be gracious to you at the sound of your cry; when he hears it, he will answer you. Though the Lord may give you the bread of adversity and waters of affliction, yet your Teacher will not hide himself any more, but your eyes shall see your Teacher. And when you turn to the right or when you turn to the left, your ears shall hear a word behind you, saying, "This is the way; walk in it."*
> *Then you will defile your silver-covered idols and your gold-plated images. You will scatter them like filthy rags; you will say to them, "Away with you!"*
> *He will give rain for the seed with which you sow the ground, and grain, the produce of the ground, which will be rich and plenteous. On that day your cattle will graze in broad pastures; and the oxen and donkeys that till the ground will eat silage, which has been winnowed with shovel and fork. On every lofty mountain and every high hill there will be brooks running with water—on a day of the great slaughter, when the towers fall. Moreover the light of the moon will be like the light of the sun, and the light of the sun will be sevenfold, like the light of seven days, on the day when the Lord binds up the injuries of his people, and heals the wounds inflicted by his blow.*
> *(Isa 30:18–26)*

The prophetic writer contends that a sense of wellbeing can be discerned from the rhythms of seedtime and harvest. Peace for humans is much like peace discerned in the natural world. People need to observe and listen to the rhythms of the world around them!

Words of Judgment for Assyria—Isaiah 30:27–33

In Scripture such as Psalms 18 and 104, Yahweh is envisioned as a holy warrior who comes on the clouds of heaven, thundering in the heavens and making his presence known like lightning. Such imagery is also found in the mythic stories about the gods of Canaan that we know from the Ugaritic sources. But in biblical poetry, it is not El or Ba'l who comes; it is clearly Yahweh. As in Isaiah 2 and 13, powerful images are used to describe Yahweh's acts of judgment. Nations both large and small experience judgment. They will be put through a sieve to sort out coarse materials. They will be given a bridle to correct them as one corrects an unruly colt. Assyria is one such arrogant empire. Babylon followed and took the same course of action. One can only wonder about how many later empires have been deceived by their own sense of power in the world.

> *See, the name of the Lord comes from far away,*
> *burning with his anger, and in thick rising smoke;*
> *his lips are full of indignation, and his tongue is like a devouring fire;*
> *his breath is like an overflowing stream that reaches up to the neck—*
> *to sift the nations with the sieve of destruction,*
> *and to place on the jaws of the peoples a bridle that leads them astray.*
>
> *You shall have a song as in the night when a holy festival is kept;*
> *and gladness of heart, as when one sets out to the sound of the flute*
> *to go to the mountain of the Lord, to the Rock of Israel.*
> *And the Lord will cause his majestic voice to be heard and the*
> *descending blow of his arm to be seen, in furious anger*
> *and a flame of devouring fire, with a cloudburst and tempest and*
> *hailstones.*

Assyria thinks it is all-powerful. But the Lord God is capable of bringing down even the mighty and the arrogant ones on the earth.

> *The Assyrian will be terror-stricken at the voice of the Lord,*
> *when he strikes with his rod. And every stroke of the staff of punishment*
> *that the Lord lays upon him will be to the sound of timbrels and lyres;*

battling with brandished arm he will fight with him. For his burning place has long been prepared; truly it is made ready for the king, its pyre made deep and wide, with fire and wood in abundance;the breath of the Lord, like a stream of sulfur, kindles it.

(Isa 30:27–33)

A funeral pyre is to be built for Assyria. The funeral will not be a time of mourning; rather it will have the joyous sounds of celebration, with timbrels and lyres as at a festival of thanksgiving! Yahweh, the divine warrior, will deal with Assyria.

Throughout the scroll, we hear repeated warnings given to small countries such as Judah about attempts to plot rebellion against an empire. This counsel comes from an awareness that such actions usually end in disaster. But as in Isaiah 10:12–19, the prophet is also convinced that even empires eventually receive punishment for arrogant and ruthless conduct. Empires rise and fall! They are not gods.

The Futility of the Alliance with Egypt—Isaiah 31:1–3

The poem picks up themes from Isaiah 30:1–5 and recalls again the dangers of placing false hope in the promises of Egypt. Later generations remember the tendency of leaders to place their trust in chariots, horsemen, and military might to achieve their goals. Looking to the Holy One of Israel means much more than prayer; it means a commitment to live by the vision that focuses on the well-being of those most in need within a community. It means exploring all options for peace before rushing off to war.

> *Alas for those who go down to Egypt for help,*
> *and who rely on horses, who trust in chariots*
> *because they are many and in horsemen*
> *because they are very strong,*
> *but do not look to the Holy One of Israel or consult the Lord!*
> *Yet he too is wise and brings disaster;*
> *he does not call back his words,*
> *but will rise against the house of the evildoers,*
> *and against the helpers of those who work iniquity.*
> *The Egyptians are human, and not God;*
> *their horses are flesh, and not spirit.*

When the Lord stretches out his hand,
the helper will stumble,
and the one helped will fall,
and they will all perish together.
(Isa 31:1–3)

A Vision of Deliverance for Jerusalem—Isaiah 31:4–9

Yahweh has good intentions for his people, Zion. This is not Zion, right or wrong. The prophet envisions a community that is seeking to live with humility and peace. When the people live with those commitments, they may trust that the Lord of hosts will protect and rescue them. In retrospect, the post-exilic community knows that some survived when destruction came. In later eras of history, these words still call people to trust and have faith.

For thus the Lord said to me,
As a lion or a young lion growls over its prey,
and—when a band of shepherds
is called out against it—
is not terrified by their shouting
or daunted at their noise,
so the Lord of hosts will come down
to fight upon Mount Zion and upon its hill.
Like birds hovering overhead,
so the Lord of hosts will protect Jerusalem;
he will protect and deliver it,
he will spare and rescue it.

Turn back to him whom you have deeply betrayed, O people of Israel.
For on that day all of you shall throw away your idols of silver and idols
of gold, which your hands have sinfully made for you.

"Then the Assyrian shall fall by a sword, not of mortals;
and a sword, not of humans, shall devour him;
he shall flee from the sword,
and his young men shall be put to forced labor.

His rock shall pass away in terror,
and his officers desert the standard in panic,"
says the Lord, whose fire is in Zion,
and whose furnace is in Jerusalem.
(Isa 31:4–9)

A Vision of an Ideal King—Isaiah 32:1–8

An ideal leader is a shelter in the midst of a windstorm. An ideal leader is a stream of fresh water in a dry place or a secure rock in a weary land. Echoing themes set forth in Isaiah 11, this poem envisions one who is a model of responsible leadership. The bitter memories heard in the call vision of chapter 6 linger over this section of the scroll. There the people and political leaders of Judah were portrayed as blind, deaf, and suffering from hardness of heart. The task of the ideal leader is to restore sight for the blind, hearing for the deaf, and good judgment for the afflicted. In chapters 36–39, Hezekiah will be remembered as a king who aspired to such virtues.

See, a king will reign in righteousness,
and princes will rule with justice.
Each will be like a hiding place from the wind,
a covert from the tempest,
like streams of water in a dry place,
like the shade of a great rock in a weary land.

Then the eyes of those who have sight will not be closed,
and the ears of those who have hearing will listen.
The minds of the rash will have good judgment,
and the tongues of stammerers
will speak readily and distinctly.

A fool will no longer be called noble,
nor a villain said to be honorable.
For fools speak folly, and their minds plot iniquity:
to practice ungodliness, to utter error concerning the Lord,
to leave the craving of the hungry unsatisfied,

and to deprive the thirsty of drink.
The villainies of villains are evil;
they devise wicked devices
to ruin the poor with lying words,
even when the plea of the needy is right.
But those who are noble plan noble things,
and by noble things they stand.
(Isa 32:1–8)

A Warning for Complacent Women—Isaiah 32:9–20

In a number of places in the Isaiah scroll, words of judgment are announced concerning wealthy women (see Is 3:16–17, 3:18–26, and 4.1). Rich women, like their husbands, grow complacent and come to feel entitled to their status in life without thought for those who are in desperate need. Isaiah boldly declares that judgment will also come for them. Then at the end of this poem, the author envisions a time when the spirit of the Lord will cause justice and righteousness to come on the earth, bringing security to the human family. Integrity and acts of human kindness will bring peace, quietness, and trust.

Rise up, you women who are at ease,
hear my voice;
you complacent daughters, listen to my speech.
In little more than a year you will shudder,
you complacent ones;
for the vintage will fail, the fruit harvest will not come.
Tremble, you women who are at ease,
shudder, you complacent ones;
strip, and make yourselves bare,
and put sackcloth on your loins.

Beat your breasts for the pleasant fields,
for the fruitful vine, for the soil of my people
growing up in thorns and briers;
yes, for all the joyous houses in the jubilant city.

For the palace will be forsaken, the populous city deserted;

the hill and the watchtower will become dens forever,

the joy of wild asses, a pasture for flocks;

until a spirit from on high is poured out on us,

and the wilderness becomes a fruitful field,

and the fruitful field is deemed a forest.

Then justice will dwell in the wilderness,

and righteousness abide in the fruitful field.

The effect of righteousness will be peace,

and the result of righteousness,

quietness and trust forever.

My people will abide in a peaceful habitation,

in secure dwellings, and in quiet resting places.

The forest will disappear completely,

and the city will be utterly laid low.

Happy will you be who sow beside every stream,

who let the ox and the donkey range freely.

(Isa 32:9–20)

Deliverance from Assyria—Isaiah 33:1–24

This chapter may originally have been a conclusion for the poetry collected in Isaiah 28–32. It opens with a word against Assyria. The prophet declares that the destroyer will in turn be destroyed. Then the mood of the poem changes abruptly to a prayer and the plea that the Lord will guide and protect those who trust in him. Zion is once again depicted as a place known for justice and righteousness.[22] Those who heard these words in the post-exilic world knew that both Assyria and Babylon had fallen. The hopes for justice and righteousness remained as powerful challenges for that restored community and they remain for later generations.

Ah, you destroyer,

who yourself have not been destroyed;

22. Childs has suggested that we hear a common thread in the concluding chapters of this section: "the stupidity and foolishness of Israel in failing to comprehend the plan of God that entails the punishment of haughty Israel, then the destruction of Assyria, and finally the exaltation of restored Zion" (Childs, *Isaiah*, 238).

you treacherous one,
with whom no one has dealt treacherously!
When you have ceased to destroy, you will be destroyed;
and when you have stopped dealing treacherously,
you will be dealt with treacherously.

Now the prayer for God's blessing begins. Even in the midst of trouble, the author expresses trust in the promises given in earlier times.

O Lord, be gracious to us;
we wait for you.
Be our arm every morning,
our salvation in the time of trouble.
At the sound of tumult, peoples fled;
before your majesty, nations scattered.
Spoil was gathered as the caterpillar gathers;
as locusts leap, they leaped upon it.
The Lord is exalted, he dwells on high;
he filled Zion with justice and righteousness;
he will be the stability of your times,
abundance of salvation, wisdom, and knowledge;
the fear of the Lord is Zion's treasure.
Listen! The valiant cry in the streets;
the envoys of peace weep bitterly.
The highways are deserted,
travelers have quit the road.
The treaty is broken, its oaths are despised,
its obligation is disregarded.
The land mourns and languishes;
Lebanon is confounded and withers away;
Sharon is like a desert;
and Bashan and Carmel shake off their leaves.

In the midst of trouble, the prophet envisions that the Lord will come and that judgment will be like fire consuming thorns!

"Now I will arise," says the Lord,
"now I will lift myself up; now I will be exalted.
You conceive chaff, you bring forth stubble;

your breath is a fire that will consume you.
And your peoples will be as if burned to lime,
like thorns cut down,
that are burned in the fire."

Hear, you who are far away, what I have done;
and you who are near, acknowledge my might.
The sinners in Zion are afraid;
trembling has seized the godless:
"Who among us can live with the devouring fire?
Who among us can live with everlasting flames?"

Now the author returns to words of promise and hope for those who walk in the way that the Lord has called them to live.

Those who walk righteously and speak uprightly,
who despise the gain of oppression,
who wave away a bribe instead of accepting it,
who stop their ears from hearing of bloodshed
and shut their eyes from looking on evil,
they will live on the heights;
their refuge will be the fortresses of rocks;
their food will be supplied, their water assured.
Your eyes will see the king in his beauty;
they will behold a land that stretches far away.
Your mind will muse on the terror:
"Where is the one who counted?
Where is the one who weighed the tribute?
Where is the one who counted the towers?"
No longer will you see the insolent people,
the people of an obscure speech that you cannot comprehend,
stammering in a language that you cannot understand.

The prophetic writer dreams of Jerusalem as a city at peace, a place where people may find rest in security and peace, a dream that has continued for centuries!

Look on Zion, the city of our appointed festivals!
Your eyes will see Jerusalem, a quiet habitation,

an immovable tent, whose stakes will never be pulled up,
and none of whose ropes will be broken.
But there the Lord in majesty will be for us
a place of broad rivers and streams,
where no galley with oars can go,
nor stately ship can pass.

For the Lord is our judge, the Lord is our ruler,
the Lord is our king;
he will save us.
Your rigging hangs loose;
it cannot hold the mast firm in its place,
or keep the sail spread out.
Then prey and spoil in abundance will be divided;
even the lame will fall to plundering.
And no inhabitant will say, "I am sick";
the people who live there will be forgiven their iniquity.
(Isa 33:1–24)

A Concluding Portrait of Judgment and Salvation—Isaiah 34–35

The twofold poem in Isaiah 34–35 forms a conclusion for the entire second section of Isaiah (Isa 13–35). In a sense, the poem summarizes what has been declared throughout the entire second section. Nations are addressed. Judgment is announced. As in Isaiah 13–14, "day of Yahweh" imagery is once again used in a prominent way to declare Yahweh's sovereignty over the entire world. The world has been filled with the horrors of war. Ruthless conduct has resulted in judgment for nations, large and small. The Lord does not allow injustice and arrogant conduct to go on forever. When nations in turn are brought low, it is God alone who remains sovereign over the earth! Yahweh is again envisioned as a mighty ruler who sets out on a new military campaign, moving from country to country and bringing down in succession the arrogant of the world. In chapter 34, Edom will be the first stop on that campaign. Edom stands as the symbol of the rebellious nation. In chapter 35, words of encouragement will be given for servants of the Lord. Zion and Jerusalem are to be a fruitful place for human and animal habitation.[23]

A Portrait of Judgment—Isaiah 34:1–17

A key for understanding the structure of this poem is to hear the four phrases repeated in a balanced way in the Hebrew text: *"for the Lord is enraged"*, *"for the Lord has a sword"*, *"for the Lord has a sacrifice"*, and finally *"for the Lord has a day of vengeance"* (or better, "vindication"). Yahweh comes to address the powers of death and destruction, powers that diminish the well-being of the human family. Isaiah 34 is primarily a commentary on the never-ending horrors of war in the world.

In contrast to the frightening vision in chapter 34, chapter 35 portrays the world that Yahweh intends for the earth and its inhabitants.

> *Draw near, O nations to hear;*
> *O peoples, give heed!*
> *Let the earth hear, and all that fills it;*
> *the world, and all that comes from it.*

THE LORD'S TIME OF RAGE[24]—ISAIAH 34:2–5

> *For the Lord is enraged against all the nations,*
> *and furious against all their hordes;*
> *he has doomed them, has given them over for slaughter.*

23. In recent scholarship, there has been considerable discussion about Isaiah 34–35. Should they be viewed together with chapters 1–33 or do they rather belong with chapters 40–66? Among the Dead Sea Scrolls, the most famous is the "Great Scroll of Isaiah" (identified as 1QIsa*a*). This scroll has been dated from the first or second century BCE and is almost a thousand years older than previously known Hebrew texts of Isaiah that formed the Masoretic Text. In the DSS scroll, there is a distinct gap of at least three lines at the bottom of a column (column 27) that separates Isaiah 33 from Isaiah 34. In my judgment, this evidence only confirms the suggestion that chapters 34–35 were at one time a separate poetic unit; it does not mean that they were originally part of chapters 40–55. See further, "On Isaiah at Qumran" by George J. Brooke in McGinnis and Tull, As *Those Who are Taught*, 69–85.

24. In the Hebrew text of Isaiah 34:1–24, the four balanced poetic clauses clearly mark off sections of the poem: 34:2: "for Yahweh has wrath" (ki *qasaph ladonai*); 34:6: "Yahweh has a sword" (*chareb ladonai*); 34:6: "for Yahweh has a sacrifice" (*ki zebach ladonai*); and 34:8: "for Yahweh has a day of vindication" (*ki yom nakam ladonai*).

Their slain shall be cast out, and the stench of their corpses shall rise;
the mountains shall flow with their blood.
All the host of heaven shall rot away, and the skies roll up like a scroll.
All their hosts shall wither like a leaf withering on a vine,
or fruit withering on a fig tree.
When my sword has drunk its fill in the heavens,
lo, it will descend upon Edom,
upon the people I have doomed to judgment.

THE LORD'S SWORD—ISAIAH 34:6A

For the Lord has a sword;
it is sated with blood, it is gorged with fat,
with the blood of lambs and goats, with the fat of the kidneys of rams.

THE LORD'S SACRIFICE—ISAIAH 34:6B–7

For the Lord has a sacrifice in Bozrah,
A great slaughter in the land of Edom.
Wild oxen shall fall with them,
and young steers with the mighty bulls.
Their land shall be soaked with blood,
and their soil made rich with fat.

THE LORD'S DAY OF VINDICATION—ISAIAH 34:8–10

For the Lord has a day of vengeance,
a year of vindication by Zion's cause.[25]
And the streams of Edom shall be turned into pitch,
and her soil into sulfur;

25. I think that in verse 34:8, the Hebrew phrase *yom nakam lathonai* should be translated "day of the vindication of Yahweh" and that the parallel phrase *shanath shelumim* should be "year of recompence."

The NRSV here translates *nakam* as "vengeance" and *shelumim* as "vindication".

her land shall become burning pitch.

Night and day it shall not be quenched;

its smoke shall go up forever.

From generation to generation it shall lie waste;

no one shall pass through it forever and ever.

THE DESERTED WASTELAND—ISAIAH 34:11–17

But the hawk and the hedgehog shall possess it;

the owl and the raven shall live in it.

He shall stretch the line of confusion over it,

and the plummet of chaos over its nobles.

They shall name it No Kingdom There,

and all its princes shall be nothing.

Thorns shall grow over its strongholds,

nettles and thistles in its fortresses.

It shall be the haunt of jackals, an abode for ostriches.

Wildcats shall meet with hyenas,

goat-demons shall call to each other;

there too Lilith shall repose, and find a place to rest.[26]

There shall the owl nest and lay and hatch and brood in its shadow;

there too the buzzards shall gather, each one with its mate.

Seek and read from the book of the Lord:

Not one of these shall be missing;

none shall be without its mate.

For the mouth of the Lord has commanded,

and his spirit has gathered them.

He has cast the lot for them,

his hand has portioned it out to them with the line;

they shall possess it forever,

26. Lilith is a female spirit mentioned only in this text in the Bible; she is associated with the creatures of the wilderness, where only death and destruction reign. See Brady, "Lilith," 810. He writes: "In medieval Jewish demonology, Lilith is identified as the "first Eve" who was created from the earth along with Adam, but refused to accept a position subservient to him. She then fled from him and roams the earth looking for newborn infants to devour."

from generation to generation they shall live in it.
(Isa 34:1–17)

The Vision of Peaceful Zion –Isaiah 35:1–10

At the conclusion of the second major section of Isaiah, we again hear words of encouragement. The poet breaks out in words of praise at what ought to be on the earth. In a world that has known all too well the horrors of war, the author urges the people to learn from the past. When people live together with respect and when justice is their guide, peace and blessing can follow. The results of peace can extend even to the animal world and to the world of nature. Eyes will be opened; ears will be unstopped; servants of the Lord will be able to hear the words: *"Strengthen the weak hands, make firm the feeble knees."* They will not fear the new challenges of life.

> *The wilderness and the dry land shall be glad,*
> *the desert shall rejoice and blossom;*
> *like the crocus it shall blossom abundantly,*
> *and rejoice with joy and singing.*
> *The glory of Lebanon shall be given to it,*
> *the majesty of Carmel and Sharon.*
> *They shall see the glory of the Lord, the majesty of our God.*

The author sets out a specific admonition. Anticipating the charge that will be given to people in Isaiah 61:1–7, the word is sounded for servants of the Lord: consider the needs of the weak and the feeble, bring encouragement and hope to others.

> *Strengthen the weak hands, and make firm the feeble knees.*
> *Say to those who are of a fearful heart,*
> *"Be strong, do not fear!*
> *Here is your God.*
> *He will come with vengeance,*
> *and with terrible recompense,*
> *He will come and save you."*
>
> *Then the eyes of the blind shall be opened,*
> *and the ears of the deaf unstopped;*

then the lame shall leap like a deer,

and the tongue of the speechless sing for joy.

For waters shall break forth in the wilderness,

and streams in the desert;

the burning sand shall become a pool,

and the thirsty ground springs of water;

the haunt of jackals shall become a swamp,

the grass shall become reeds and rushes.

A highway shall be there, and it shall be called the Holy Way;

the unclean shall not travel on it,

but it shall be for God's people;

no traveler, not even fools, shall go astray.

No lion shall be there, nor shall any ravenous beast come up on it;

they shall not be found there, but the redeemed shall walk there.

And the ransomed of the Lord shall return,

and come to Zion with singing;

everlasting joy shall be upon their heads;

they shall obtain joy and gladness,

and sorrow and sighing shall flee away.

(Isa 35:1–10)

4.

The Narrative Interlude—Memories of King Hezekiah

Isaiah 36–39

INTRODUCTION

CHAPTERS 36–39 SEEM TO be purposely located at the center of the Isaiah scroll. The memories preserved are dated from 701 BCE, the *"fourteenth year of King Hezekiah"* (Isa 36:1). It is striking that these chapters appear in a prose narrative rather than as a new collection of poetic oracles. With only slight differences, this narrative also appears in 2 Kings 18:13 and 2 Kings 18:17–20:19. Three important verses in 2 Kings 18:14–16 are not included in the Isaiah text. Whether they were deleted from the Isaiah scroll or added to the Kings text has been a subject of widespread debate.[1]

1. The great difficulty in determining what actually happened in the assault by Sennacherib on Jerusalem in 701 BCE stems in large part from the three verses found in 2 Kings 18:14–16. If they are accurate, then it would be difficult to view the departure of the Assyrians as a miracle or as an act of divine deliverance. Those three verses report: *"King Hezekiah sent to the king of Assyria at Lachish, saying, "I have done wrong; withdraw from me; whatever you impose on me I will bear." The king of Assyria demanded of King Hezekiah of Judah three hundred talents of silver and thirty talents of gold. Hezekiah gave him all the silver that was found in the house of the Lord and in the treasuries of the king's house. At that time Hezekiah stripped the gold from the doors of the temple of the Lord, and from the doorposts that King Hezekiah of Judah had overlaid and gave it to the king of Assyria."* A similar account is preserved in the Annals of

The three verses that are present in 2 Kings report that during a military crisis, Judah suffered huge losses and the text strongly suggests that the leaders in Jerusalem surrendered. They suggest that King Hezekiah and Jerusalem survived only by paying a large tribute to the Assyrian emperor, Sennacherib. The account in 2 Kings is also supported by a report preserved in the Annals of Sennacherib.[2] For whatever reason, the Isaiah narrative does not include that report and focuses rather on the miraculous deliverance of the city. This might suggest that the author is recalling a separate or later event. But the contrast between the two accounts, in 2 Kings 18 and in Isaiah 36, may also help us to reflect on what exactly is being emphasized in the Isaiah scroll. In Isaiah, a strong contrast is set out between the memories of Ahaz, a faithless king, and his son Hezekiah, who is remembered as a model for good leadership. Whatever happened in the crisis of 701 BCE with Sennacherib, even if Hezekiah paid tribute, he still could be remembered by later generations for his personal character and for saving the city from destruction.

SENNACHERIB OF ASSYRIA THREATENS JUDAH AND JERUSALEM—ISAIAH 36:1-22

In Isaiah 7, Ahaz was remembered as a poor king. He did not trust in the promises of God or live by the counsel of the prophet. In contrast, King Hezekiah is now portrayed as a "man of God." He responds in a time of crisis with an attitude of reverence and humility. He puts on sackcloth and makes a plea for mercy. During the assault on Jerusalem, an Assyrian official known as the Rabshakeh came as a spokesperson or herald for the king of Assyria. He stands outside of the city wall and addresses the aides to King Hezekiah in the presence of other people on the wall. The location is by the conduit of the upper pool on the highway to the Fuller's Field, exactly the same place where Isaiah went with his son to confront Ahaz, according to chapter 7. The mention of this location suggests that the reaction of Hezekiah is to be understood in striking contrast with the earlier reaction of his father, Ahaz.

Sennacherib, which has led many scholars to trust that the 2 Kings record is probably a more accurate record of what actually happened in 701. The contrasting views suggest that the Isaiah scroll is purposely preserving an ideal portrait of Hezekiah as a model to give encouragement and guidance for servants of the Lord.

2. See Pritchard, *Ancient Near Eastern Texts,* 287–88.

*In the fourteenth year of King Hezekiah, King Sennacherib of As-
syria came up against all the fortified cities of Judah and captured
them. The king of Assyria sent the Rabshakeh from Lachish to
King Hezekiah at Jerusalem with a great army. He stood by the
conduit of the upper pool on the highway to the Fuller's Field. And
there came out to him Eliakim son of Hilkiah, who was in charge
of the palace, and Shebna the secretary, and Joah son of Asaph,
the recorder.*

*The Rabshakeh said to them, "Say to Hezekiah: Thus says the
great king, the king of Assyria: On what do you base this confidence of yours? Do you think that mere words are strategy and
power for war? On whom do you now rely, that you have rebelled
against me? See, you are relying on Egypt, that broken reed of a
staff, which will pierce the hand of anyone who leans on it. Such is
Pharaoh king of Egypt to all who rely on him. But if you say to me,
'We rely on the Lord our God,' is it not he whose high places and
altars Hezekiah has removed, saying to Judah and to Jerusalem,
'You shall worship before this altar'? Come now, make a wager
with my master the king of Assyria: I will give you two thousand
horses if you are able on your part to set riders on them. How then
can you repulse a single captain among the least of my master's
servants, when you rely on Egypt for chariots and for horsemen?
Moreover, is it without the Lord that I have come up against this
land to destroy it? The Lord said to me, Go up against this land,
and destroy it."*

*Then Eliakim, Shebna, and Joah said to the Rabshakeh,
"Please speak to your servants in Aramaic, for we understand it;
do not speak to us in the language of Judah within the hearing of
the people who are on the wall." But the Rabshakeh said, "Has my
master sent me to speak these words to your master and to you,
and not to the people sitting on the wall, who are doomed with you
to eat their own dung and drink their own urine?"*

*Then the Rabshakeh stood and called out in a loud voice in
the language of Judah, "Hear the words of the great king, the king
of Assyria! Thus says the king: 'Do not let Hezekiah deceive you,
for he will not be able to deliver you. Do not let Hezekiah make
you rely on the Lord by saying, The Lord will surely deliver us; this
city will not be given into the hand of the king of Assyria.' Do not
listen to Hezekiah; for thus says the king of Assyria: 'Make your
peace with me and come out to me; then every one of you will
eat from your own vine and your own fig tree and drink water
from your own cistern, until I come and take you away to a land
like your own land, a land of grain and wine, a land of bread
and vineyards. Do not let Hezekiah mislead you by saying, The*

Lord will save us. Has any of the gods of the nations saved their land out of the hand of the king of Assyria? Where are the gods of Hamath and Arpad? Where are the gods of Sepharvaim? Have they delivered Samaria out of my hand? Who among all the gods of these countries have saved their countries out of my hand, that the Lord should save Jerusalem out of my hand?

But they were silent and answered him not a word, for the king's command was, "Do not answer him." Then Eliakim son of Hilkiah, who was in charge of the palace, and Shebna the secretary, and Joah son of Asaph, the recorder, came to Hezekiah with their clothes torn, and told him the words of the Rabshakeh.

(Isa 36:1–22)

Three issues merit comment. First, we have before us the incredible drama of a herald speaking on behalf of a king. That herald role is the model for understanding the work of a prophet in ancient Israel. We can almost hear the Rabshakeh declaring: "Thus says Sennacherib, the great Lord of the Assyrian world, the ruler of all the lands of the empire!" With the same kind of royal herald or messenger speech, we hear the prophets of ancient Israel as they declare: "Thus says the Lord, the ruler of heaven and earth!"

Second, we hear the Rabshakeh focus the situation for Hezekiah with the question: "On whom do you now rely?" Isaiah had urged Ahaz "to rely on the Lord" by seeking a sign or listening to prophetic counsel (Isa 7:10–17). We know that Ahaz refused that plea. Now Hezekiah is remembered as faithfully relying on the word of the Lord.

Finally, the herald boasts that the king of Assyria has brought destruction to Hamath, Arpad, and Sepharvaim, cities whose gods could not deliver them. He taunts the people in Jerusalem about the belief that their God, Yahweh, can save them. At the same time, the author suggests that the Assyrians have heard of the warnings spoken by Isaiah or other prophetic figures. The Rabshakeh actually uses the words spoken by Isaiah to declare that the king of Assyria has a command from Yahweh to destroy Jerusalem.

HEZEKIAH CONSULTS WITH ISAIAH—ISAIAH 37:1–7

Tensions are high within Jerusalem. The city is under siege. Assyria will not tolerate rebellion or an alliance with Egypt. The narrative account suggests a direct reversal of the earlier encounter that Isaiah had with Ahaz (Isa 7:1–25). In that earlier encounter, it was Isaiah who had to seek out and confront Ahaz. Now it is the other way around; King Hezekiah summons Isaiah. King Ahaz had earlier responded to Isaiah with a sense of impatience and annoyance; now Hezekiah listens carefully. He demonstrates an attitude of humility as he seeks out the best course of action for the city, even donning sackcloth as a sign of mourning.

> When King Hezekiah heard it, he tore his clothes, covered himself with sackcloth, and went into the house of the Lord. And he sent Eliakim, who was in charge of the palace, and Shebna the secretary, and the senior priests, covered with sackcloth, to the prophet Isaiah son of Amoz. They said to him,"Thus says Hezekiah, This day is a day of distress, of rebuke, and of disgrace; children have come to the birth, and there is no strength to bring them forth. It may be that the Lord your God heard the words of the Rabshakeh, whom his master the king of Assyria has sent to mock the living God, and will rebuke the words that the Lord your God has heard; therefore lift up your prayer for the remnant that is left."
>
> When the servants of King Hezekiah came to Isaiah, Isaiah said to them, "Say to your master, 'Thus says the Lord: Do not be afraid because of the words that you have heard, with which the servants of the king of Assyria have reviled me. I myself will put a spirit in him, so that he shall hear a rumor, and return to his own land; I will cause him to fall by the sword in his own land.'"

(Isa 37:1–7)

The imagery of mourning in the poem is striking. The city is likened to a woman in labor who does not have strength to complete her delivery! After hearing so many words announcing judgment from Isaiah, it seems almost remarkable that here he is remembered as giving a word of hope to the king. Isaiah declares that the siege will be lifted and the Assyrians will return to their own land.

KING SENNACHERIB SENDS A MESSAGE TO KING HEZEKIAH—ISAIAH 37:8-13

Despite the fact that Isaiah has given Hezekiah a word of hope, the Assyrian army has not yet lifted the siege. The Rabshakeh comes a second time and again taunts those on the city wall. The Assyrians have learned that the Egyptian pharaoh, Tirhakah, and the forces of Ethiopia have joined the rebellion and they are waging a siege also against Libnah, a city in southern Judah. Sennacherib sends messengers to remind Hezekiah of his past military conquests. He asks how Hezekiah expects to stand against his overwhelming power and might.

> *The Rabshakeh returned, and found the king of Assyria fighting against Libnah; for he had heard that the king had left Lachish. Now the king heard concerning King Tirhakah of Ethiopia, "He has set out to fight against you." When he heard it, he sent messengers to Hezekiah, saying, "Thus shall you speak to king Hezekiah of Judah: Do not let your God on whom you rely deceive you by promising that Jerusalem will not be given into the hand of the king of Assyria. See, you have heard what the kings of Assyria have done to all lands, destroying them utterly. Shall you be delivered? Have the gods of the nations delivered them, the nations that my predecessors destroyed, Gozan, Haran, Rezeph, and the people of Eden who were in Telassar? Where is the king of Hamath, the king of Arpad, the king of the city of Sepharvaim, the king of Hena, or the king of Ivvah?*

> *(Isa 37:8–13)*

HEZEKIAH'S PRAYER—ISAIAH 37:14-20

Hezekiah is faced with a very difficult dilemma. He may in fact have initi-ated or supported policies that caused the national crisis. But here, he demonstrates his faith and trust in the Lord; his response is understood to be the critical factor for the outcome of the crisis. By his ability to pray, he reveals the depth of his faith. The prayer rightly includes matters of lament as well as praise. This is the first of three prayers that Hezekiah offers in this section of the scroll. He acknowledges his own weaknesses and seeks guidance. Like the ideal leader portrayed in Isaiah 11 and 32, Hezekiah speaks now and acts as a wise ruler.

> *Hezekiah received the letter from the hand of the messengers and read it; then Hezekiah went up to the house of the Lord and spread it before the Lord. And Hezekiah prayed to the Lord, saying: "O Lord of hosts, God of Israel, who are enthroned above the cheru-bim, you are God, you alone, of all the kingdoms of the earth; you have made heaven and earth. Incline your ear, O Lord, and hear; open your eyes, O Lord, and see; hear all the words of Sen-nacherib, which he has sent to mock the living God. Truly, O Lord,*

*the kings of Assyria have laid waste all the nations and their lands,
and have hurled their gods into the fire, though they were no gods,
but the work of human hands—wood and stone—and so they
were destroyed. So now, O Lord our God, save us from his hand,
so that all the kingdoms of the earth may know that you alone are
the Lord."*

(Isa 36:14–20)

THE LORD'S RESPONSE TO KING HEZEKIAH —ISAIAH 37:21-29

Isaiah is able to give Hezekiah a further word of encouragement and
hope. The word comes in the form of an address to Sennacherib, the arrogant king of Assyria, who seems to delight in destroying cities.

> *Then Isaiah son of Amoz sent to Hezekiah, saying: "Thus says the
> Lord, the God of Israel: Because you have prayed to me concerning
> King Sennacherib of Assyria, this is the word that the Lord has
> spoken concerning him:*
> *She despises you,*
> *she scorns you—virgin daughter Zion;*
> *she tosses her head—behind your back,*
> *daughter Jerusalem.*
> *"Whom have you mocked and reviled?*
> *Against whom have you raised your voice*
> *and haughtily lifted your eyes?*
> *Against the Holy One of Israel!*

What follows is a classic statement of the "arrogance of power" theme first
set forth regarding emperors and empires in Isaiah 10:5–19. Sennacherib
has "played God" in the world and now, with the destruction of his army
(probably involving disease of some sort among his deployed troops),
will come to realize the truth that people, even warriors prepared for
battle, are still mortal human beings. God alone is God and is the author
of Sennacherib's energy and strength, even when he does not know that.

> *By your servants you have mocked the Lord,*
> *and you have said,*
> *'With my many chariots I have gone up*

the heights of the mountains, to the far recesses of Lebanon;
I felled its tallest cedars, its choicest cypresses;
I came to its remotest height, its densest forest.
I dug wells, and drank waters,
I dried up with the sole of my foot all the streams of Egypt.'
"Have you not heard that I determined it long ago?
I planned from days of old what now I bring to pass,
that you should make fortified cities crash into heaps of ruins,
while their inhabitants, shorn of strength, are dismayed and confounded;
they have become like plants of the field and like tender grass,
like grass on the housetops, blighted before it is grown."
"I know your rising up and your sitting down,
your going out and coming in, and your raging against me.

Sennacherib has accomplished results from wisdom granted from his creator.

He alone bears responsibility for how he has used that wisdom. Now, because of arrogance, he will experience judgment. Like a fish, he will have a hook placed in his nose. Like a horse, he will have a bit put into his mouth. He will return by the way that he has come.

Because you have raged against me
and your arrogance has come to my ears,
I will put my hook in your nose and my bit in your mouth;
I will turn you back on the way by which you came."
(Isa 37:21–29)

A PROMISE OF FUTURE HOPE FOR A REMNANT PEOPLE—ISAIAH 37:30-36

The memory preserved here is from the era when Sennacherib was threatening Jerusalem, when deliverance was promised to the people of Judah. A promise is given that people who trust and live by the promises of the Lord will within three years sow, reap, plant vineyards, and eat their own fruit, once again finding joy in life. For those who heard these words in the post-exilic era, hope is grounded in the same conviction that the God of history intends that people should know and experience peace and prosperity.

"And this shall be the sign for you: This year eat what grows of itself, and in the second year what springs from that; then in the third year sow, reap, plant vineyards, and eat their fruit. The surviving remnant of the house of Judah shall again take root downward, and bear fruit upward; for from Jerusalem a remnant shall go out, and from Mount Zion a band of survivors. The zeal of the Lord of hosts will do this."

"Therefore thus says the Lord concerning the king of Assyria: He shall not come into this city, shoot an arrow there, come before it with a shield, or cast up a siege ramp against it. By the way that he came, by the same he shall return; he shall not come into this city, says the Lord. For I will defend this city to save it, for my own sake and for the sake of my servant David."

(Isa 37:30–35)

THE REPORT OF SENNACHERIB'S DEFEAT AND DEATH—ISAIAH 37:36-38

A miracle is remembered! A prophetic word is given to Hezekiah concerning Sennacherib and that word becomes reality. In the Isaiah scroll, the crisis involving Sennacherib (at about 701 BCE) is remembered as a time not of judgment but of amazing deliverance. The army of Assyria lifted the siege and returned home.

Then the angel of the Lord set out and struck down one hundred eighty-five thousand in the camp of the Assyrians; when morning dawned, they were all dead bodies. Then King Sennacherib of Assyria left, went home, and lived at Nineveh. As he was worshiping in the house of his god Nisroch, his sons Adram-melech and Sharezer killed him with the sword, and they escaped into the land of Ararat. His son Esar-haddon succeeded him.

(Isa 37:36–38)

The report suggests that a plague swept through the Assyrian camp; whatever happened, later generations remembered that there had been a sudden withdrawal of Assyrian forces. The prayers of a good king made a difference. Disaster was averted! Isaiah's word of promise for Hezekiah came to pass as the enemy departed and the king of Assyria, Sennacherib, died at the hand of his own sons.[3]

HEZEKIAH'S ILLNESS AND A SECOND PRAYER—ISAIAH 38:1-8

The memory in Isaiah 38:1-8 preserves an account from a time when Hezekiah had grown older and became ill. He wants to live and his new prayer to Yahweh is characterized by both candor and contrition. In the Torah, the command is given: *"You shall love the Lord your God with all your heart, and with all your soul, and with all your might"* (Deut 6:5). Hezekiah is portrayed as one who seeks to live by that command. In response to his prayer, Isaiah is able to tell Hezekiah that he will have another fifteen years of life.

> *In those days Hezekiah became sick and was at the point of death. The prophet Isaiah son of Amoz came to him, and said to him,*
> *"Thus says the Lord: Set your house in order,*
> *for you shall die; you shall not recover."*
> *Then Hezekiah turned his face to the wall, and prayed to the Lord:*
> *"Remember now, O Lord, I implore you, how I have walked before you in faithfulness with a whole heart, and have done what is good in your sight." And Hezekiah wept bitterly.*
> *Then the word of the Lord came to Isaiah: "Go and say to Hezekiah, Thus says the Lord, the God of your ancestor David: I have heard your prayer, I have seen your tears; I will add fifteen years to your life. I will deliver you and this city out of the hand of the king of Assyria, and defend this city.*
> *"This is a sign to you from the Lord, that the Lord will do this thing that he has promised: See, I will make the shadow cast by the declining sun on the dial of Ahaz turn back ten steps." So the sun turned back on the dial the ten steps by which it had declined.*[4]

(Isa 38:1-8)

3. It is interesting to speculate that Isaiah 22:1-14 may have originally been a memory of the same events of 701 BCE from quite a different perspective. In that account, the prophet recalls severe fighting and loss of life. And yet it also presupposes that the enemy has left without destroying Jerusalem. Isa 22:1-14 seems more compatible with the memories preserved in the 2 Kings 18 narrative.

4. In his "Hymn in Honor of Our Ancestors," dated from about 200 BCE, the author of the apocryphal book of Sirach remembers this event as the first word in his

A THIRD PRAYER OF HEZEKIAH—ISAIAH 38:9-22

The prayers of King Hezekiah in the Isaiah scroll are among the most moving poems in the entire Bible. The third prayer describes a monarch who is fully prepared to acknowledge the mistakes he has made as a king. He listens to the counsel of the prophet and prays to God for guidance and deliverance. The prayer is a model for all people of faith who face difficulties and troubles in various stages of life.

A writing of King Hezekiah of Judah, after he had been sick and had recovered from his sickness:

I said: In the noontide of my days I must depart;
I am consigned to the gates of Sheol
for the rest of my years.
I said, I shall not see the Lord in the land of the living;
I shall look upon mortals no more among the inhabitants of the world.
My dwelling is plucked up and removed from me like a shepherd's tent;
like a weaver I have rolled up my life;
he cuts me off from the loom;
from day to night you bring me to an end;
I cry for help until morning;
like a lion he breaks all my bones;
from day to night you bring me to an end.
Like a swallow or a crane I clamor, I moan like a dove.
My eyes are weary with looking upward.
O Lord, I am oppressed; be my security!
But what can I say? For he has spoken to me,
and he himself has done it.

All my sleep has fled because of the bitterness of my soul.
O Lord, by these things people live,
and in all these is the life of my spirit.
Oh, restore me to health and make me live!
Surely it was for my welfare that I had great bitterness;
but you have held back my life from the pit of destruction,

---

tribute to Isaiah: "In Isaiah's days the sun went backward, and he prolonged the life of the king. By his dauntless spirit he saw the future, and comforted mourners in Zion. He revealed what was to occur to the end of time, and the hidden things before they happened" (see Sirach 48:23–25).

THE NARRATIVE INTERLUDE—MEMORIES OF KING HEZEKIAH

for you have cast all my sins behind your back.

For Sheol cannot thank you,

death cannot praise you;

those who go down to the Pit

cannot hope for your faithfulness.

The living, the living, they thank you as I do this day;

fathers make known to children your faithfulness.

The Lord will save me,

and we will sing to stringed instruments

all the days of our lives,

at the house of the Lord.

    Now Isaiah had said, "Let them take a lump of figs, and apply it to the boil, so that he may recover. Hezekiah also had said, "What is the sign that I shall go up to the house of the Lord?"

(Isa 38:9–22)

The last lines in this section seem out of place. In 2 Kings 20:1–11, the reference to treating a boil with a lump of figs comes before Hezekiah's prayer (2 Kgs 20:7). Could it be that a scribe simply added this detail at the end of this account because it was included in the 2 Kings account?[5] Throughout history, people have tested and lived by various remedies and cures for physical problems such as boils. But the power of prayer is still at the center of this text. The prayer is set in the context of healing and restoration. While the memory focuses on the life of an individual king, the prayer seems to be preserved as a model for all people in later generations who long for physical health and healing.

MESSENGERS COMING FROM BABYLON —ISAIAH 39:1–8

The final chapter of this narrative interlude is filled with intrigue. Why would Hezekiah show guests from the province of Babylon the valuables in the temple and in his armory? The Babylonian king, Merodach-baladan, is remembered from a time at about 705–701 BCE, well before the era when Babylon became a world empire some ninety years later, around 612 BCE. Those who collected the memories in the Isaiah scroll included this narrative, fully aware that it was Babylon that devastated

---

5. See further, Tucker, *The Book of Isaiah 1–39*, 301.

Jerusalem in both 598 and 587 BCE. This report recalls that Isaiah told Hezekiah that a day would come when Babylon would destroy Jerusalem, deport many people, and bring an end to the Davidic line of monarchy in Judah.

> At that time King Merodach-baladan son of Baladan of Babylon sent envoys with letters and a present to Hezekiah, for he heard that he had been sick and had recovered. Hezekiah welcomed them; he showed them his treasure house, the silver, the gold, the spices, the precious oil, his whole armory, all that was found in his storehouses. There was nothing in his house or in all his realm that Hezekiah did not show them. Then the prophet Isaiah came to King Hezekiah and said to him, "What did these men say? From where did they come to you?" Hezekiah answered, "They have come to me from a far country, from Babylon." He said "What have they seen in your house?" Hezekiah answered, "They have seen all that is in my house; there is nothing in my storehouses that I did not show them."

(Isa 39:1–4)

The text is filled with puzzling questions. Why would Hezekiah share his state secrets with the officials from Babylon? And why would those who later collected Isaiah's writings have chosen to preserve this historical memory? The account records that Hezekiah was told that at a future time, Babylon would conquer Jerusalem and deport people, including his sons. The author of this account reports that Hezekiah somehow felt a certain degree of relief after hearing that word, trusting that at least he would have peace in his own time.

> Then Isaiah said to Hezekiah, "Hear the word of the Lord of hosts: Days are coming when all that is in your house, and that which your ancestors have stored up until this day, shall be carried to Babylon; nothing shall be left, says the Lord. Some of your own sons who are born to you shall be taken away; they shall be eunuchs in the palace of the king of Babylon." Then Hezekiah said to Isaiah, "The word of the Lord that you have spoken is good." For he thought, "There will be peace and security in my days."

(Isa 39:1–8)

Those in the post-exilic era who set chapters 36–39 in the heart of the Isaiah scroll knew that Assyria and Babylon had risen to power and that they had both fallen from power. There is a sense in which chapters

36–39 provide a break or a pause between the "bitter memories" of those past eras of history and the new hopeful eras that is to come. New eras of history provide the setting for Isaiah 40–55 and 56–66.

5.

The Hopeful Memories
Isaiah 40–55

INTRODUCTION

"COMFORT, O COMFORT MY people, says your God!" With these words, a new section of the Isaiah scroll begins. After the prose narrative in Isaiah 36–39, a message of comfort is set forth for people who have known the death-like experience of exile. The lyric poetry in these chapters recalls a particular time in the history of Israel. It was a time when Babylon was no longer to be feared. The poetry is filled with the hopeful expectations that a new era is emerging in history with the rise of Cyrus of Persia. A "new thing" is happening. Chapters 1–12 are crafted with the knowledge that Jerusalem had been destroyed. The prophetic words of warning remembered there came to pass with the fall of Jerusalem. Judgment came for Judah! Chapters 13–35 preserve memories of the horrors of past warfare including the fall of Assyria, the rise and fall of Babylon, and other warfare that devastated many small countries. Now chapters 40–55 focus not on the past but on hope for the future. In the years between 550 and 539 BCE, Cyrus of Persia conquered vast territory and allowed captive peoples to return to their homelands. Hebrew captives in Babylon could anticipate that they would also be allowed to return home. The authors of the poetry in the Isaiah scroll understood these events to be in accord with an essential part of Isaiah's vision that the world can be redeemed.

Life can be renewed. When leaders appear in the world who are sensitive to human need, they give evidence of Yahweh's spirit at work, bringing hope through their acts of compassion and justice in the world.

Because of his actions, Cyrus will be described as a servant carrying out the will of Yahweh. And in fact, in 539 BCE, he issued a formal degree that allowed exiles to return to their homelands. The lyric poetry preserved in this section celebrates that historic era. The poetry is like fresh cool water on a very warm day. It is like delightful "sweet water."[1] Like King Hezekiah, described in Isaiah 36–39, many within the community knew the experience of being near death. Like Hezekiah, those captive people and others who later preserved the poetry in the Isaiah scroll knew that their calling was to be faithful servants of the Lord. Over the centuries, people have continued to find new strength and energy for living from these words with trust and hopeful expectations about the future.

WORDS OF COMFORT AND HOPE—ISAIAH 40-48

Comfort for Weary People!—Isaiah 40:1–5

At the heart of the Torah are the words, *"You shall have no other gods before me!"* (Exod 20:3; Deut 5:7). That declaration does not deny the existence of other divine powers; it simply puts other powers in their proper place. In this introductory poem, the scene is once again the heavenly court. It is the same setting in which Yahweh brought suit against a rebellious people in the opening chapter of the scroll. Isaiah was remembered standing in the heavenly courtroom when he received his commission

---

1. The contrasts between "bitter" and "sweet" in the Bible recall the sojourn in the wilderness of Shur described in Exodus 15:22–25. Three days into the wilderness, the community found no water; at Marah, they could not drink the water because it was *mar* ("bitter"). Moses cried out to the Lord, who showed him a piece of wood; when Moses threw it into the water, the water became *matoq* ("sweet"). In Isaiah, the contrast is used in the woe oracle in 5:20: *"Ah, you who call evil good and good evil, who put darkness for light and light for darkness, who put bitter for sweet and sweet for bitter!"* The bitter memories of the fall of Jerusalem are expressed in Lamentations 1:4: *"*The roads to Zion mourn, for no one comes to the festivals; all her gates are desolate, her priests groan; her young girls grieve, and her lot is bitter!" Similarly, in Isaiah 24:5, destruction is likened to the silencing of the timbrel and lyre and to strong drink becoming "bitter." And in Isaiah 22:4, the author deplores the behavior of people and declares: *"Look away from me, let me weep bitter tears."* The message of Isaiah 40–55 is that the past era of bitterness and grieving is coming to an end.

(Isa 6:1–13). Now, we hear Yahweh addressing the heavenly court with a wonderful new word of instruction. The imperatives are plural: all who are assembled are told that they should bring comfort to those who are in exile and distress. While the words are addressed to members of the heavenly court, it is clear that they are also intended for later generations of the human family who will hear them:

> Comfort, O comfort my people,
> says your God.
> Speak tenderly to Jerusalem, and cry to her that she has served her term,
> that her penalty is paid,
> that she has received from the Lord's hand double for all her sins.

> A voice cries out:
> "In the wilderness prepare the way of the Lord,
> make straight in the desert a highway for our God.
> Every valley shall be lifted up,
> and every mountain and hill be made low;
> the uneven ground shall become level,
> and the rough places a plain.

> Then the glory of the Lord shall be revealed,
> and all people shall see it together,
> for the mouth of the Lord has spoken."
> (Isa 40:1–5)

The author presupposes that the experiences of exile have transformed people. Arrogance has been replaced by humility. False pretense has been replaced by a more modest and humble spirit. This transformation makes possible the declaration that past sins are forgiven and that a time of captivity should end.[2] The poet envisions a highway that will allow the "glory of the Lord" to return to its proper place. That proper place was within the temple of the Lord at Jerusalem, where people believed that

2. See further, Childs, *Isaiah*, 297: "An immediate elaboration of the message of comfort follows with three announcements of change in the divine purpose, each introduced with a ki "that her term of service is over," "that her iniquity has been pardoned," and "that she has received double from the Lord's hand for all her sins". The reference to "double for all her sins" is not to suggest that Israel received more punishment than deserved, but rather the author makes use of a legal image already found in Exodus 22:3 (4), which requires a guilty one to restore double for a crime."

it had dwelt ever since the completion of the temple during the era of Solomon (1 Kings 8:1–13).[3] Now a poet envisions that Yahweh will once again dwell in Jerusalem among people. With the return of the "glory of the Lord," God will once again be *Immanuel*, God with us![4]

The Enduring Word of the Lord—Isaiah 40:6–8

People are like grass, declares the poet. Amid all of the changing fortunes of time and history, generations of people come and go. The poet contends that what remains constant and enduring in life is the word of Yahweh. That is a gracious word of the Creator that endures forever.

> *A voice says: 'Cry out!"*
> *And I said, "What shall I cry?"*
> *All people are grass, their constancy is like the flower of the field.*
> *The grass withers, the flower fades, when the breath of the Lord blows upon it;*
> *surely the people are grass.*
> *The grass withers, the flower fades;*
> *but the word of our God will stand forever.*
> *(Isa 40:6–8)*

The poet invites reflection on these questions: What counts in life? What ultimately brings meaning to life? By what word can people live? In Isaiah's vision, the word becomes visible in actions that demonstrate compassion, mercy, and goodness. Such actions have lasting value because they mirror the will of the Creator of heaven and earth. When actions are humane, God's presence is affirmed. And it is through such activity

---

3. In the book of Ezekiel, great attention is given to the poetry of the "glory of the Lord." It is depicted as a bright light or fiery presence that reflects the divine presence of God which resided in the Holy of Holies within the temple in Jerusalem. In Ezekiel 8–11, the "glory of the Lord" departs from Jerusalem; this is a powerful way by which the prophet announces judgment upon the city, declaring that without the presence of Yahweh, they are totally vulnerable to enemy attack and destruction. In Ezekiel 40–48, the prophetic collection concludes with a word of hope, envisioning the return of the "glory of the Lord" to the temple (see Ezek 43:1–5).

4. In the New Testament, the evangelist Mark quotes from this text to speak of the coming of John the Baptist and the "good news" (gospel) of God's love proclaimed by Jesus (Mark 1:1–3 and 1:14).

that people are capable of achievements that last far beyond their own lifetimes![5]

The Proclamation of Good Tidings!—Isaiah 40:9–11

The author is leading up to a complex debate about idols. Already he has declared that among the heavenly assembly, Yahweh is not to be feared as a fickle or remote god. Rather, Yahweh is like a shepherd who cares for those who know weariness and trouble.

> *Get you up to a high mountain, O Zion, herald of good tidings;*
> *lift up your voice with strength, O Jerusalem, herald of good tidings,*
> *lift it up, do not fear;*
> *say to the cities of Judah;*
> *"Here is your God!"*
> *See, the Lord God comes with might, and his arm rules for him;*
> *his reward is with him, and his recompense before him.*
> *He will feed his flock like a shepherd;*
> *he will gather the lambs in his arms,*
> *and carry them in his bosom,*
> *and gently lead the mother sheep.*
> *(Isa 40:9–11)*

Humility remains a key for understanding this section of the scroll. The memories of the destruction of Jerusalem and the difficult aspects of life

---

5. In our time, one cannot help but think about the role model of Nelson Mandela, who suffered years of imprisonment during the era of apartheid in South Africa and then became the "father of South Africa" as the first elected president after apartheid was abolished. We can also think of the poet, Vaclav Havel, who suffered imprisonment under the communist rule in Czechoslovakia and then became president of the Czech Republic; it is most interesting to ponder how his country separated peacefully into two countries, the Czech Republic and the Slovakian Republic, rather than going to war to preserve a strangely unified country. We can also think of the heroic life of Dietrich Bonhoeffer, who chose deliberately to leave New York to return to his homeland to speak out against Adolf Hitler, to combat the forces of Nazi power, and to die as a martyr in Germany. We can remember the heroic work of Mother Theresa in India. In the United States, we can recall the work of Sojourner Truth, Harriet Tubman, Susan B. Anthony, Harriet Beecher Stowe, and others who spoke out for justice in matters such as ending slavery and giving equal rights to women. And we remember Marin Luther King for his courageous life and for his voice speaking truth to power on behalf of justice for all people.

in exile have brought a sense of humility within the community, whether they wished for it or not. Some among the deportees had come to possess wealth and position. But for many others, the situation in Babylon was difficult and oppressive. In this section, we no longer hear words of warning to the community about arrogant conduct as in the earlier sections of the scroll. Humble people are now to be comforted!

Yahweh as Creator of Heaven and Earth—Isaiah 40:12–17

The announcement of restoration has been made. A new era is coming. To support his case, the author draws from the traditions about the creation of the world, stories known from the Torah. In Genesis, God created the earth and charged humanity to be the caretakers of the earth. In Exodus, God created a people, bringing them out of bondage in Egypt. Yahweh is remembered both as creator of heaven and earth and as the source of redemption and renewal in the world. The artistic blending of creation traditions and memories of the exodus is a hallmark within this collection of poetry.

The four rhetorical questions posed in the poem all focus on the same theme: God is God; humans are not! Humans want to create their own gods, carving them out with their own wishful imagination, at times out of fear or greed. When they do so, humans are in fact "playing God;" they're going it on their own and making decisions about priorities in life quite removed from matters of righteousness and justice.

> Who has measured the waters in the hollow of his hand
> and marked off the heavens with a span,
> enclosed the dust of the earth in a measure,
> and weighed the mountains in scales
> and the hills in a balance?
> Who has directed the spirit of the Lord,
> or as his counselor has instructed him?
> Whom did he consult for his enlightenment,
> and who taught him the path of justice?
> Who taught him knowledge, and showed him the way of understanding?
> Even the nations are like a drop from a bucket,
> and are accounted as dust on the scales;
> see, he takes up the isles like fine dust.

Lebanon would not provide fuel enough,
nor are its animals enough for a burnt offering.
All the nations are as nothing before him;
they are accounted by him as less than nothing and emptiness.
(Isa 40:12–17)

The Problem with Idols—Isaiah 40:18–26

Jerusalem lies in ruins! The temple has been destroyed! And the royal house and line of David has been cut off! Where is there any evidence that the God of Abraham is still active in the world? Where was Yahweh when it seemed that Israel or Judah most needed loving care and protection? For an answer, the poet turns to ancient traditions of Yahweh as creator. In Psalm 8, the author declares that God had created humans just *"a little lower than God, and had crowned them with glory and honor,"* charging them to exercise care and dominion over all creatures and things of the earth (Ps 8:5–6). In Isaiah, this understanding of the role of humanity becomes the basis for rejecting the practices of idol worship so prevalent in Babylon and Canaan.

The folly of "bowing down to idols" is the theme of five different poems in this section of the scroll (Isa 40:18–26, 41:6–7, 44:9–20, 45:20–25, and 46:1–13). How will people understand their relationships in life? What will they fear and what will they worship? The poet is concerned that humans find ways to live with courage and joy, fearing only their Creator and taking responsibility for the earth.

To whom then will you liken God,
or what likeness compare with him?
An idol?—A workman casts it,
and a goldsmith overlays it with gold,
and casts for it silver chains.
As a gift one chooses mulberry wood
—wood that will not rot—
then seeks out a skilled artisan
to set up an image that will not topple.
Have you not known? Have you not heard?
Has it not been told you from the beginning?
Have you not understood from the foundations of the earth?

It is he who sits above the circle of the earth,
and its inhabitants are like grasshoppers;
who stretches out the heavens like a curtain,
and spreads them like a tent to live in;
who brings princes to naught,
and makes the rulers of the earth as nothing.
Scarcely are they planted, scarcely sown,
scarcely has their stem taken root in the earth,
when he blows upon them, and they wither,
and the tempest carries them off like stubble.

To whom will you compare me, or who is my equal?
says the Holy One.
Lift up your eyes on high and see:
Who created these?
He who brings out their host and numbers them, calling them all by
name;
because he is great in strength, mighty in power,
not one is missing.
(Isa 40:18–26)

Strength for the Weary—Isaiah 40:27–31

The poetry raises again the question of how people choose to walk. God does not intend that people should walk in dread or in fear of what idols, or the gods whom they represent, may do to them or for them. God intends that people should live with confidence and trust in all stages of their life, even when their physical conditions or social situations change. "Waiting for the Lord" means living with hope, reflecting confidence born of trust. "Walking in the light of the Lord" means living with confidence, accepting responsibility for compassionate and joyous community life with others.

Why do you say, O Jacob, and speak, O Israel,
"My way is hidden from the Lord,
and my right is disregarded by my God"?

Have you not known? Have you not heard?
The Lord is the everlasting God,
the Creator of the ends of the earth.
He does not faint or grow weary;
his understanding is unsearchable.
He gives power to the faint, and strengthens the powerless.

Even youths shall faint and be weary, and the young will fall exhausted;
but those who wait for the Lord shall renew their strength,
they shall mount up with wings like eagles,
they shall run and not be weary,
they shall walk and not faint.
(Isa 40:27–31)

A New Summons and the Introduction of Cyrus—41:1–5

The vision of the heavenly court scene continues. Yahweh reigns over the powers of heaven and earth. Kings and rulers of the earth may not know that their actions will affirm or defy the will of their Creator. Like all other people on earth, they have freedom to choose what actions they will take. But political leaders often wield such enormous authority that their decisions can directly affect the lives of many other people, for better or for worse. When a ruler like Cyrus of Persia is seen to be a redemptive force in the world, there is great joy in the heavenly realms. In the court scene, an announcement is given. Yahweh has *"roused a victor from the east and summoned him to his service"*.

Listen to me in silence, O coastlands;
let the peoples renew their strength;
let them approach, then let them speak;
let us together draw near for judgment.

Who has roused a victor from the east,
summoned him to his service?
He delivers up nations to him,
and tramples kings under foot;
he makes them like dust with his sword,

like driven stubble with his bow.
He pursues them and passes on safely,
scarcely touching the path with his feet.
Who has performed and done this,
calling the generations from the beginning?
I, the Lord, am first and will be with the last.
The coastlands have seen and are afraid,
the ends of the earth tremble;
they have drawn near and come.
(Isa 41:1–5)

Cyrus will not be mentioned by name until the end of Isaiah 44; then he will be mentioned by name again on two different occasions in chapter 45 (See Isa 44:28, 45:1, and 45:13). But there can be no mistaking the allusions in this text. It was the new ruler of Persia who transformed the world by his actions.

Again, the Human Problem: Creating Idols—Isaiah 41:6–7

Warnings were given in Isaiah 40:18–26; now, a taunt song is set forth with a detailed picture of idol-makers who expend great energy creating weighty objects for people. There is both humor and sarcasm in this passage. After working diligently to create the image of a god, people must find nails to prop it up so that it will not topple over! It is the same with the gods that are represented by idols.

Each one helps the other, saying to one another,
"Take courage!"
The artisan encourages the goldsmith,
and the one who smooths with the hammer
encourages the one who strikes the anvil, saying of the sodering,
"It is good";
and they fasten it with nails so that it cannot be moved.
(Isa 41:6–7)

The same sense of humor and irony will be evident in the discourses on idols found in Isaiah 44:9–20, 45:20–25, and 46:1–13. People are created in the image of God; they do not need to manufacture and then prop up images of various gods.

Israel, My Servant—Isaiah 41:8–10

Drawing from the traditions about creation and from memories of Abraham and Jacob, the author reminds the audience that they are a servant people amid the nations of the world. Their calling is not to dominate or to rule harshly over others. The audience is called to be servant people, both individually and as a community. They are called to be examples of justice, upright conduct, humility, and hope. These are the fruits that demonstrate trust in the promises of God, even when the world seems filled with hostility or despair.

> But you, Israel, my servant,
> Jacob, whom I have chosen,
> the offspring of Abraham, my friend;
> you whom I took from the ends of the earth,
> and called from its farthest corners, saying to you,
> "You are my servant,
> I have chosen you and not cast you off";
> do not fear, for I am with you,
> do not be afraid, for I am your God;
> I will strengthen you, I will help you,
> I will uphold you with my victorious right hand.
> (Isa 41:8–10)

The promise is made to people who seek to live in the light of the Lord. They may know that Yahweh is not far from them! The imagery in this text is intended to give reassurance of God's presence and help.

I Will Help You!—Isaiah 41:11–13

The servant community is to draw courage and confidence from the promises of God. There will be new challenges and new difficulties in life. Powers will arise that will seem like brutal enemies. But a word of encouragement is sounded for a new generation in a new era of history: "*Do not fear, I will help you.*" In Isaiah's vision, these words are like a sturdy shelter.

> Yes, all who are incensed against you
> shall be ashamed and disgraced;

those who strive against you
shall be as nothing and shall perish.
You shall seek those who contend with you,
but you shall not find them;
those who war against you
shall be as nothing at all.
For I, the Lord your God, hold your right hand;
it is I who say to you,
"Do not fear, I will help you."
(Isa 41:11–13)

You Shall Rejoice in the Lord!—Isaiah 41:14–16

In Isaiah 40:3–4, the poet speaks of the construction of a highway in the wilderness that will allow captive people to return to Jerusalem. He speaks of the valleys being filled and the mountains and hills being brought low. It is interesting that in this poetry, the author suggests that the servant people will be like a threshing sledge to be used in crushing the mountains and turning hills to chaff. With new energy and power, people will rejoice in their creator as a new era of history comes to reality. Faith makes possible such hopeful expectations concerning the future.

Do not fear, you worm, Jacob,
you insect Israel!
I will help you, says the Lord;
your Redeemer is the Holy One of Israel.
Now, I will make of you a threshing sledge,
sharp, new, and having teeth;
you shall thresh the mountains and crush them,
and you shall make the hills like chaff.
You shall winnow them and the wind shall carry them away,
and the tempest shall scatter them.
Then you shall rejoice in the Lord;
in the Holy One of Israel, you shall glory.
(Isa 41:14–16)

Water for Those Who Thirst—Isaiah 41:17–20

The poet now focuses on "sweet water" that is not bitter or stale. The poet envisions the transformation of the wilderness into a world where pools of fresh water will abound and where an abundance of trees—cedars, acacia, myrtle, olive, and cypress—will provide shade and comfort for the weary. Those who thirst and feel parched in the midst of life are reminded that Yahweh, the author and creator of the world, is the source of good water and also the source of redemption and renewal in the world.[6] We can sense the power and hope that the poet feels, convinced that a new era is coming with the rise of Cyrus of Persia.

> *When the poor and the needy seek water,*
> *and there is none,*
> *and their tongue is parched with thirst,*
> *I the Lord will answer them,*
> *I the God of Israel will not forsake them.*
>
> *I will open rivers on the bare heights,*
> *and fountains in the midst of valleys;*
> *I will make the wilderness a pool of water,*
> *and the dry land springs of water.*
>
> *I will put in the wilderness the cedar,*
> *the acacia, the myrtle, and the olive;*
> *I will set in the desert the cypress,*
> *the plane and the pine together,*
> *so that all may see and know,*
> *all may consider and understand,*
> *that the hand of the Lord has done this,*
> *the Holy One of Israel has created it.*
> *(Isa 41:17–20)*

---

6. Note the striking contrast between the poetry in this chapter and the references to people as "bitter fruit" in the "Song of the Vineyard" allegory in Isaiah 5:1–7.

Set Forth Your Case!—Isaiah 41:21–24

In a bold statement, the author declares that Yahweh is not to be discovered in cultic rituals but rather, through careful reflection on past history. It is in the world that God's activity, for good or for evil, can be discerned. Gods that are represented by idols are challenged to do something! Otherwise, they are declared to be powerless, as impotent as the wood or stone from which those idols have been made.

> *Set forth your case, says the Lord;*
> *bring your proofs, says the King of Jacob.*
> *Let them bring them, and tell us what is to happen.*
> *Tell us the former things,*
> *what they are,*
> *so that we may consider them,*
> *and that we may know their outcome;*
> *or declare to us the things to come.*
> *Tell us what is to come hereafter,*
> *that we may know that you are gods;*
> *do good, or do harm,*
> *that we may be afraid and terrified.*
> *You, indeed, are nothing*
> *and your work is nothing at all;*
> *whoever chooses you is an abomination.*
> *(Isa 41:21–24)*

The vision of Isaiah relates directly to the questions of how human people will choose to live. In the parable of the vineyard in Isaiah 5:1–7, people were to live in such ways that they would bear good fruit. When the vineyard proved to be worthless, destruction was seen as the necessary act for redeeming the land. Now that vineyard was gone; Jerusalem and Judah lay in ruins. Yahweh's earlier announcement of judgment, spoken by Isaiah, had thus been confirmed. God has been active in history. The author challenges the gods of the idols to show something similar in the real world of past history. The author also knows that Isaiah also spoke words of hope for the future. Now those words are coming to pass!

Cyrus as the Instrument of God—Isaiah 41:25–29

With the advances of Cyrus, Isaiah's earlier words of hope have become visible. Those prophetic words of hope are also trustworthy. The poetry in this chapter now concludes with a theological reflection on Cyrus and his military conquests. Yahweh is speaking:

> *I stirred up one from the north, and he has come,*
> *from the rising of the sun he was summoned by name.*
> *He shall trample on rulers as on mortar,*
> *as the pottter treads clay.*
> *Who declared it from the beginning, so that we might know,*
> *and beforehand, so that we might say,*
> *"He is right"?*
> *There was no one who declared it, none who proclaimed,*
> *none who heard your words.*
> *I first have declared it to Zion,*
> *and I give to Jerusalem a herald of good tidings.*
> *But when I look there is no one;*
> *among these there is no counselor*
> *who, when I ask, gives an answer.*
> *No, they are all a delusion;*
> *their works are nothing;*
> *their images are empty wind.*
> *(Isa 41:25–29)*

In the drama of human history, the poet can speak of the freedom and the responsibility of kings and emperors to plan and carry out their own activities. Kings may choose to assume their responsibility for the welfare of people, or they may be corrupt or self-centered. When they choose this latter course of action, they join the rulers of arrogant Assyria and Babylon, leaving only a legacy of ruthless deeds that lead eventually to disaster. And they are unloved by later generations. On the other hand, when national leaders act in humane ways, they leave a legacy of blessing for the world. In Isaiah, Cyrus is remembered as bringing a blessing.

The Summons to Servant Life—Isaiah 42:1–4

The community has already been addressed collectively as a "servant" in Isaiah 41:8. Now we hear more about the role of servant people who seek to live by Isaiah's vision.

> Here is my servant, whom I uphold,
> my chosen, in whom my soul delights;
> I have put my spirit upon him;
> he will bring forth justice to the nations.
> He will not cry or lift up his voice,
> or make it heard in the street;
> a bruised reed he will not break,
> and a dimly burning wick he will not quench;
> he will faithfully bring forth justice.
> He will not grow faint or be crushed
> until he has established justice in the earth;
> and the coastlands wait for his teaching.
> (Isa 42:1–4)

The servant is to bring forth justice (*mishpat*). Throughout the scroll, justice refers specifically to respectful relationships between individuals and groups. Here the servant is charged to be about the task of pursuing justice. Where there is an unfair distribution of wealth in the world, the servant is to speak on behalf of Yahweh. For it seems quite evident that Yahweh sees the world most clearly from the vantage point of the poor. They are the repeated focus of his special concern. From their perspective, patterns of greed are most evident in the world.

Of special interest here is the description of how the servant lives and works in the world. The servant figure does not seem to be a military king. Rather, the servant will work quietly and patiently. The servant can pass through a field so carefully that even a bruised reed will not be broken; the servant can pass by a candle so carefully that the flame will not be extinguished!

The Servant: A Light to the Nations—Isaiah 42:5–8

The work of the servant has an international context. The situation of Judah is understood to be intertwined with surrounding nations. So the task of the servant is not confined to the community in exile. Rather, the servant is to be an example within the community of nations. His calling is to live by righteousness (meaning uprightness or integrity) and he is to be a light for the nations. The servant calls people from captivity to freedom and from blindness to sight. Both the community as a whole and individuals within the community are to draw strength from the promises of the Lord as they seek to live as servants in the world.[7]

> *Thus says God, the Lord,*
> *who created the heavens and stretched them out,*
> *who spread out the earth and what comes from it,*
> *who gives breath to the people upon it*
> *and spirit to those who walk in it:*
> *I am the Lord,*
> *I have called you in righteousness,*
> *I have taken you by the hand and kept you;*
> *I have given you as a covenant to the people,*
> *a light to the nations,*
> *to open the eyes that are blind,*
> *to bring out the prisoners from the dungeon,*
> *from the prison those who sit in darkness.*
> *I am the Lord, that is my name;*
> *my glory I give to no other,*
> *nor my praise to idols.*
> *(Isa 42:5–8)*

The Former Things and the New Things—Isaiah 42:9

The poem concludes by declaring that the former things have come to pass. The prophetic warnings have come to pass. Judah has been punished but Assyria and Babylon have also fallen. The prophetic word has been confirmed by events that have happened. The new things relate to

7. Bernard Duhm first isolated four particular poems within this section of Isaiah as "servant songs": Isaiah 42.1–4, 49.1–6, 50.4–11 and 52.12–53.11. The basic problem with isolating those four poems is that a passage such as Isa. 41.1–10, in which collective Israel is clearly identified as the servant, is disregarded in favor of a view of the servant as an individual. See C.R. North, *The Servant in Deutero Isaiah* for an extended summary of different interpretations of the Servant Songs.

the new world situation created by Cyrus. History is the arena in which God's promise of redemption and hope will come to pass. The prophet declares that life involves new chapters. This poem declares that people stand at the beginning of a new chapter or era of history.

> See, the former things have come to pass,
> and new things I now declare;
> before they spring forth, I tell you of them.
> (Isa 42:9)

Sing to the Lord A New Song!—Isaiah 42:10–13

A hymn of praise similar to the doxologies in Isaiah 12 now follows. In anticipation of Yahweh's new intervention in the world, people of faith are summoned to celebrate! The warfare envisioned in the poem is now on behalf of captive Israel, not against her.

> Sing to the Lord a new song,
> his praise from the end of the earth!
>
> Let the sea roar and all that fills it,
> the coastlands and their inhabitants.
> Let the desert and its towns lift up their voice,
> the villages that Kedar inhabits;
> let the inhabitants of Sela sing for joy,
> let them shout from the tops of the mountains.
>
> Let them give glory to the Lord,
> and declare his praise in the coastlands.
> The Lord goes forth like a soldier,
> like a warrior he stirs up his fury;
> he cries out, he shouts aloud,
> he shows himself mighty against his foes.
> (Isa 42:10–13)

Gasping like a Woman in Labor!—Isaiah 42:14–17

The poet speaks now of the suffering that Yahweh has felt concerning the suffering of people during their time in exile. Yahweh has suffered in silence but now must cry out like a woman in labor. The work of liberation will be as difficult as childbirth. But it will happen.

> *For a long time I have held my peace,*
> *I have kept still and restrained myself;*
> *now I will cry out like a woman in labor,*
> *I will gasp and pant.*
> *I will lay waste mountains and hills,*
> *and dry up all their herbage;*
> *I will turn the rivers into islands,*
> *and dry up the pools.*
> *I will lead the blind by a road they do not know,*
> *by paths they have not known*
> *I will guide them.*
> *I will turn the darkness before them into light,*
> *the rough places into level ground.*
> *These are the things I will do,*
> *and I will not forsake them.*
> *They shall be turned back and utterly put to shame—*
> *those who trust in carved images,*
> *who say to cast images,*
> *"You are our gods."*
> *(Isa 42:14–17)*

What has changed, we might ask? The answer seems to be that the experience of exile caused people to think, to act, and to behave in a more appropriate manner. They understood that life is filled with uncertainties. Exile has given people a clearer perspective on what it means to be human. Servant people, here still remembered as blind and deaf, are summoned to discover new pathways in life where Yahweh will guide them. Darkness will become light and the rough places will turn to level ground.

Learning from Past History—Isaiah 42:18–25

Throughout the Isaiah scroll, we have heard that war is the most shattering reality that can come for a nation or people. War is not heroic. Most often, war leaves behind a legacy of death, disease, wounds, and lingering illness. War pollutes land and destroys the fabric of community structures. In the concluding lines of this poem, two rhetorical questions are posed: Who allowed Jacob or Judah to fall before Babylon? And who gave up Israel, the northern kingdom, to the horrors of the Assyrian army? The poet then answers his own questions. It was not just Assyria or Babylon; it was Yahweh. Yahweh brought punishment upon the people because they did not walk in the way of the Lord and their actions led to warfare. War is understood as the sad consequence of the failures of earlier generations. A community must learn from the horrors of war.

Listen, you that are deaf;
and you that are blind, look up and see!
Who is blind but my servant,
or deaf like my messenger whom I send?
Who is blind like my dedicated one,
or blind like the servant of the Lord?

He sees many things but does not observe them;
his ears are open, but he does not hear.
The Lord was pleased,
for the sake of his righteousness,
to magnify his teaching and make it glorious.

But this is a people robbed and plundered,
all of them trapped in holes and hidden in prisons;
they have become a prey with no one to rescue,
a spoil with no one to say, "Restore!"
Who among you will give heed to this,
and who will attend and listen
for the time to come?

Who gave up Jacob to the spoiler, and Israel to the robbers?
Was it not the Lord, against whom we have sinned,

in whose ways they would not walk,
and whose law they would not obey?

So he poured upon him the heat of his anger
and the fury of war;
it set him on fire all around, but he did not understand;
it burned him, but he did not take it to heart.
(Isa 42:18–25)

The Redemption of a People—Isaiah 43:1–7

The past "bitter era" is over. The Babylonian power has diminished; a whole new world of hope has opened. People were counting the days. Life is not a matter to be determined by the fickle whims of small deities that jealously claim control over various aspects of human life. Life takes on a larger perspective when God is trusted as the source of all creativity and energy in the world. Because God is one, humanity is one. Humans, created in the image of God, are to care for the earth and all creatures on the earth. As they do so, they reflect the love and will of their Creator!

But now thus says the Lord, he who created you, O Jacob,
he who formed you, O Israel:
Do not fear, for I have redeemed you;
I have called you by name, you are mine.
When you pass through the waters,
I will be with you;
and through the rivers, they shall not overwhelm you;
when you walk through fire you shall not be burned,
and the flame shall not consume you.
For I am the Lord your God,
the Holy One of Israel, your Savior.
I give Egypt as your ransom,
Ethiopia and Seba in exchange for you.
Because you are precious in my sight,
and honored, and I love you,
I give people in return for you,
nations in exchange for your life.

Do not fear, for I am with you;
I will bring your offspring from the east, and from the west
I will gather you; I will say to the north,
"Give them up,"
and from the south,
"Do not withhold;
bring my sons from far away
and my daughters from the end of the earth—
everyone who is called by my name,
whom I created for my glory,
whom I formed and made."
(Isa 43:1–7)

Witnesses to a New Chapter in Life—Isaiah 43:8–13

The poet now enters into a legal dispute with those who cannot find hope in their situation. There are some who simply cannot see or hear what is happening in the world. They still seem to be blind and deaf. Apart from anything of their doing, Yahweh is about to be vindicated by the actions of a foreign king and his government.

Bring forth the people who are blind, yet have eyes,
who are deaf, yet have ears!
Let all the nations gather together, and let the peoples assemble.
Who among them declared this and foretold to us the former things?
Let them bring their witnesses to justify them,
and let them hear and say,
"It is true,"
You are my witnesses, says the Lord,
and my servant whom I have chosen,
so that you may know and believe me
and understand that I am he.
Before me no god was formed,
nor shall there be any after me.
I, I am the Lord
and besides me there is no savior.

I declared and saved and proclaimed,
when there was no strange god among you;
and you are my witnesses, says the Lord.
I am God, and also henceforth I am He;
there is no one who can deliver from my hand;
I work and who can hinder it?
(Isa 43:8–13)

I Am About to Do Something New!—Isaiah 43:14–21

A time comes when memories of tragic events should no longer control or dominate one's understanding of life. A time comes when future hope should bring liberation from past troubles and sorrows.[8] The author declares *"Do not remember the former things, or consider the things of old. I am about to do a new thing: now it springs forth, do not you perceive it?"* Past memories are important. Lessons are to be learned. But life can have new chapters! God's presence in the world is not just to be discerned in past history; it is also to be discerned in the present and in new hopes for the future.

Thus says the Lord,
your Redeemer, the Holy One of Israel:
For your sake I will send to Babylon and break down all the bars,
and the shouting of the Chaldeans will be turned into lamentation.
I am the Lord, your Holy One,
the Creator of Israel, your King.
Thus says the Lord, who makes a way in the sea,
a path in the mighty waters, who brings out chariot and horse,
army and warrior:
they lie down, they cannot rise,
they are extinguished, quenched like a wick:
Do not remember the former things, or consider the things of old.

8. No one can dictate or prescribe how long a person should mourn after the death of a loved one or the end of a loving relationship through divorce or separation. Grief runs its own course and sometimes can bring very real depression and sorrow. But for many, a time comes when sad memories are overtaken by new hope for the future. When that time comes, it can almost be difficult to experience happiness and joy again in life. But that is precisely the reality of hope of which this text speaks.

I am about to do a new thing, now it springs forth,
do you not perceive it?
I will make a way in the wilderness and rivers in the desert.
The wild animals will honor me,
the jackals and the ostriches;
for I give water in the wilderness, rivers in the desert,
to give drink to my chosen people,
the people whom I formed for myself
so that they might declare my praise.
(Isa. 43:14–21)

Burdened with Sins—Isaiah 43:22–28

The legal dispute continues. Yahweh faults the human family for their lack of proper sacrificial offerings in life. People have wearied God not with sacrificial offerings but with their sins. But even without remorse from the human family, the poet declares that Yahweh is now forgiving sins in order to renew life. The experience of exile can accomplish this miracle.

Yet you did not call upon me, O Jacob;
but you have been weary of me, O Israel!
You have not brought me your sheep
for burnt offerings,
or honored me with your sacrifices.
I have not burdened you with offerings,
or wearied you with frankincense.
You have not bought me sweet cane with money,
or satisfied me with the fat of your sacrifices.
But you have burdened me with your sins;
you have wearied me with your iniquities.
I, I am He
who blots out your transgressions for my own sake,
and I will not remember your sins.

Accuse me, let us go to trial;
set forth your case, so that you may be proved right.

Your first ancestor sinned,
and your interpreters transgressed against me.
Therefore I profaned the princes of the sanctuary,
I delivered Jacob to utter destruction,
and Israel to reviling.
(Isa 43:22–28)

Water for a Thirsty Land—Isaiah 44:1–5

Amid the bitter memories from the past, the reality of drought has been present. Drought recalls the work of Mot, the Cananite god of death, whose presence results in the realities of suffering, hunger, thirst, and death. Now the promise of rain is announced like a gracious gift from Yahweh. Streams and rivers renew the earth and allow willows, green tamarisk plants, and other good fruits to grow and prosper. They in turn allow life to prosper and flourish. It is the Creator who is the source of renewal in life. This is a "sweet water" memory.[9]

But now hear, O Jacob my servant,
Israel whom I have chosen!
Thus says the Lord who made you,
who formed you in the womb and will help you:
Do not fear, O Jacob my servant,
Jeshurun whom I have chosen.
For I will pour water on the thirsty land,
and streams on the dry ground;
I will pour my spirit upon your descendants,
and my blessing on your offspring.

They shall spring up like a green tamarisk,
like willows by flowing streams,
This one will say,
"I am the Lord's,"
another will be called by the name of Jacob,
yet another will write on the hand,
"The Lord's,"

9. In contrast, see the "bitter memory" in Isaiah 5.

and adopt the name of Israel.
(Isa 44:1–5)

The Lord Alone is God—Isaiah 44:6–8

The overriding concern in the Isaiah scroll is with how people will live. What values will they take as the foundation for life? How will they view the earth and its resources? And what things in life will they fear? The myriad of Babylonian and Canaanite gods draws people into patterns of thinking that remain primarily selfish and self-centered. How do I get ahead? How do I ward off trouble? How do I gain blessing?

The Isaiah scroll sets out an invitation to live without fearing things of this earth; the fear of the Lord is sufficient. With a fundamental sense of reverence for the creator, people are called to be good stewards and caretakers of the earth and the human family.[10]

> *Thus says the Lord, the King of Israel,*
> *and his Redeemer, the Lord of hosts:*
> *I am the first and I am the last;*
> *besides me there is no god.*
> *Who is like me? Let them proclaim it,*
> *let them declare and set it forth before me.*
> *Who announced from of old the things to come?*
> *Let them tell us what is yet to be.*
> *Do not fear, or be afraid;*
> *have I not told you from of old and declared it?*
> *You are my witnesses!*
> *Is there any god beside me?*
> *There is no other rock;*
> *I know not one.*
> *(Isa 44:6–8)*

10. It is interesting to reflect on the parallels between ancient polytheism and the modern-day gambling industry, especially as people become addicted to gambling. Like gambling, ancient polytheistic systems lured people with the promises of potential blessing (prosperity) that would result from generous sacrificial offerings.

A Third Commentary on Idols—Isaiah 44:9–20

The text continues the debate set forth in Isaiah 40:18–26 and 41:6–7. The gods of the nations are like the images that are carved or created to represent them; they are worthless because they have no power in and of themselves. Yahweh is not to be seen in a carved image but in the realities of righteousness and justice whenever and wherever they are apparent in the world. In this narrative, we hear a detailed description of how graven images were made for different classes of people. The rich could afford ornately decorated idols while the poor had to make do with simple images. In the end, however, they are all deemed to be the same. A fine cedar log may be cut in two: half may be carved into an idol and the remainder used to cook food or heat a house. At least the remainder serves some purpose, providing heat on a cold day. The poet wonders why people want to bow down to an idol that is no more active than a dead log or a hunk of wood. The deeper question is what the god, represented by the idol, has done by way of judgment or saving activity in the world.[11]

> All who make idols are nothing,
> and the things they delight in do not profit;
> their witnesses neither see nor know.
> And so they will be put to shame.
> Who would fashion a god or cast an image that can do no good?
> Look, all its devotees shall be put to shame;
> the artisans too are merely human.
> Let them all assemble, let them stand up;
> they shall be terrified,
> They shall all be put to shame.
> The ironsmith fashions it and works it over the coals,
> shaping it with hammers,
> and forging it with his strong arm;
> he becomes hungry and his strength fails,
> he drinks no water and is faint.

11. This text demonstrates the difficulty of discerning between Hebrew prose and poetry. Following the common Hebrew text, the NRSV translates this poem as a prose satire on the absurdity of idolatry. In keeping with the vivid imagery that is present and in light of the other texts dealing with the folly of idol-worship in this section of the scroll, I have presented it here as poetry.

The carpenter stretches a line, marks it out with stylus,
fashions it with planes, and marks it with a compass;
he makes it in human form, with human beauty,
to be set up in a shrine.
He cuts down cedars or chooses a holm tree or an oak
and lets it grow strong among the trees of the forest.
He plants a cedar and the rain nourishes it.
Then it can be used as fuel.
Part of it he takes and warms himself;
he kindles a fire and bakes bread.
Then he makes a god and worships it,
makes it a carved image and bows down before it.
Half of it he burns in the fire;
over this half he roasts meat, eats it and is satisfied.
He also warms himself and says,
"Ah, I am warm, I can feel the fire!"
The rest of it he makes into a god, his idol, bows down to it
and worships it;
he prays to it and says,
"Save me, for you are my god!"
They do not know, nor do they comprehend;
for their eyes are shut, so that they cannot see,
and their minds as well, so that they cannot understand.
No one considers, nor is there knowledge or discernment to say,
"Half of it I burned in the fire;
I also baked bread on its coals, I roasted meat and have eaten.
Now shall I make the rest of it an abomination?
Shall I fall down before a block of wood?
He feeds on ashes;
a deluded mind has led him astray,
and he cannot save himself, or say,
"Is not this thing in my right hand a fraud?"
(Isa 44:9–20)

Remember These Things, O Jacob—Isaiah 44:21–22

As commentary on the previous narrative, the poet offers words to reassure his audience of Yahweh's steadfast love and their calling to be servant people in the world.

> Remember these things, O Jacob,
> and Israel, for you are my servant;
> I formed you, you are my servant;
> O Israel, you will not be forgotten by me.
> I have swept away your transgressions like a cloud,
> and your sins like mist;
> return to me, for I have redeemed you.
> (Isa 44:21–22)

Sing, O Heavens—Isaiah 44:23

Then, in a pattern that is familiar within the lyric poetry in Isaiah, the author breaks out into a hymn of praise.

> Sing, O heavens, for the Lord has done it;
> shout, O depths of the earth;
> break forth into singing, O mountains,
> O forest, and every tree in it!
> For the Lord has redeemed Jacob,
> and will be glorified in Israel.
> (Isa 44:23)

I will Raise Up their Ruins—Isaiah 44:24–28

The chapter concludes with words of reassurance. A spirit of hopefulness has the power to renew confidence and bring new energy for facing future challenges. Yahweh will be there in the new era. Five specific words are set forth: the first is about Jerusalem; the second, a reminder of the exodus when a pathway was made through the sea and when God triumphed over chaos. The third word, located at the center of this text, speaks of Cyrus, who is now mentioned by name for the first time. He is heralded as a "shepherd of Yahweh" who carries out the purpose of

Yahweh. The fourth word is another declaration about Jerusalem; the fifth and final word is about the restoration of the temple.

> *Thus says the Lord, your Redeemer,*
> *who formed you in the womb:*
> *I am the Lord, who made all things,*
> *who alone stretched out the heavens,*
> *who by myself spread out the earth;*
> *who frustrates the omens of liars,*
> *and makes fools of diviners;*
> *who turns back the wise,*
> *and makes their knowledge foolish;*
> *who confirms the word of his servant,*
> *and fulfills the prediction of his messengers;*
> *who says of Jerusalem,*
> *"It shall be inhabited,"*
> *and of the cities of Judah*
> *"They shall be rebuilt, and I will raise up their ruins";*
> *who says of the deep,*
> *"Be dry—I will dry up your rivers";*
> *who says of Cyrus,*
> *"He is my shepherd, and he shall carry out all my purpose";*
> *and who says of Jerusalem,*
> *"It shall be rebuilt,"*
> *and of the temple,*
> *"Your foundation shall be laid."*
> *(Isa 44:24–28)*

Though You Do Not Know Me, Cyrus—45:1–7

This is one of the most striking poems in the entire Hebrew Bible. The author declares that the new emperor of the Near Eastern world, Cyrus of Persia, is not just a servant but is also a *messiah* ("an anointed one") of Yahweh, the God of Israel, appointed to bring liberation for captive peoples. Twice, the poet declares that this is what is happening, even though Cyrus has no knowledge of Yahweh. Cyrus is a servant and a *messiah* of Yahweh because he is part of the human family. Yahweh can call Cyrus by name because he is the Creator of all. Yahweh is the source of light and darkness at the creation and the source of life for the human family. Yahweh's presence is evident in the world when people show mercy by their actions.

> *Thus says the Lord to his anointed, to Cyrus,*
> *whose right hand I have grasped*
> *to subdue nations before him and strip kings of their robes,*
> *to open doors before him—and the gates shall not be closed;*
> *I will go before you and level the mountains,*
> *I will break in pieces the doors of bronze and cut through the bars of iron,*
> *I will give you the treasures of darkness and riches hidden in secret places,*
> *so that you may know that it is I, the Lord,*
> *the God of Israel, who call you by your name.*
> *For the sake of my servant Jacob, and Israel my chosen,*
> *I call you by your name, I surname you,*
> *though you do not know me.*
> *I am the Lord, and there is no other;*
> *beside me there is no god.*
> *I arm you, though you do not know me, so that they may know,*
> *from the rising of the sun and from the west,*
> *that there is no one beside me;*
> *I am the Lord, and there is no other.*
> *I form light and create darkness,*
> *I make weal and create woe;*
> *I the Lord do all these things.*
> *(Isa 45:1–7)*

Shower, O Heavens!—Isaiah 45:8

Again, after a bold proclamation, the poet breaks into a word of praise. The poem is a directive from Yahweh to the heavens; rains are commanded to come so that salvation and righteousness, like good vines, may spring up in abundance to bring fruit for people on earth.

> *Shower, O heavens, from above,*
> *and let the skies rain down righteousness;*
> *let the earth open, that salvation may spring up,*

and let it cause righteousness to sprout up also;
I the Lord have created it.
(Isa. 45:8)

The Clay and the Potter—Isaiah 45:9-13

Words of woe are now set forth for those who abuse their freedom and defy God's way of creating the world. Humans are, after all, life-clay: they have been fashioned and created by their Creator.[12] Interspersed with the woes are rhetorical questions as people are challenged to reflect on their own mortality. Then in the midst of this discussion, the author returns again to Cyrus as a clear example of one who is doing God's will in the world.

Woe to you who strive with your Maker,
earthen vessels with the potter!
Does the clay say to the one who fashions it,
"What are you making"?
or
"Your work has no handles"?
Woe to anyone who says to a father,
"What are you begetting?"
or to a woman,
"With what are you in labor?"
Thus says the Lord,
the Holy One of Israel, and its Maker:
Will you question me about my children, or command me
concerning the work of my hands?
I made the earth, and created humankind upon it;
it was my hands that stretched out the heavens,
and I commanded all their host.
I have aroused Cyrus in righteousness,
and I will make all his paths straight;
he shall build my city and set my exiles free,
not for price or reward,

---

12. An interesting contrast to the pottery imagery is present in Psalm 139:13-18, where God's creative activity is likened to that of a weaver.

says the Lord of hosts.
(Isa 45:9–13)

Heavens and Earth: Not Created for Chaos—Isaiah 45:14–19

Now the poet dreams of a future reversal of fortune. The people can feel
that they were sent into exile in disgrace among the nations of the earth.
The opposite will happen: an abundance of wealth shall one day flow to
Zion! A time will come when the God of Israel will be vindicated, when
his people, Israel, will no longer feel shame or confusion. The basis for
this reasoning is set forth at the end of this poem. God did not create
the earth for chaos. Rather, God created the earth intending that its inhabitants would bring blessing and order to the world. God's intention is
harmony and *shalom,* that is, peace and proper functioning, not chaos.[13]

> *Thus says the Lord:*
> *The wealth of Egypt and the merchandise of Ethiopia,*
> *and the Sabeans, tall of stature,*
> *shall come over to you and be yours,*
> *they shall follow you;*
> *they shall come over in chains and bow down to you.*
> *They will make supplication to you, saying,*
> *"God is with you alone, and there is no other;*
> *there is no god besides him."*
> *Truly, you are a God who hides himself,*
> *O God of Israel, the Savior.*
> *All of them are put to shame and confounded,*
> *the makers of idols go in confusion together.*
> *But Israel is saved by the Lord*
> *with everlasting salvation;*
> *You shall not be put to shame*
> *or confounded to all eternity.*

13. While I was still in high school, I accompanied a farmer friend on a mid-winter
visit to a neighbor's machine shed, where two brothers had overhauled an old diesel
tractor. One of them leaned over from behind the steering wheel and shouted through
the din of the roaring machine, "Listen, she's purring like a kitten!" The tractor had
been restored to its original proper functioning. I have found this story to be very
helpful when explaining the Hebrew term *shalom* or "peace."

For thus says the Lord, who created the heavens
(he is God!)
who formed the earth and made it
(he established it; he did not create it a chaos,
he formed it to be inhabited!):
I am the Lord, and there is no other,
I did not speak in secret, in a land of darkness;
I did not say to the offspring of Jacob,
"Seek me in chaos,"
I the Lord speak the truth, I declare what is right.
(Isa 45:14–19)

Assemble Yourselves and Come Together—Isaiah 45:20–25

Again the poet warns of the dangers of idol worship. The problem was evidently troublesome for the author. The lure of idolatry was compelling. People were living in a culture in which small gods were associated with various aspects of life. Some promised protection for animals, protection against sterility, protection against illness, and blessings for crops, fertility, and long life. The variety of shrines probably seemed harmless enough. But they encouraged a view of the world in which life was understood primarily as a matter of chance. Sacrifice was the means of warding off evil and gaining rewards. But even with generous sacrifices, one could never know for sure how much was expected. The deeper problem was that polytheism encouraged a world of thinking in which people manipulate their gods. The one who sacrifices could believe that an offering might influence divine powers to ward off evil or bring blessing. In contrast, the poet declares that righteous deeds performed out of thankfulness for the gift of life are the activities that please God.

Assemble yourselves and come together,
draw near, you survivors of the nations!
They have no knowledge—
those who carry about their wooden idols,
and keep on praying to a god that cannot save.
Declare and present your case;
let them take counsel together!

Who told this long ago?
Who declared it of old?
Was it not I, the Lord?
There is no other god beside me,
a righteousness God and a Savior;
there is no one beside me.
Turn to me and be saved,
all the ends of the earth!
For I am God, and there is no other.
By myself I have sworn,
from my mouth has gone forth in righteousness
a word that shall not return:
"To me every knee shall bow, every tongue shall swear."

Only in the Lord, it shall be said of me,
are righteousness and strength;
all who were incensed against him
shall come to him and be ashamed.
In the Lord all the offspring of Israel
shall triumph and glory.
(Isa 45:20–25)

It is rather remarkable that this poem includes an invitation to all the peoples of the earth: *"Turn to me and be saved, all the ends of the earth!"* In keeping with the declarations about Cyrus, the poet suggests that in the coming new era, a new community will be formed, based not on ethnicity but rather on righteous conduct. The *"offspring of Israel"* will be known for their commitment to righteousness.

Religion: Like a Burden on a Weary Animal—Isaiah 46:1–4

A sad scene from Babylon is remembered. Marduk-bel and Nebo were powerful gods within Babylonian religious tradition. But something has happened! A situation has come in which the idols representing these gods have been loaded on weary animals. They have become *"burdens tied on weary animals"*. We are to feel sorry for an overloaded donkey. Wherever the people are going, they dare not leave behind their sacred images. The poet uses this picture to declare that faith should not be a burden. Yahweh does not need to be carried like a heavy weight. Rather, Yahweh is a source of energy and strength for people in all stages of their life. Four declarations are used to convey the distinctive reality about Yahweh. In contrast to the gods represented by idols, Yahweh declares: "*I have made, and I will bear; I will carry and will save!*"

> *Bel bows down, Nebo stoops,*
>
> *their idols are on beasts and cattle;*
>
> *these things you carry are loaded as burdens on weary animals.*
>
> *They stoop, they bow down together;*
>
> *they cannot save the burden, but themselves go into captivity.*
>
> *Listen to me, O house of Jacob,*
>
> *all the remnant of the house of Israel,*
>
> *who have been borne by me from your birth,*
>
> *carried from the womb;*
>
> *even to your old age I am he,*
>
> *even when you turn gray*
>
> *I will carry you.*
>
> *I have made, and I will bear;*
>
> *I will carry and will save.*
>
> *(Isa 46:1–4)*

Once Again, The Folly of Idol Worship!—Isaiah 46:5–13

The poem continues reflection on the differences between those caught up in the world of idol worship and those who trust in Yahweh. Skilled craftsmen carved idols and adorn them with gold, silver, or other ornaments. Regardless of the ornaments, the images of various gods need to be propped up or they will fall over. The poet challenges his audience to explain where, when, and how those gods demonstrate any power or make any difference in world affairs. That is the realm where Yahweh's presence can be discerned.[14]

---

14. Advocates of the gods of Babylon or Canaan would have an answer for the poet in Isaiah 46. They would explain the world of fortune and misfortune from their own perspective, based on life as they had understood it before or after offering sacrifices to their gods. In Jeremiah 44:15–20, the response of certain women who fled to Egypt during the exilic era is reported. They are upset with the words that Jeremiah continued to proclaim and offer their own response to him: *"As for the word that you have*

To whom will you liken me and make me equal,
and compare me, as though we were alike?
Those who lavish gold from the purse,
and weigh out silver in the scales—
they hire a goldsmith, who makes it into a god;
then they fall down and worship!
They lift it to their shoulders, they carry it,
they set it in its place, and it stands there;
it cannot move from its place.
If one cries out to it, it does not answer
or save any one from trouble.

Remember this and consider,
recall it to mind, you transgressors,
remember the former things of old;
for I am God, and there is no other;
I am God, and there is no one like me,
declaring the end from the beginning
and from ancient times things not yet done, saying,
"My purpose shall stand,
and I will fulfill my intention,"
calling a bird of prey from the east,
the man for my purpose from a far country.
I have spoken, and I will bring it to pass;
I have planned, and I will do it.

Listen to me, you stubborn of heart,
you who are far from deliverance:
I will bring near my deliverance,
it is not far off, and my salvation will not tarry;

---

spoken to us in the name of the Lord, we are not going to listen to you. Instead, we will do everything that we have vowed, make offerings to the queen of heaven and pour out libations to her, just as we and our ancestors, our kings and our officials, used to do in the towns of Judah and in the streets of Jerusalem. We used to have plenty of food, and prospered, and saw no misfortune. But from the time we stopped making offerings to the queen of heaven and pouring out libations to her, we have lacked everything and have perished by the sword and by famine."

I will put salvation in Zion, for Israel my glory.
(Isa 46:5–13)

A Taunt Song: "Sit in the Dust, Proud Daughter Babylon!" —Isaiah 47:1–7

The taunt song provides an insight into the rage that some within the exilic community felt concerning the rude and insensitive behavior of Babylonian officials. Babylon is depicted as an arrogant queen who is about to experience a dramatic change or reversal in fortune. Babylon was certain that her power could last forever. But the arrogant one has been brought low!

Come down and sit in the dust,
virgin daughter Babylon!
Sit on the ground without a throne,
daughter Chaldea!
For you shall no more be called tender and delicate,
Take the millstones and grind meal,
remove your veil, strip off your robe,
uncover your legs, pass through the rivers.
Your nakedness shall be uncovered,
and your shame shall be seen.
I will take vengeance, and I will spare no one.
Our Redeemer—the Lord of hosts is his name—
is the Holy One of Israel.

Sit in silence, and go into darkness, daughter Chaldea!
For you shall no more be called the mistress of kingdoms.
I was angry with my people, I profaned my heritage;
I gave them into your hand, you showed them no mercy;
on the aged you made your yoke exceedingly heavy.
You said, "I shall be mistress forever,"
so that you did not lay these things to heart
or remember their end.
(Isa 47:1–7)

Like empires before and after her, Babylon "played God" in the world. Throughout the centuries, empires have believed that ultimately "might makes right" in the world. The vision of Isaiah contends that this simply is not true. Sooner or later, history demonstrates that it is righteous and just conduct that prevails. The arrogant use of power leads to feelings of resentment among others that can smolder and grow until a time when the arrogant power can be brought low. It is difficult to think of a tyrant leader or nation whose legacy has been appreciated by a later generation.

No One Sees Me!—Isaiah 47:8–15

Empires presume that they bear special responsibilities for keeping order and peace in the world. The Roman empire created a certain Pax Romana, a peace that extended throughout their vast empire. But that peace was based on strict military rule and the oppression of minority groups. It is interesting to reflect on how quickly an empire can justify covert actions or torture, certain that in the long run those actions will benefit all people. "*No one sees me!*" writes the poet, describing actions taken by an empire. Plans made in secret have a strange way of most benefiting those who are in power; all too often, the pain and distress of those in greatest need are not matters of major concern.

> *Now therefore hear this, you lover of pleasures,*
> *who sit securely, who say in your heart,*
> *"I am, and there is no one beside me;*
> *I shall not sit as a widow or know the loss of children"—*
> *both these things shall come upon you*
> *in a moment, in one day:*
> *the loss of children and widowhood*
> *shall come upon you in full measure,*
> *in spite of your many sorceries*
> *and the great power of your enchantments.*
> *You felt secure in your wickedness;*
> *you said, "No one sees me."*
> *Your wisdom and your knowledge led you astray,*
> *and you said in your heart,*
> *"I am, and there is no one beside me."*
> *But evil shall come upon you,*

which you cannot charm away;
disaster shall fall upon you,
which you will not be able to ward off;
and ruin shall come on you suddenly,
of which you know nothing.
Stand fast, in your enchantments and your many sorceries,
with which you have labored from your youth;
perhaps you may be able to succeed,
perhaps you may inspire terror.

You are wearied with your many consultations;
let those who study the heavens stand up and save you,
those who gaze at the stars, and at each new moon
predict what shall befall you.
See, they are like stubble, the fire consumes them;
they cannot deliver themselves from the power of the flame.
No coal for warming oneself is this, no fire to sit before!
Such to you are those with whom you have labored,
who have trafficked with you from your youth;
they all wander about in their own paths;
there is no one to save you.
(Isa 47:8–15)

Praise for the Creator of Heaven and Earth—Isaiah 48:1–13

After the words directed to Babylon, the poet now focuses on the lesson that hearers should take from these warnings. History demonstrates the truth of the claim: tyrants are not gods; they are mortal beings who hold power for a time but then fall, without being loved or cherished by later generations. Praise should be directed not to them but to the source of righteousness and justice.

Hear this, O house of Jacob,
who are called by the name of Israel,
and who came forth from the loins of Judah;
who swear by the name of the Lord,
and invoke the God of Israel,

but not in truth or right.
For they call themselves after the holy city,
and lean on the God of Israel;
the Lord of hosts is his name.
The former things I declared long ago,
they went out from my mouth and I made them known;
then suddenly I did them and they came to pass.
Because I know that you are obstinate,
and your neck is an iron sinew and your forehead brass,
I declared them to you from long ago,
before they came to pass I announced them to you,
so that you would not say,
"My idol did them, and my carved image
and my cast image commanded them."
You have heard; now see all this;
and will you not declare it?

From this time forward
I make you hear new things, hidden things
that you have not known.
They are created now, not long ago;
before today you have never heard of them,
so that you could not say,
"I already knew them."
You have never heard,
you have never known,
from of old your ear has not been opened.
For I knew that you would deal very treacherously,
and that from birth you were called a rebel.

For my name's sake I defer my anger,
for the sake of my praise I restrain it for you,
so that I may not cut you off.
See, I have refined you, but not like silver;
I have tested you in the furnace of adversity.
For my own sake, for my own sake, I do it,
for why should my name be profaned?

My glory I will not give to another.

Listen to me, O Jaocb,
and Israel, whom I called;
I am He; I am the first, and I am the last.
My hand laid the foundation of the earth,
and my right hand spread out the heavens;
when I summon them, they stand at attention.
(Isa 48:1–13)

A New Courtroom Assembly—Isaiah 48:14–22

The setting is again a courtroom setting. In a summary statement for this portion of the scroll, the poet presents evidence from the events of the world. Babylon is falling as Cyrus and Persia come to aid in the restoration of people who have been in bondage. A new exodus is about to happen in history. Yahweh, who led Moses and the people through the wilderness and provided them manna and water in their time of need, is now enabling a new exodus event.

Assemble, all of you, and hear!
Who among them has declared these things?
The Lord loves him;
he shall perform his purpose on Babylon,
and his arm shall be against the Chaldeans.
I, even I, have spoken and called him,
I have brought him, and he will prosper in his way.
Draw near to me, hear this!
From the beginning
I have not spoken in secret,
from the time it came to be I have been there.
And now the Lord God has sent me and his spirit.
Thus says the Lord, your Redeemer,
the Holy One of Israel:
I am the Lord your God,
who teaches you for your own good,
who leads you in the way you should go.

O that you had paid attention to my commandments!
Then your prosperity would have been like a river,
and your success like the waves of the sea;
your offspring would have been like the sand,
and your descendants like its grains;
their name would never be cut off
or destroyed from before me.
(Isa. 48.14–19)

Go Out from Babylon!—Isaiah 48:20–22

Those in bondage are to summon courage and make plans for a new future with a sense of celebration and joy. Life is a gift from God to be nurtured and cherished!

Go out from Babylon, flee from Chaldea,
declare this with a shout of joy, proclaim it,
send it forth to the end of the earth; say,
"The Lord has redeemed his servant Jacob!"
They did not thirst when he led them through the deserts;
he made water flow for them from the rock;
he split open the rock and the water gushed out.
"There is no peace," says the Lord,
"for the wicked."
(Isa 48:20–22)

Readers of the scroll in the post-exilic era know that a second exodus actually happened. These words were also confirmed by history. With the fall of Babylon and the return of people to Judah, the prophetic word of hope has also been confirmed. But the challenges of living with justice and righteousness will continue.

BRINGING LIGHT TO THE NATIONS—ISAIAH 49–55

In Isaiah 49–55, the poetry focuses even more specifically on the life of faith, both for individuals and for the community as a whole. There is increased focus on Zion, the special name for Jerusalem and the temple mount, described now as an abandoned mother whose children are about to return home.[15]

The Servant and the Nations—Isaiah 49:1–6

The servant of the Lord speaks in this poem. He speaks of his twofold mission: to restore the tribes of Judah and to be a light to the nations. His speech will be like a sharp sword. He likens his relationship to God like that of a polished arrow kept in the quiver of the Lord. Like an archer, the Lord will give the servant power and direction. The servant reports what Yahweh has said: *"You are my servant, you are Israel, in whom I will be glorified."* Whether understood as words from an individual or collectively from the community, the author affirms that it is through people that Yahweh is glorified on earth! The servant is to restore the remnant of Israel; more than that, however, as in Isaiah 42:5–8, the servant is instructed to be a light to the nations, so that the gifts offered by Yahweh can also extend to all peoples.

> *Listen to me, O coastlands,*
> *pay attention, you peoples from far away!*
> *The Lord called me before I was born,*
> *while I was in my mother's womb he named me.*
> *He made my mouth like a sharp sword,*
> *in the shadow of his hand he hid me;*
> *he made me a polished arrow,*
> *in his quiver he hid me away,*
> *And he said to me, "You are my servant,*
> *Israel, in whom I will be glorified."*
> *But I said, "I have labored in vain,*
> *I have spent my strength for nothing and vanity;*
> *yet surely my cause is with the Lord,*
> *and my reward with my God."*
> *And now, the Lord says,*
> *who formed me in the womb to be his servant,*

15. The terms "Jacob" and "Israel" do not appear after Isaiah 48:14: they are now replaced by the personified woman, Zion, sometimes portrayed as a "daughter," a "mother," or a "wife." Five times in the first chapter of the book of Lamentations, we hear a similar refrain concerning Zion: *"she has no one to comfort her"* (Lam 1:2, 1:9, 1:16, 1:17, and 1:21.)

to bring Jacob back to him,
and that Israel might be gathered to him,
for I am honored in the sight of the Lord,
and my God has become my strength—he says,
"It is too light a thing that you should be my servant
to raise up the tribes of Jacob and to restore the survivors of Israel;
I will give you as a light to the nations,
that my salvation may reach to the end of the earth."
(Isa 49:1–6)

One Deeply Despised and Abhorred by the Nations—Isaiah 49:7

Yahweh now speaks a word to the servant, who feels despised and abhorred by the nations. One day there will be a reversal of fortunes. Kings and princes will prostrate themselves before the servant. One day, the word about justice and peace will be understood by the kings and princes of the world.

Thus says the Lord,
the Redeemer of Israel and his Holy One,
to one deeply despised, abhorred by the nations, the slave of rulers,
"Kings shall see and stand up,
princes, and they shall prostrate themselves,
because of the Lord, who is faithful,
the Holy One of Israel, who has chosen you."
(Isa 49:7)

The Promise of a Homecoming—Isaiah 49:8–13

The poem concludes with a deep sense of hopefulness and joy about the future. The future will be a time when prisoners will be released and those in darkness discover light. There will be food and springs of good water that can sustain life. This is a sweet memory intended to renew hope and courage for all who have known the feelings of exile.

Thus says the Lord:
In a time of favor I have answered you,

on a day of salvation I have helped you;
I have kept you and given you
as a covenant to the people, to establish the land,
to apportion the desolate heritages;
saying to the prisoners,
"Come out,"
to those who are in darkness,
"Show yourselves."
They shall feed along the ways,
on all the bare heights shall be their pasture;
they shall not hunger or thirst,
neither scorching wind nor sun
shall strike them down,
for he who has pity on them will lead them,
and by springs of water will guide them.
And I will turn all my mountains into a road,
and my highways shall be raised up.
Lo, these shall come from far away,
and lo, these from the north and from the west,
and these from the land of Syrene.
Sing for joy, O heavens,
and exult, O earth;
break forth, O mountains, into singing!
For the Lord has comforted his people,
and will have compassion on his suffering ones.
(Isa 49:8–13)

The Lord has Forsaken Me!—Isaiah 49:14–23

Now the focus shifts again from the servant of the Lord to the woman Zion. The poet anticipates a mood of pessimism among those who will hear this word. There are those who want to interpret past history and current political events in other ways. They want to persist in contending that God has simply forgotten his people. The poet poses a frightening question: Can a mother forget her nursing child? The question is meant to shock! The poet answers his own question and declares: Yes! This reality has in fact happened. There have been mothers who have been known to neglect or forget their own nursing children. But this will not happen with Zion. Yahweh has not forgotten her! Zion is inscribed like a tattoo on the hand of Yahweh. And Zion will see her children returning to her in such numbers that they will say: "The place is too crowded for me!"

> But Zion said,
> "The Lord has forsaken me,
> my Lord has forgotten me."
> Can a woman forget her nursing child,
> or show no compassion for the child of her womb?
> Even these may forget,
> yet I will not forget you.
> See, I have inscribed you on the palms of my hands;
> your walls are continually before me.
> Your builders outdo your destroyers,
> and those who laid you waste go away from you.
> Lift up your eyes all around and see;
> they all gather, they come to you.
> As I live, says the Lord,
> You shall put all of them on like an ornament,
> and like a bride you shall bind them on.
> Surely your waste and your desolate places
> and your devastated land—
> surely now you will be too crowded for your inhabitants,
> and those who swallowed you up will be far away.
>
> The children born in the time of your bereavement
> will yet say in your hearing:
> "The place is too crowded for me;
> make room for me to settle."

Mother Zion, Jerusalem, will ask when these exiled peoples return: "Where did all of these children come from?" And when exiles return home, that will be evidence that the Lord continues to be present in the world. "Then you will know that I am the Lord!"

> Then you will say in your heart,
> "Who has borne me these?

I was bereaved and barren, exiled and put away—
so who has reared these?
I was left all alone—where then have these come from?
Thus says the Lord God:
I will soon lift up my hand to the nations,
and raise my signal to the peoples;
and they shall bring your sons in their bosom,
and your daughters shall be carried on their shoulders.
Kings shall be your foster fathers,
and their queens your nursing mothers.
With their faces to the ground they shall bow down to you,
and lick the dust of your feet.
Then you will know that I am the Lord;
those who wait for me shall not be put to shame.
(Isa 49:14–23)

Can Prey be Taken from the Mighty?—Isaiah 49:24–26

Now a second rhetorical question is posed. Can prey be taken from the mighty? The world may say that this cannot happen. But the poet's answer again is: Yes; this also can happen! Prey can be taken from the mighty and captive people can be rescued from a tyrant empire. Yahweh has the power to deliver people from oppression and trouble.

Can the prey be taken from the mighty,
or the captives of a tyrant be rescued?
But thus says the Lord:
Even the captives of the mighty shall be taken,
and the prey of the tyrant be rescued;
for I will contend with those who contend with you,
and I will save your children.
I will make your oppressors eat their own flesh,
and they shall be drunk with their own blood as with wine.
Then all flesh shall know that I am the Lord your Savior,
and your Redeemer, the Mighty One of Jacob.
(Isa 49:24–26)

Where is your Mother's Bill of Divorce?—Isaiah 50:1–3

The poet now employs the imagery of a marriage vow. To make the point that God is still faithful to Zion, he explains that it was because of transgressions and arrogant conduct that she was punished for violating covenant expectations. The author uses this imagery to affirm that Yahweh has not given up on his people.

> *Thus says the Lord:*
> *Where is your mother's bill of divorce*
> *with which I put her away?*
> *Or which of my creditors is it to whom I have sold you?*
> *No, because of your sins you were sold,*
> *and for your transgressions your mother was put away.*
> *Why was no one there when I came?*
> *Why did no one answer when I called?*
> *Is my hand shortened, that it cannot redeem?*
> *or have I no power to deliver?*
> *By my rebuke I dry up the sea, I make the rivers a desert;*
> *their fish stink for lack of water, and die of thirst.*
> *I clothe the heavens with blackness,*
> *and make sackcloth their covering.*
> *(Isa 50:1–3)*

The Difficult Role of the Servant—Isaiah 50:4–11

Now the servant speaks again. He describes the gifts that he has received from the Lord; they are the gifts of a teacher who can sustain weary people. As in Isaiah 49, we sense here that the author may be describing his own difficult role as a servant within the larger community. Or he may be describing some other individual who remained patient and courageous despite suffering persecution and abuse. Even when struck by those who persecuted him or when he had hair pulled from his beard, the servant was able to endure suffering by recalling the promises of the Lord God.

While the poem seems to have been inspired by the pain of an individual, it still may well be also intended as a description of the community of faithful people in exile, those who collectively endured persecution and oppression from their captors. Particularly striking is the description

of the nonviolent response of the servant, a response that is born of faithful obedience to the word of the Lord.[16]

> *The Lord God has given me the tongue of a teacher,*
>
> *that I may know how to sustain the weary with a word.*
>
> *Morning by morning he wakens—*
>
> *wakens my ear to listen as those who are taught.*
>
> *The Lord God has opened my ear,*
>
> *and I was not rebellious,*
>
> *I did not turn backward.*
>
> *I gave my back to those who struck me,*
>
> *and my cheeks to those who pulled out the beard;*
>
> *I did not hide my face from insult and spitting.*
>
> *The Lord God helps me;*
>
> *therefore I have not been disgraced;*
>
> *therefore I have set my face like flint,*
>
> *and I know that I shall not be put to shame;*
>
> *he who vindicates me is near.*

The poem concludes with a deep expression of frustration. Adversaries
have not come forward to openly accuse the servant of misdeeds. By deceit or by false reports, people have been spreading words of contempt
about him. The servant asks for openness rather than false witness.

> *Who will contend with me?*
>
> *Let us stand up together.*
>
> *Who are my adversaries?*
>
> *Let them confront me.*
>
> *It is the Lord God who helps me;*
>
> *who will declare me guilty?*
>
> *All of them will wear out like a garment;*
>
> *the moth will eat them up.*
>
> *Who among you fears the Lord*
>
> *and obeys the voice of his servant,*
>
> *who walks in darkness and has no light,*
>
> *yet trusts in the name of the Lord*

16. One could contend that the reactions of the servant here were still largely pragmatic; a powerless person may have no other choice. A larger ethical question comes
for those who have power to choose between violent and nonviolent responses in life.

and relies upon his God?
But all of you are kindlers of fire,
lighters of firebrands.
Walk in the flame of your fire,
and among the brands that you have kindled!
This is what you shall have from my hand:
you shall lie down in torment.
(Isa 50:4–11)

Look to the Rock from which You were Hewn—Isaiah 51:1–3

Anyone who has walked in a rock quarry gains a sense of past history from the layers evident in a rock wall. The poet uses this imagery to suggest that people can draw strength by recalling the courage of Abraham and Sarah, the rock and the quarry from which they are dug. Trusting in the Lord, Sarah and Abraham left their home country and family and journeyed to a new land, where their descendants were to become a people and a blessing for all the families of the earth (Gen 12:1–3). A similar challenge is now given to those in captivity in Babylon.

Listen to me, you that pursue righteousness,
you that seek the Lord.
Look to the rock from which you were hewn,
and to the quarry from which you were dug.
Look to Abraham your father
and to Sarah who bore you;
for he was but one when I called him,
but I blessed him and made him many.
For the Lord will comfort Zion;
he will comfort all her waste places,
and will make her wilderness like Eden,
her desert like the garden of the Lord;
joy and gladness will be found in her,
thanksgiving and the voice of song.
(Isa 51:1–3)

My Justice: A Light to the Peoples—Isaiah 51:4–6

Echoes of Isaiah 40:6–8 are heard in this text. There the author speaks of grass that withers, flowers that fade, and of people whose lives are like grass, before declaring that it is the word of the Lord that stands forever. Here the poet suggests that even if the heavens and the earth should pass away and even if inhabitants of the earth die like gnats, the promises of salvation are still certain. With that sense of security, people are summoned to face new challenges with trust and hope. The vision of justice and deliverance is to be a light for all peoples.

> Listen to me, my people,
> and give heed to me, my nation;
> for a teaching will go out from me,
> and my justice for a light to the peoples.
> I will bring near my deliverance swiftly,
> my salvation has gone out and my arms will rule the peoples;
> the coastlands wait for me, and for my arm they hope.
>
> Lift up your eyes to the heavens,
> and look at the earth beneath;
> for the heavens will vanish like smoke,
> the earth will wear out like a garment,
> and those who live on it will die like gnats;
> but my salvation will be forever,
> and my deliverance will never be ended.
> (Isa 51:4–6)

Withstanding Those Who Scorn—Isaiah 51:7–8

The poet declares a word of counsel from Yahweh for those who seek to live with the vision of justice and righteousness: Do not fear when other people offer criticism and speak scornfully!

> Listen to me, you who know righteousness,
> you people who have my teaching in your hearts;
> do not fear the reproach of others,
> and do not be dismayed when they revile you.

For the moth will eat them up like a garment,

and the worm will eat them like wool;

but my deliverance will be forever,

and my salvation to all generations.

(Isa 51:7-8)

The word is spoken directly to the audience that will hear and ponder what it means to walk in the light of the Lord. Times and situations in the world may change. What remains is the invitation to walk with integrity and compassion. That is what it means to know righteousness (*sedekah*) and to have the teaching of the Lord in one's heart. Those who have the teaching of the Lord in their hearts have a treasure that will endure through the ages.

Yahweh and the Chaos Monster, Rahab—Isaiah 51:9-11

This is a remarkable poem. We have seen how themes of creation and redemption are woven together throughout the Isaiah scroll. In earlier poetry, the "arm of the Lord" is stretched out in judgment over his own people. Now the poet calls on Yahweh to awaken and prepare for battle with the chaos-monster known as Rahab. In various countries throughout the ancient Near East, mythic stories tell of the struggle between a god of order and the chaos-monster. As we have heard in earlier texts, it is not Marduk or Ba'l who does battle with chaos; it is Yahweh, creator of the heavens who set the heavens as a tent or as a canopy over the earth. Here the author links the creation myth with memories of the exodus, the time when waters were cut and a dry pathway formed to allow for the creation and deliverance of a new community under Moses. The poet again envisions a "new exodus" in which the ransomed of the Lord, the exiles in Babylon, will return from captivity to Zion to find what God intends for all people, a world of joy and gladness, a place where sorrow and sighing flee away.

Awake, awake, put on strength, O arm of the Lord!

Awake, as in days of old, the generations of long ago!

Was it not you who cut Rahab in pieces, who pierced the dragon?

Was it not you who dried up the sea, the waters of the great deep;

who made the depths of the sea a way for the redeemed to cross over?

So the ransomed of the Lord shall return,

and come to Zion with singing;
everlasting joy shall be upon their heads;
they shall obtain joy and gladness,
and sorrow and sighing shall flee away.
(Isa 51:9–11)

The Promise of Comfort—Isaiah 51:12–16

"Why then are you afraid of a mere mortal who must die?" This is the question posed by the poet. Throughout history, people have known all too well why they live with fear of a tyrant. Tyrant leaders are unpredictable and can be extremely violent. But a time has come when people are to have a new sense of confidence even as they wait for a new era. God does not intend that people should be dominated by fear. Instead, the oppressed are to have the right of finding bread for living, freedom from oppression, and a meaningful life within the created orders of the world. This is the will of the Creator who speaks this word of comfort.

I, I am he who comforts you;
why then are you afraid of a mere mortal who must die,
a human being who fades like grass?
You have forgotten the Lord, your Maker,
who stretched out the heavens
and laid the foundations of the earth.
You fear continually all day long
because of the fury of the oppressor,
who is bent on destruction.
But where is the fury of the oppressor?
The oppressed shall speedily be released;
they shall not die and go down to the Pit,
nor shall they lack bread.
For I am the Lord your God,
who stirs up the sea so that its waves roar—
the Lord of hosts is his name.
I have put my words in your mouth,
and hidden you in the shadow of my hand,
stretching out the heavens

and laying the foundations of the earth,
and saying to Zion,
"You are my people."
(Isa 51:12–16)

The Word for Jerusalem—Isaiah 51:17–23

Several prophetic writers used the imagery of a "cup of wrath" to reflect on the seemingly endless cycle of wars throughout the Near East. War was like a cup of poison that was passed around among nations. It seemed to the prophets that nations in turn were forced to drink from this bitter cup as a consequence of arrogant and ruthless conduct. This was part of their attempt to interpret past history. In retrospect, the prophet declares in this poem that Judah and Jerusalem were also forced to drink from this terrible cup. But now there is a new reality for Jerusalem. Yahweh has taken away the *"cup of staggering"* and has passed it on to another country.[17]

Rouse yourself, rouse yourself!
Stand up, O Jerusalem,
you have drunk at the hand of the Lord the cup of his wrath,
who have drunk to the dregs the bowl of staggering.
There is no one to guide her
among all the children she has borne;
there is no one to take her by the hand
among all the children she has brought up.
These two things have befallen you
—who will grieve with you?—
devastation and destruction,
famine and sword—
who will comfort you?
Your children have fainted,
they lie at the head of every street like an antelope in a net;
they are full of the wrath of the Lord,

---

17. See Jeremiah 25:15–29, 51:6–10, and Habakkuk 2:15–16. The "cup of wrath" poetry is similar to "day of the Lord" poetry in which prophetic writers interpret various events of war as divine punishment or judgment.

the rebuke of your God.

Therefore hear this, you are who wounded,
who are drunk, but not with wine;
Thus says your Sovereign, the Lord,
your God, who pleads the cause of his people;
See, I have taken from your hand the cup of staggering;
you shall drink no more from the bowl of my wrath.
And I will put it into the hand of your tormentors,
who have said to you,
"Bow down, that we may walk on you";
and you have made your back like the ground
and like the street for them to walk on.
(Isa 51:17–23)

The Redemption of Jerusalem—Isaiah 52:1–2

Jerusalem, depicted in Isaiah 51:17 as a woman in mourning, is now told to put on her finest garments. The city is to prepare for a new era.

Awake, awake,
put on your strength, O Zion!
Put on your beautiful garments,
O Jerusalem, the holy city;
for the uncircumcised and the unclean
shall enter you no more.
Shake yourself from the dust, rise up,
O captive Jerusalem;
loose the bonds from your neck,
O captive daughter Zion!
(Isa 52:1–2)

Sold and Redeemed without Money!—Isaiah 52:3–6

Captive people in Babylon have waited patiently, wondering if indeed justice and righteousness can prove stronger than the oppressive rule of

Babylon. If people want to discern Yahweh's presence in the world, they are instructed to look at the political events of their time. Where they see liberation and restoration of human dignity, they are to discern the presence of Yahweh, the great "I Am" who is the creative force and source of energy for good in the created world.

> *For thus says the Lord:*
> *You were sold for nothing,*
> *and you shall be redeemed without money.*
> *For thus says the Lord God:*
> *Long ago, my people went down into Egypt*
> *to reside there as aliens;*
> *the Assyrian, too, has oppressed them without cause.*
> *Now therefore what am I doing here, says the Lord,*
> *seeing that my people are taken away without cause?*
> *Their rulers howl, says the Lord,*
> *and continually, all day long, my name is despised.*
> *Therefore my people shall know my name;*
> *therefore in that day they shall know that it is I who speak;*
> *here am I.*
> *(Isa 52:3–6)*

The Messenger who Brings Good Tidings!—Isaiah 52:7–10

We are invited to reflect on the most joyous moments in life. I sat one morning in a hospital waiting room and a doctor arrived to tell me: "You have a son!" Two years later, in another waiting room, another doctor simply asked: "Would you settle for a second son?" And four years later, a third doctor said to me: "You have a new daughter!" I have never felt more joyous than at those moments. In this passage, the poet recalls the sense of joy that people in Jerusalem had experienced when watchmen on the towers discerned that a particular runner was coming with news of victory from a battlefield. Because a particular runner was designated for carrying good news, victory could be celebrated even before the runner arrived. In this poem, joy is expressed with the words: *"How beautiful . . . are the feet of a messenger . . . who comes with good news!"* The poet is declaring that peace and well-being are the will of the Creator for all people.

How beautiful upon the mountains
are the feet of the messenger who announces peace,
who brings good news, who announces salvation,
who says to Zion, "Your God reigns."
Listen! Your sentinels lift up their voices,
together they sing for joy;
for in plain sight they see the return of the Lord to Zion.
Break forth together into singing, you ruins of Jerusalem;
for the Lord has comforted his people,
he has redeemed Jerusalem.
The Lord has bared his holy arm before the eyes of all the nations;
and all the ends of the earth shall see the salvation of our God.
(Isa 52:7–10)

You Shall Not Go Out in Haste—Isaiah 52:11–12

The poet now offers counsel about the preparations of people as they prepare to leave bondage and captivity. The promise is given that in this act of liberation, the Lord God will be their guide and their rearguard. One cannot help but think of the unbelievable changes that came in South Africa with the release of Nelson Mandela from prison and the relatively peaceful end of apartheid. While there was some violence, the overall transition from a minority white government to a new era of rule by the black majority in South Africa remains a miracle of our modern era. In such moments where justice and righteousness triumph, the authors who contributed to the Isaiah scroll would contend that God is most visible in the world.

Depart, depart, go out from there!
Touch no unclean thing;
go out from the midst of it, purify yourselves,
you who carry the vessels of the Lord.
For you shall not go out in haste,
and you shall not go in flight;
for the Lord will go before you,
and the God of Israel will be your rear guard.
(Isa 52:11–12)

The Servant Who Suffers—Isaiah 52:13—53:12

This poem is one of the best known and perhaps the most controversial poem in the entire Isaiah scroll. Interpreters have offered widely differing interpretations of the servant of the Lord described in this text. In Isaiah 41:8, the servant figure was clearly introduced and identified as the remnant community by being called by the names Israel and Jacob. The poet was addressing a group of faithful people within the community who had known the loss of their homeland and the pain of life in exile in a far country, and who now faced the prospect and challenges of new life with a return to Judah. As in any community, there were others who did not share in the vision set forth in the Isaiah scroll. This explains why the poet repeatedly addresses the issue of idolatry and seems to despair over the lack of faith demonstrated by some within the community. The poet can thus describe the task of the servant in terms of restoring Judah and Israel to their place of proper relationship with Yahweh. Hebrew poetry allowed an author to use servant imagery to refer either to an individual or to the larger community. In this poem, the imagery is so detailed that it seems possible that the author was also thinking about a particular individual, someone who had experienced persecution, torture, and even death during the exile. The poem breaks into three parts: A) the future exaltation of the servant (Isa 52:13–15), B) the suffering experienced by the servant (Isa 53:1–10), and C) vicarious suffering on behalf of others (Isa 53:10–12).[18]

The Future Exaltation of the Servant—Isaiah 52:13–15

In this first section, the Lord God praises the life and work of the servant who suffered on behalf of the community.

> *See, my servant shall prosper;*
> *he shall be exalted and lifted up, and shall be very high.*
> *Just as there were many who were astonished at him—*

18. All four New Testament evangelists, Matthew, Mark, Luke, and John, use this poetry to describe and interpret the suffering, death, and resurrection of Jesus in the New Testament. It is clear that for them, as well as for Paul and other New Testament writers, Jesus was to be understood in the context of the "suffering servant of the Lord" tradition as described here by Isaiah. He is also understood in terms of the messianic prophetic texts as an "ideal king", although his kingship is quite different from that of ancient kings in Israel or Judah. See also the reference in Acts 8:32–35.

so marred was his appearance, beyond human semblance,
and his form beyond that of mortals—
so, he shall startle many nations;
kings shall shut their mouths because of him;
for that which had not been told them they shall see,
and that which they had not heard they shall contemplate.
(Isa 52:13–15)

The Suffering Experienced by the Servant—Isaiah 53:1–9

In this second section of the poem, it is the poet author who is speaking. The servant did not seem to be anyone very special in appearance or personality. And yet in retrospect the author declares that this servant suffered on behalf of the community, apparently being punished and tortured. Scholars have long debated whether the servant was actually dead at the time when this poem was written. Or is that reference to being *"cut off from the land of the living"* only a figure of speech? In any case, the servant is remembered as one who was truthful and without deceit in his actions.

Who has believed what we have heard?
And to whom has the arm of the Lord been revealed?
For he grew up before him like a young plant,
and like a root out of dry ground;
he had no form or majesty that we should look at him,
nothing in his appearance that we should desire him.
He was despised and rejected by others;
a man of suffering and acquainted with infirmity;
and as one from whom others hide their faces
he was despised, and we held him of no account.
Surely he has borne our infirmities and carried out diseases;
yet we accounted him stricken, struck down by God, and afflicted.
But he was wounded for our transgressions,
crushed for our iniquities;
upon him was the punishment that made us whole,
and by his bruises we are healed.
All we like sheep have gone astray;

we have all turned to our own way,
and the Lord has laid on him the iniquity of us all.
He was oppressed, and he was afflicted,
yet he did not open his mouth;
like a lamb that is led to the slaughter,
and like a sheep that before its shearers is silent,
so he did not open his mouth.

By a perversion of justice he was taken away.
Who could have imagined his future?
For he was cut off from the land of the living,
stricken for the transgression of my people.
They made his grave with the wicked
and his tomb with the rich,
although he had done no violence,
and there was no deceit in his mouth.
(Isa 53:1–9)

Vicarious Suffering on Behalf of Others—Isaiah 53:10–12

In this third part of the poem, the author declares that the servant vicariously suffered on behalf of others, bearing the sins of many and interceding for other people.

Yet it was the will of the Lord to crush him with pain.
When you make his life an offering for sin,
he shall see his offspring, and shall prolong his days;
through him the will of the Lord shall prosper.
Out of his anguish he shall see light;
he shall find satisfaction through his knowledge.
The righteous one, my servant, shall make many righteous,
and he shall bear their iniquities.
Therefore I will allot him a portion with the great,
and he shall divide the spoil with the strong;
because he poured out himself to death,
and was numbered with the transgressors;
yet he bore the sin of many,

and made intercession for the transgressors.
(Isa 53:10–12)

Sing, O Barren One!—Isaiah 54:1–10

After the moving portrait of the servant who suffers in Isaiah 53, the focus shifts once again to Mother Zion. Although she is not mentioned by this name, we recognize her as the personification of Jerusalem. In Isaiah 52:1–12, she was told to put on her finest garments. Now she is to break out in song in anticipation of what is coming. Her focus is on the future that is promised. God, who is her husband, has not abandoned her despite all appearances to the contrary. One can almost sense the poet struggling with the imagery of marriage. Yahweh declares: *"In overflowing wrath for a moment I hid my face from you, but with everlasting love* [hesed] *I will have compassion on you."*

> *Sing, O barren one who did not bear;*
> *burst into song and shout,*
> *you have not been in labor!*
> *For the children of the desolate woman will be more*
> *than the children of her that is married,*
> *says the Lord.*
> *Enlarge the size of your tent,*
> *and let the curtains of your habitations be stretched out;*
> *do not hold back;*
> *Lengthen your cords and strengthen your stakes.*
> *For you will spread out to the right and to the left,*
> *and your descendants will possess the nations*
> *and will settle the desolate towns.*
> *Do not fear, for you will not be ashamed;*
> *do not be discouraged,*
> *for you will not suffer disgrace;*
> *for you will forget the shame of your youth,*
> *and the disgrace of your widowhood*
> *you will remember no more.*
> *For your Maker is your husband,*
> *the Lord of hosts is his name;*

the Holy One of Israel is your Redeemer,
the God of the whole earth he is called.

For the Lord has called you
like a wife forsaken and grieved in spirit,
like the wife of a man's youth when she is cast off,
says your God.
For a brief moment I abandoned you,
but with great compassion I will gather you.
In overflowing wrath for a moment I hid my face from you,
but with everlasting love I will have compassion on you,
says the Lord, your Redeemer.

Now the Lord God reminds people of the era of Noah. The author is clearly struggling. In Isaiah 54:7–8, he has announced Yahweh's word: *"for a brief moment, I abandoned you"* and *"In overflowing wrath for a moment, I hid my face from you."* But in that poem as well as in this declaration, the poet reminds people that Yahweh gave the rainbow as a sure and steadfast sign of divine love. Even while the Lord God was angry, his steadfast love did not depart from people of faith.

This is like the days of Noah to me:
Just as I swore that the waters of Noah would never again go over the earth,
So I have sworn that I will not be angry with you
and will not rebuke you.
For the mountains may depart and the hills be removed,
but my steadfast love shall not depart from you,
and my covenant of peace shall not be removed,
says the Lord,
who has compassion on you.
(Isa 54:1–10)

The Heritage of the Servants of the Lord—Isaiah 54:11–17

The rainbow promise of the Noah story is recalled to assure the woman Zion of the continuing great compassion (*hesed*) of Yahweh. Jerusalem is to be rebuilt and adorned with precious stones: sapphires, rubies, jewels, and precious gems. Of even more importance, righteousness will be established as a norm within the restored city and the fear of violence will seem far away. And now, we hear reference not to the "servant" but to "servants of the Lord" who are to bring a new era of peace and justice.[19] This is a rather dramatic change. Throughout chapters 56–66, further charges to "servants of the Lord" will be given (Isa 63:17; 65:8–9, 65: 13–15; 66:14).

> *O afflicted one, storm-tossed, and not comforted,*
> *I am about to set your stones in antimony,*
> *and lay your foundations with sapphires.*
> *I will make your pinnacles of rubies, your gates of jewels,*
> *and all your wall of precious stones.*
> *All your children shall be taught by the Lord,*
> *and great shall be the prosperity of your children.*
> *In righteousness you shall be established;*
> *you shall be far from oppression,*
> *for you shall not fear;*
> *and from terror, for it shall not come near you.*
> *If anyone stirs up strife, it is not from me;*
> *whoever stirs up strife with you shall fall because of you.*
> *See it is I who have created the smith who blows the fire of coals,*
> *and produces a weapon fit for its purpose;*
> *I have also created the ravager to destroy.*
> *No weapon that is fashioned against you shall prosper,*
> *and you shall confute every tongue that rises against you in judgment.*
> *This is the heritage of the servants of the Lord*
> *and their vindication from me,*
> *says the Lord.*
> *(Isa 54:11–17)*

---

19. Brevard Childs offers the interesting suggestion that there is a direct link between Isaiah 53 and 54. He writes: "The suffering innocent one of chapter 53 is seen as having his life, in some way, extended and incorporated through the suffering by those who are now designated "the servants of the Lord". They are the bearers of the true faith to the next generation" (Childs, *Isaiah*, 430).

A Doxology: The Vision of Peaceful Life—Isaiah 55:1–13

Isaiah 40–55 are like sweet memories written in an era of great hope and anticipation. The Hebrew term for sweetness (*matoq*) is used in Psalm 19 to praise the words of the Torah. There the psalmist declares that the commandments and ordinances are *"more to be desired than fine gold, even much fine gold; sweeter also than honey, and drippings of the honeycomb"* (Ps 19:10). In Proverbs 16:24, an author declares: *"Pleasant words are like a honeycomb, sweetness to the soul and health to the body."* In this concluding chapter of Isaiah, water is envisioned as "sweet water." The words suggest fresh water that can renew life for the earth and for people. The chapter sets out a vision of what the future can be as servants of the Lord seek to live as responsible people in community.

> *Ho, everyone who thirsts, come to the waters;*
> *and you that have no money, come, buy and eat!*
> *Come, buy wine and milk without money and without price.*
> *Why do you spend your money*
> *for that which is not bread,*
> *and your labor for that which does not satisfy?*
> *Listen carefully to me, and eat what is good,*
> *and delight yourselves in rich food.*
> *Incline your ear, and come to me;*
> *listen, so that you may live.*

In the following section of the poem, it is significant to hear the reference to the covenant with David. Kingship in Judah ended with the fall of Jerusalem. But here the theme of the restoration of ideal leadership is sounded: David is recalled, along with the themes in Isaiah 11 and 32, and the memories of Hezekiah preserved in chapters 36–39. It is possible to question if the covenant promises made with David are compatible with the depictions of the servant set forth in chapters 41–43, 49–50, and 52–53. But the virtues of integrity, humility, and reverence are held up both for leaders and for servant members of a community.

> *I will make with you an everlasting covenant,*
> *my steadfast, sure love for David.*
> *See, I made him a witness to the peoples,*
> *a leader and commander for the peoples.*
> *See, you shall call nations that you do not know,*

and nations that do not know you shall run to you,
because of the Lord your God,
The Holy One of Israel, for he has glorified you.

Seek the Lord while he may be found,
call upon him while he is near;
let the wicked forsake their way,
and the unrighteous their thoughts;
let them return to the Lord,
that he may have mercy on them,
and to our God,
for he will abundantly pardon.
For my thoughts are not your thoughts,
nor are your ways my ways,
says the Lord.

Again the poet recalls the rhythms of nature. The Lord God declares that just as rain and snow make the earth fertile, so also the word of the Lord is to bring forth fruitfulness, prosperity, and joy on the earth.

For as the heavens are higher than the earth,
so are my ways higher than your ways
and my thoughts than your thoughts.
For as the rain and the snow come down from heaven,
and do not return there until they have watered the earth,
making it bring forth and sprout,
giving seed to the sower and bread to the eater,
so shall my word be that goes out from my mouth;
it shall not return to me empty,
but it shall accomplish that which I purpose,
and succeed in the thing for which I sent it.

For you shall go out in joy, and be led back in peace;
the mountains and the hills before you shall burst into song,
and all the trees of the field shall clap their hands.
Instead of the thorn shall come up the cypress;
instead of the brier shall come up the myrtle;
and it shall be to the Lord for a memorial,

for an everlasting sign that shall not be cut off.
(Isa 55:1–13)

The "bitter memories" (Isa 2–12 and 13–35) provide a backdrop from an earlier era for these chapters. These hopeful or "sweet memories" (Isa 40–55) take center stage in the drama of the Isaiah scroll. They present a picture of life born of faith and trust as intended by Yahweh. Through pain and suffering, people in exile have learned a degree of humility that has allowed them to move from arrogance toward a spirit of humane and sensitive life as their Creator intended. In the following section of the scroll (Isa 56–66), Isaiah's vision will be given further interpretation from the perspective of a later generation that struggled with new challenges of life. But chapters 40–55 remain the centerpiece for the fabric that is woven together in this scroll. These chapters set out a focus for confident hope, calling people to walk in the light of the Lord. Almost as an echo to that opening word of the scroll, the author declares: *"Seek the Lord while he may be found, call upon him while he is near"* (Isa 55:6).

6.

Living with the Vision
Isaiah 56–65

INTRODUCTION

IN THE OPENING LINES of this section of the scroll, the author speaks of
the charge which Isaiah's vision brings for those who hear and care about
it. The author declares: *"Maintain justice* [mishpat] *and do what is right!"*
The words "righteousness" (*sedekah*) and "justice" (*mishpat*) appear a
number of times throughout the Isaiah scroll. In the introduction and
in the first parts of the scroll (Isa 1 and Isa 2–12, respectively) where the
two terms are frequently linked, grief is expressed about the fact that the
faithful city which once was full of righteousness and justice had become
corrupted by greed and arrogance (Isa 1:21–25). The human community
described as a vineyard in Isaiah 5:1–7 had produced bitter fruit. With
the destruction of Jerusalem, a terrible price has been paid. But already
in the opening chapter of Isaiah, a second theme was set forth: some in
Zion (Jerusalem) would be redeemed by justice and righteousness while
rebels and sinners would be destroyed (Isa 1:28).

Now, with a new era of history and the rise of the Persian empire,
the term "righteousness" (*sedekah)* is used to describe God's activity and
is linked with the term "salvation" (*yeshuah*). Salvation is declared to
be the activity of a loving and faithful God, who is the ultimate author
and source of all righteousness. Hope is held out for a new era of life.

In this concluding section of the scroll, we now hear references not to a "servant" but rather to "servants of the Lord," people who in their daily life are recognized by their integrity and by their acts of compassion and justice among people on earth.[1]

The words of promise spoken about Cyrus in chapters 44–45 have come to pass. People have returned to their homeland in and around Jerusalem. It is important to note that in fact, only a portion of the people deported to Babylon chose to return. Many had evidently grown accustomed to life in Babylon and chose to remain there. But the Isaiah scroll preserves a view of the world from the perspective of those who returned to Judah and Jerusalem.

Those who returned had to contend with enormous challenges: rebuilding homes, re-establishing villages, and restoring the city of Jerusalem from ruins. Poverty was widespread. Many had to endure hostility from neighboring communities. And there were new religious challenges, including questions about rebuilding the temple and proper observance of the Sabbath. In addition, there were questions about intermarriages, determining what people should be properly included in the community.

Both the bitter memories in chapters 1–12 and 13–35 and the hopeful memories in chapters 40–55 provide the context for understanding the poetry in this final section of the scroll. In a way, the closing chapters present a more muted or perhaps a more realistic view of life than is set forth in chapters 40–55. At times, the tone is somber. Living with the vision involves discipline and patience. The conviction about God's steadfast love is understood to be the power that brings new meaning and joy in life. The challenge to be servants of the Lord is a unifying theme within these final chapters.

MAINTAIN JUSTICE AND DO WHAT IS RIGHT —ISAIAH 56-59

Maintain Justice—Isaiah 56:1-8

How much from earlier temple traditions and priestly rites should be restored? And what should the community say about foreigners who have intermarried with people from the Jewish community? Just as complex

---

1. See further, Rendtorff, "Isaiah 56.1 as a Key to the Formation of the Book of Isaiah," 181–89. Rendtorff sees the charge to "Maintain justice and do what is right" as a basic theme of the entire Isaiah scroll.

were the questions about what the community should say about eunuchs, some of whom may have served in religious or political spheres of life in Babylon?

This opening passage sets forth an all-embracing view of community life. All who keep Sabbath and refrain from doing evil may be included. Even foreigners and eunuchs who maintain justice and observe the Sabbath are welcomed! This remarkable perspective evidently represented only one view within the community debate. It would not become the norm for everyone in the post-exilic community.[2]

> *Thus says the Lord:*
> *Maintain justice, and do what is right,*
> *for soon my salvation will come,*
> *and my deliverance be revealed.*
>
> *Happy is the mortal who does this,*
> *the one who holds it fast,*
> *who keeps the sabbath, not profaning it,*
> *and refrains from doing any evil.*
> *Do not let the foreigner joined to the Lord say,*
> *"The Lord will surely separate me from his people";*
> *and do not let the eunuch say,*
> *"I am just a dry tree."*
> *For thus says the Lord:*
> *To the eunuchs who keep my sabbaths,*
> *who choose the things that please me*
> *and hold fast my covenant,*
> *I will give, in my house and within my walls,*
> *a monument and a name*
> *better than the sons and daughters;*
> *I will give them an everlasting name that shall not be cut off.*
> *And the foreigners who join themselves to the Lord,*
> *to minister to him, to love the name of the Lord,*

2. For a different perspective on the debate, see the concluding chapters of Ezra, where men who have married foreign women are charged to send them away. The book of Ezra ends with a formal listing of all of those who had married foreign women; the book ends with the sad note: *"All these married foreign women, and they sent them away with their children"* (Ezra 10:44).

and to be his servants,
all who keep the sabbath, and do not profane it,
and hold fast my covenant—
these I will bring to my holy mountain,
and make them joyful in my house of prayer;
their burnt offerings and their sacrifices
will be accepted on my altar;
for my house shall be called a house of prayer
for all peoples.
Thus says the Lord God,
who gathers the outcasts of Israel,
I will gather others to them
besides those already gathered.
(Isa 56:1–8)

A Critique of Judah's Rulers—Isaiah 56:9–12

The text presupposes that people are back in Jerusalem. Here there is no idealistic dream about a return to the homeland. Rather, the author expresses disappointment and even frustration at the human frailties and limitations of "sentinels" or "shepherds", evidently references to city guards and political officials. The sentinels are blind. They seem to act without knowledge! The shepherds turn too quickly to strong drink without listening to the community. They are not much different from wild dogs that roam through desert ruins!

All you wild animals,
all you wild animals in the forest,
come to devour!
Israel's sentinels are blind,
they are all without knowledge;
they are all silent dogs that cannot bark;
dreaming, lying down, loving to slumber.
The dogs have a mighty appetite;
they never have enough.
The shepherds also have no understanding;
they have all turned to their own way,

to their own gain, one and all.
"Come," they say, "let us get wine;
let us fill ourselves with strong drink.
And tomorrow will be like today, great beyond measure."
(Isa 56:9–12)

A New Critique of the Community—Isaiah 57:1–13

Evidently, some who returned to their homeland reverted back to idol worship. People went back to using sacred objects which they believed could bring them good luck or could ward off trouble. In so doing, they reverted to an understanding of worship that was self-centered. And consequently, declares the poet, they lost sight of what it meant to be servants of the Lord.

The righteous perish, and no one takes it to heart;
the devout are taken away, while no one understands.
For the righteous are taken away from calamity,
and they enter into peace;
those who walk uprightly will rest on their couches.
But as for you, come here, you children of a sorceress,
you offspring of an adulterer and a whore.
Whom are you mocking?
Against whom do you open your mouth wide
and stick out your tongue?
Are you not children of transgression, the offspring of deceit—
you that burn with lust among the oaks, under every green tree;
you that slaughter your children in the valleys, under the clefts of the rocks?
Among the smooth stones of the valley is your portion;
they, they, are your lot;
to them you have poured out a drink offering,
you have brought a grain offering.
Shall I be appeased for these things?
Upon a high and lofty mountain you have set your bed,
and there you went up to offer sacrifice.
Behind the door and the doorpost

you have set up your symbol;
for, in deserting me, you have uncovered your bed,
you have gone up to it,
you have made it wide;
and you have made a bargain for yourself with them,
you have loved their bed, you have gazed on their nakedness.

Some people even went back to the practices of child sacrifice, offering children to the god of death, Moloch, seeking both to avoid illness and to gain long life for themselves. The Lord God is angry and disappointed, even as he concedes that some have done good and gracious deeds.

You journeyed to Molech with oil, and multiplied your perfumes;
you sent your envoys far away, and sent down even to Sheol.
You grew weary from your many wanderings,
but you did not say,
"It is useless."
You found your desire rekindled and so you did not weaken.

Whom did you dread and fear so that you lied,
and did not remember me or give me a thought?
Have I not kept silence and closed my eyes,
and so you do not fear me?
I will concede your righteousness and your works,
but they will not help you.
When you cry out, let your collection of idols deliver you!
The wind will carry them off,
a breath will take them away.
But whoever takes refuge in me shall possess the land
and inherit my holy mountain.
(Isa 57:1–13)

Words of Comfort and Assurance—Isaiah 57:14–21

After the harsh word in the previous poem, the poet now addresses the righteous. His word is that God, who seems far away, is to be found among those who have the gift of humility. The wicked are like the tossing sea;

they do not know peace. But those who are contrite and humble in spirit are promised a spirit of peace and comfort.

> It shall be said,
> "Build up, build up, prepare the way,
> remove every obstruction from my people's way."
>
> For thus says the high and lofty one
> who inhabits eternity, whose name is Holy:
> I dwell in the high and lofty place,
> and also with those who are contrite
> and humble in spirit,
> to revive the spirit of the humble,
> and to revive the heart of the contrite.
> For I will not continually accuse,
> nor will I always be angry;
> for then the spirits would grow faint before me,
> even the souls that I have made.
> Because of their wicked covetousness I was angry;
> I struck them, I hid and was angry;
> but they kept turning back to their own ways.
> I have seen their ways, but I will heal them;
> I will lead them and repay them with comfort,
> creating for their mourners the fruit of the lips.
>
> Peace, peace, to the far and the near,
> says the Lord;
> and I will heal them.
> But the wicked are like the tossing sea
> that cannot keep still;
> its waters toss up mire and mud.
> There is no peace, says my God, for the wicked.
> (Isa 57:14–21)

Problems with Worship—Isaiah 58:1–14

This poem speaks again to the heart of Isaiah's vision. In the parable of the vineyard in Isaiah 5:1–17, Yahweh declared that his chosen people were to be like a vineyard, lush with good fruit and beauty. For reasons of greed and other problems within human nature, the vineyard became overgrown with thorns and weeds and produced only sour, bitter fruit, bringing destruction.

Now the poet draws from the memory of that parable to suggest that patterns of greed have once again appeared within the community. People ask: Why do we keep the fast and deprive our bodies? Does God even notice? The poet declares that upright conduct is what God sees. It is through upright conduct that people live out the vision of Isaiah. Let worship be authentic. Do not engage in meaningless ritual.

> Shout out, do not hold back!
> Lift up your voice like a trumpet!
> Announce to my people their rebellion,
> to the house of Jacob their sins.
> Yet day after day they seek me
> and delight to know my ways,
> as if they were a nation
> that practiced righteousness
> and did not forsake the ordinance of their God;
> they ask of me righteous judgments,
> they delight to draw near to God,
> "Why do we fast, but you do not see?
> Why humble ourselves, but you do not notice?"
>
> Look, you serve your own interest on your fast day,
> and oppress all your workers.
> Look, you fast only to quarrel and to fight
> and to strike with a wicked fist.
> Such fasting as you do today
> will not make your voice heard on high.
> Is such the fast that I choose,
> a day to humble oneself?
> Is it to bow down the head like a bulrush,

and to lie in sackcloth and ashes?
Will you call this a fast,
a day acceptable to the Lord?

Now the poet shares the word of the Lord concerning what it means to keep a proper fast or to offer proper sacrifice. In a word for the ages to servants of the Lord, the charge is set forth: share bread with the hungry, welcome the homeless, cover the naked, watch out for hypocrisy, and care for the needy! It is by such actions that a community can again be like a watered garden. With such actions, the community will find joy and meaning that will last.

Is not this the fast that I choose:
to loose the bonds of injustice,
to undo the thongs of the yoke,
to let the oppressed go free,
and to break every yoke?
Is it not to share your bread with the hungry,
and bring the homeless poor into your house;
when you see the naked, to cover them,
and not to hide yourself from your own kin?
Then your light shall break forth like the dawn,
and your healing shall spring up quickly;
your vindicator shall go before you,
the glory of the Lord shall be your rear guard.
Then you shall call, and the Lord will answer;
you shall cry for help, and he will say,
Here I am.
If you remove the yoke from among you,
the pointing of the finger, the speaking of evil,
if you offer your food to the hungry
and satisfy the needs of the afflicted,
then your light shall rise in the darkness
and your gloom be like the noonday.

The Lord will guide you continually
and satisfy your needs in parched places,
and make your bones strong;

and you shall be like a watered garden,
like a spring of water,
who waters never fail.
Your ancient ruins shall be rebuilt;
you shall raise up the foundations
of many generations;
you shall be called the repairer of the breach,
the restorer of streets to live in.
If you refrain from trampling the Sabbath,
from pursuing your own interests on my holy day;
if you call the Sabbath a delight
and the holy day of the Lord honorable;
if you honor it, not going your own ways,
serving your own interests,
or pursuing your own affairs;
then you shall take delight in the Lord,
and I will make you ride upon the heights of the earth;
I will feed you with the heritage of your ancestor Jacob,
for the mouth of the Lord has spoken.
(Isa 58:1–14)

Discerning the Ways of Peace—Isaiah 59:1–8

Some within the community still charge that God does not have the power to save. They contend that God does not listen to prayers. The author responds by suggesting that it is the sin of the people that has become a barrier between God and the people. The passage is reminiscent of the world described in Isaiah 2–12; the poet describes people running to evil, rushing to shed innocent blood, and speaking falsely.

See, the Lord's hand is not too short to save,
nor his ear too dull to hear.
Rather, your iniquities have been barriers
between you and your God,
and your sins have hidden his face from you
so that he does not hear.
For your hands are defiled with blood,

and your fingers with iniquity;
your lips have spoken lies,
your tongue mutters wickedness.
No one brings suit justly,
no one goes to law honestly;
they rely on empty pleas, they speak lies,
conceiving mischief and begetting iniquity.
They hatch adders' eggs,
and weave the spider's web;
whoever eats their eggs dies,
and the crushed egg hatches out a viper.
Their webs cannot serve as clothing;
they cannot cover themselves
with what they make.
Their works are works of iniquity,
and deeds of violence are in their hands.
Their feet run to evil,
and they rush to shed innocent blood;
their thoughts are thoughts of iniquity,
desolation and destruction are in their highways.

We can only wonder at what prompted the author to give such a sad poetic description. Clearly, the people described did not live by the vision of Isaiah as preserved by this writer and the scroll. The tragic reality is that such behavior is clearly the preface to new acts of hostility, pain, and war.

The way of peace they do not know,
and there is no justice in their paths.
Their roads they have made crooked;
no one who walks in them knows peace.
(Isa 59:1–8)

The Loss of Justice … and Truth! Isaiah 59:9–15a

The loss of justice is so often linked with the loss of truth. The poem opens with the lament that *"justice is far from us."* But the lament turns to a confession with the words: *"our transgressions before you are many."* Thus, declares the author, *"truth stumbles in the public square."* And when truth is lacking, all sorts of injustice can follow, often justified by government or other public officials. People are left to growl like bears or moan like mournful doves!

> *Therefore justice is far from us,*
> *and righteousness does not reach us;*
> *we wait for light, and lo! there is darkness;*
> *and for brightness, but we walk in gloom.*
> *We grope like the blind along a wall,*
> *groping like those who have no eyes;*
> *we stumble at noon as in the twilight,*
> *among the vigorous as though we were dead.*
>
> *We all growl like bears;*
> *like doves we moan mournfully.*
> *We wait for justice, but there is none;*
> *for salvation but it is far from us.*
> *For our transgressions before you are many,*
> *and our sins testify against us.*
> *Our transgressions indeed are with us,*
> *and we know our iniquities;*
> *transgressing, and denying the Lord,*
> *and turning away from following our God,*
> *talking oppression and revolt,*
> *conceiving lying words*
> *and uttering them from the heart.*
> *Justice is turned back,*
> *and righteousness stands at a distance;*
> *for truth stumbles in the public square,*
> *and uprightness cannot enter.*
> *Truth is lacking,*
> *and whoever turns from evil is despoiled.*
> *(Isa 59:9–15a)*

The Divine Warrior and a new "Day of Yahweh"!
—Isaiah 59:15b–20

Destructive conduct can be tolerated by God for only so long! There will come again a new time of reckoning, a time when the sovereignty of God will be reaffirmed in the world. If there is no leader who will strive for justice and righteousness, Yahweh must put on his armor and once again venture forth as the divine warrior. When we hear rhetoric describing Yahweh preparing to go forth to war, we understand that the poet fears that a new time of judgment, a new "day of the Lord," is coming. Yahweh's coat of mail is righteousness; his helmet is salvation; his garments are vengeance or vindication; his robe is zeal or righteous anger.

> *The Lord saw it, and it displeased him*
> *that there was no justice.*
> *He saw that there was no one,*
> *and was appalled that there was no one to intervene;*
> *so his own arm brought him victory,*
> *and his righteousness upheld him.*
> *He put on righteousness like a breastplate,*
> *and a helmet of salvation on his head;*
> *he put on garments of vengeance for clothing,*
> *and wrapped himself in fury as in a mantle.*
> *According to their deeds, so will he repay;*
> *wrath to his adversaries,*
> *requital to his enemies;*
> *to the coastlands*
> *he will render requital.*
> *So those in the west*
> *shall fear the name of the Lord,*
> *and those in the east, his glory;*
> *for he will come like a pent-up stream*
> *that the wind of the Lord drives on.*
> *And he will come to Zion as Redeemer,*
> *to those in Jacob who turn from transgression,*
> *says the Lord.*
> *(Isa 59:15b–20)*

A Benediction—Isaiah 59:21

A prose benediction brings closure for this collection of poems. The prayer is a request that covenant blessings may be a reality for those who hear, for their children, and for their grandchildren:

> *And as for me, this is my covenant with them, says the Lord: my spirit that is upon you, and my words that I have put in your mouth, shall not depart out of your mouth, or out of the mouths of your children, or out of the mouths of your children's children, says the Lord, from now on and forever.*
>
> *(Isa 59:21)*

CELEBRATING ZION—ISAIAH 60-62

There are reasons to believe that one author wrote the poems that follow in Isaiah 60-62. They have a cohesive nature and celebrate the new community life that is envisioned for the servants of the Lord. They reflect the same spirit of optimism, majesty, and lyric beauty found in the poetry in chapters 40-55.[3]

Arise, Shine, for Your Light has Come!—Isaiah 60:1–16

What is it that allows a person to feel centered and authentic in the midst of the strains and stress of life? Here it is clearly the promise that Yahweh will be with servants of the Lord as a gracious and good friend, amid all joys and sorrows of life.

> *Arise, shine; for your light has come,*
> *and the glory of the Lord has risen upon you.*
> *For darkness shall cover the earth,*
> *and thick darkness the peoples;*
> *but the Lord will arise upon you,*
> *and his glory will appear over you.*
> *Nations shall come to your light,*

---

3. A number of scholars have suggested a tripartite arrangement in chapters 56–66, with chapters 60–62 at the center and calling particular attention to 61:1–3 as a central point for the entire collection. See esp. Blenkinsopp, *Isaiah 56–66*, 60.

and kings to the brightness of your dawn.
Lift up your eyes and look around;
they all gather together,
they come to you;
your sons shall come from far away,
and your daughters shall be carried
upon their nurses' arms.
Then you shall see and be radiant;
your heart shall thrill and rejoice,
because the abundance of the sea
shall be brought to you,
the wealth of the nations shall come to you.
A multitude of camels shall cover you,
the young camels of Midian and Ephah;
all those from Sheba shall come.
They shall bring gold and frankincense,
and shall proclaim the praise of the Lord.
All the flocks of Kedar shall be gathered to you,
the rams of Nebaioth shall minister to you;
they shall be acceptable on my altar,
and I will glorify my glorious house.

There is a confident expectation that a time of despair, sadness, and poverty is about to end. People who have known exile and despair may dream of having their own place of security and confidence. One day, they will again feel authentic among peoples of the world.

Who are these that fly like a cloud,
and like doves to their windows?
For the coastlands shall wait for me,
the ships of Tarshish first,
to bring your children from far away,
their silver and gold with them,
for the name of the Lord your God,
and for the Holy One of Israel,
because he has glorified you.

Foreigners shall build up your walls,

and their kings shall minister to you;
for in my wrath I struck you down,
but in my favor I have had mercy on you.
Your gates shall always be open;
day and night they shall not be shut,
so that nations shall bring you their wealth,
with their kings led in procession.
For the nation and kingdom that will not serve you shall perish;
those nations shall be utterly laid waste.

The glory of Lebanon shall come to you,
the cypress, the plane, and the pine,
to beautify the place of my sanctuary;
and I will glorify where my feet rest.
The descendants of those who oppressed you
shall come bending low to you,
and all those who despised you
shall bow down at your feet;
they shall call you the City of the Lord,
the Zion of the Holy One of Israel.
Whereas you have been forsaken and hated,
with no one passing through,
I will make you majestic forever,
a joy from age to age.
You shall suck the milk of nations,
you shall suck the breasts of kings;
and you shall know that I, the Lord, am your Savior
and your Redeemer, the Mighty One of Jacob.
(Isa 60:1–16)

People who live in relative comfort within an empire must reflect carefully on this text. This word is not spoken to people who know power, luxury, and comfort. It is a word intended for people who know illness, poverty, loss of a position, aging, or the sense of helplessness that comes when life involves constant help from others. Those who enjoy health and relative prosperity may need to identify with someone in the world who is in a marginal situation to appreciate and understand this text.

Peace and Righteousness—Isaiah 60:17–22

Zion is again envisioned as a center for peace and understanding in the world. This theme, first set out in Isaiah 2:1–5, has been echoed a number of times throughout the scroll. A time is again envisioned when violence will disappear. That will happen when peace and righteousness become the guidelines for the human family. The walls of the new community will be known as Salvation and her gates as Praise.

> *Instead of bronze I will bring gold,*
> *instead of iron I will bring silver;*
> *instead of wood, bronze, instead of stones, iron.*
>
> *I will appoint Peace as your overseer*
> *and Righteousness as your taskmaster.*
> *Violence shall no more be heard in your land,*
> *devastation or destruction within your borders;*
> *you shall call your walls Salvation, and your gates Praise.*
> *The sun shall no longer be your light by day,*
> *nor for brightness shall the moon*
> *give light to you by night;*
> *but the Lord will be your everlasting light,*
> *and your God will be your glory.*
> *Your sun shall no more go down,*
> *or your moon withdraw itself,*
> *for the Lord will be your everlasting light,*
> *and your days of mourning shall be ended.*
> *Your people shall all be righteous;*
> *they shall possess the land forever.*
> *They are the shoot that I planted,*
> *the work of my hands,*
> *so that I might be glorified.*
> *The least of them shall become a clan,*
> *and the smallest one a mighty nation;*
> *I am the Lord;*
> *in its time I will accomplish it quickly.*
> *(Isa 60:17–22)*

The Role of Servants of the Lord—Isaiah 61:1-7

This is a very special poem. It is one of the best known and loved hall-marks of the Isaiah scroll. With great clarity, the author states what it means to be a servant of the Lord. The servant will bring good news to the oppressed, bind up the broken-hearted, and proclaim liberty and release to captive peoples. The servant will comfort all who mourn, give garlands instead of ashes, and the oil of gladness instead of mourning.

> *The spirit of the Lord God is upon me,*
> *because the Lord has anointed me;*
> *he has sent me to bring good news to the oppressed,*
> *to bind up the brokenhearted,*
> *to proclaim liberty to the captives,*
> *and release to the prisoners;*
> *to proclaim the year of the Lord's favor,*
> *and the day of vindication[4] of our God;*
> *to comfort all who mourn;*
> *to provide for those who mourn in Zion—*
> *to give them a garland instead of ashes,*
> *the oil of gladness instead of mourning,*
> *the mantle of praise instead of a faint spirit.*

Servants assume their proper posture in life when they can acknowledge thanks for all of the gifts of life with a sense of confidence rather than with a faint spirit. When they do so, such people will be called "oaks of righteousness" and they will reflect the glory of their creator.[5]

> *They will be called oaks of righteousness,*

4. I again translate the Hebrew term *nakam* here as "vindication" rather than as "vengeance" in keeping with the full dual meaning of the term, involving both judgment and rescue.

5. The evangelist Luke reports that when Jesus returned to his home village of Nazareth and visited the synagogue, he read a portion of this passage (Luke 4:14-29). Luke contends that Jesus understood his own calling in terms of the "servant of the Lord" tradition. He was explaining that servant work is what his ministry was all about when he declared *"Today this Scripture has been fulfilled in your hearing."* See also the parallels in Matthew 13:53-58 and Mark 6:1-6a. In the passage in Luke, it is interesting that those who heard him are reported first to have spoken well of him but become angry with him when he refers to Elijah bringing bread to a foreigner, the widow at Zarephath in Sidon (1 Kgs 17:1-16) and to Elisha, who cured Naaman the Syrian (2 Kgs 5:1-14).

the planting of the Lord, to display his glory.
They shall build up the ancient ruins,
they shall raise up the former devastations;
they shall repair the ruined cities,
the devastations of many generations.
Strangers shall stand and feed your flocks,
foreigners shall till your land and dress your vines;
but you shall be called priests of the Lord,
you shall be named ministers of our God;
you shall enjoy the wealth of the nations,
and in their riches you shall glory.
Because their shame was double,
and dishonor was proclaimed as their lot,
therefore they shall possess a double portion,
everlasting joy shall be theirs.
(Isa 61:1–7)

A Bride Adorned with Jewels—Isaiah 61:8–11

The poem continues. Yahweh speaks of an everlasting covenant with future descendants who will live as servants.

For I the Lord love justice,
I hate robbery and wrongdoing;
I will faithfully give them their recompense,
and I will make an everlasting covenant with them.
Their descendants shall be known among the nations,
and their offspring among the peoples;
all who seek them shall acknowledge
that they are a people
whom the Lord has blessed.

Then the servant responds, celebrating like a bridegroom or a bride. Righteousness and praise will be the fruit in a newly envisioned garden on earth as a model for all nations.

I will greatly rejoice in the Lord,
my whole being shall exult in my God;

for he has clothed me
with the garments of salvation,
he has covered me with the robe of righteousness,
as a bridegroom decks himself with a garland,
and as a bride adorns herself with her jewels.
For as the earth brings forth its shoots,
and as a garden causes what is sown in it to spring up,
so the Lord God will cause righteousness and praise
to spring up before all the nations.
(Isa 61:8–11)

The Vindication of Zion—Isaiah 62:1–12

The restoration of Zion is the focus for the hopes and dream of the poet. A day will come when desolation and forsakenness will only be memories from the distant past. Marriage imagery proclaims that God has not forsaken his people; people are to be known by the name Hephzibah, "My Delight is in Her," and the land is to be called Beulah, "Married." The vision urges people to retain courage and trust as they face the difficult challenges of rebuilding a city and a country. The author draws from themes in Isaiah 40 to declare: build up a highway and prepare for the Lord who brings salvation.

For Zion's sake I will not keep silent,
and for Jerusalem's sake I will not rest,
until her vindication shines out like the dawn,
and her salvation like a burning torch.
The nations shall see your vindication,
and all the kings your glory;
and you shall be called by a new name
that the mouth of the Lord will give.
You shall be a crown of beauty in the hand of the Lord,
and a royal diadem in the hand of your God.
You shall no more be termed Forsaken (Azubah),
and your land shall no more be termed Desolate (Shemamah);
but you shall be called My Delight is in Her (Beulah),
and your land Married (Hephzibah);

for the Lord delights in you,
and your land shall be married.
For as a young man marries a young woman,
so shall your builder marry you,
and as the bridegroom rejoices over the bride,
so shall your God rejoice over you.

Earlier in Isaiah 56:9–12, sentinels or guards were chastised for being blind and for not performing their appointed tasks. Now in contrast, the Lord God declares that new sentinels have been appointed who will make life secure and good for those within the walls of the city.

Upon your walls, O Jerusalem, I have posted sentinels;
all day and all night they shall never be silent.
You who remind the Lord, take no rest,
and give him no rest until he establishes Jerusalem
and makes it renowned throughout the earth.
The Lord has sworn by his right hand
and by his mighty arm:
I will not again give your grain
to be food for your enemies,
and foreigners shall not drink the wine
for which you have labored;
but those who garner it shall eat it
and praise the Lord,
and those who gather it shall drink it in my holy courts.

Go through, go through the gates,
prepare the way for the people;
build up, build up the highway,
clear it of stones,
lift up an ensign over the peoples.

The Lord has proclaimed to the end of the earth:
Say to daughter Zion,
"See, your salvation comes;
his reward is with him,
and his recompense before him."

They shall be called "The Holy People,
The Redeemed of the Lord";
and you shall be called "Sought Out,
A City Not Forsaken."
(Isa 62:1–12)

NEW "DAYS OF THE LORD"—ISAIAH 63–65

The Divine Warrior Coming from Bozrah—Isaiah 63:1–6

In the poem in Isaiah 59:15b–20, Yahweh was seen donning armor for his work as the divine warrior. Now, after the interlude provided by the poetry in chapters 60–62, we hear of Yahweh's return from battle.

Isaiah 63 is a new "day of Yahweh" poem. An event of war has happened. The twofold character of this "day" is now evident. The "day" poetry envisions a time of punishment for evildoers. But this event also brings redemption for those who are faithful and just. When such an event happens in the world, Yahweh's sovereignty is most clearly revealed and vindicated. This passage comes into focus when considered in light of earlier references to "day of Yahweh" poetry in Amos 5:18–20 (judgment for northern Israel) as well as in Isaiah 2:6–22 (judgment for Judah); Isaiah 13–14 (judgment for Babylon), Isaiah 22:1–14 (a close call for Judah), Isaiah 34 (judgment for Edom), and Isaiah 61:1–11(salvation for Judah). "Day of Yahweh" poetry was at times used to describe a distant future event but it could also be used as powerful poetic rhetoric to describe a number of different historic events (most often war) that could change the course of history or life in decisive ways.[6]

The imagery of "stamping out the vintage" is particularly compelling in this text. The time for harvesting grapes was a particularly joyous occasion in ancient Israel. Men would gather in a stone pit to stomp on the vintage, that is, the new crop of grapes. As they stomped, their feet and legs turned red from the fruit of the vine. At the lowest end of the vat, an opening would allow grape juice to be gathered in jugs for fermentation and preservation. When the harvest was good, this would be a time

---

6. The "day of Yahweh" tradition seems also to have provided the background for Mary's song (the Magnificat) recorded in the Gospel of Luke, especially in Luke 2:52–53: *"He has brought down the powerful from their thrones, and lifted up the lowly; he has filled the hungry with good things, and sent the rich away empty."*

of great joy and celebration (See Judges 9:27; Isaiah 9:4; Psalms 67 and 126.[7] Such is the joyful background for the imagery in this poem.

But in this text the imagery has a somber character. Yahweh returns from a "day of the Lord." He is all alone, spattered with what appears to be red wine. We are to realize, however, that his garment is covered not with wine but with blood. An event of war has taken place with the loss of human life. As in Isaiah 34, Edom is mentioned here, most probably as a symbol of a ruthless nation, now destroyed by war. God is there even amid the sadness and horror of war.

> *I have trodden the wine press alone,*
>
> *and from the peoples no one was with me;*
>
> *I trod them in my anger and trampled them in my wrath;*
>
> *their juice spattered on my garments, and stained all my robes.*
>
> *For the day of vengeance was in my heart,*
>
> *and the year for my redeeming work had come.*
>
> *I looked, but there was no helper;*
>
> *I stared, but there was no one to sustain me;*
>
> *so my own arm brought me victory,*
>
> *and my wrath sustained me.*
>
> *I trampled down peoples in my anger,*
>
> *I crushed them in my wrath,*
>
> *and I poured out their lifeblood on the earth."*
>
> *(Isa 63:1–6)*

The mysteries of evil and war haunt the world in every era of history. "Day of Yahweh" poetry invites reflection on the disastrous consequences of war as well as on the reasons why people so often feel compelled to wage war.

A Community Lament—Isaiah 63:7–19

It is not difficult to understand the patriotic feelings and the aspirations of leaders in small countries or city-states to break free from the tyranny

---

7. The imagery from this poem and from related psalms provided the inspiration for the words of the hymn, *The Battle Hymn of the Republic*: "Mine eyes have seen the glory of the coming of the Lord; he is stamping out the vintage where the grapes of wrath are stored . . ."

of empires such as Assyria or Babylon. Nationalism was then and is still today a powerful force that binds people to their homelands.

Economic hardships, drought, plagues of locusts or swarms of other insects can provide ample reasons for giving voice to a lament. The poet asks: Where in the world can your presence be discerned, O Lord? How long are you going to allow a community to hang on the edge of starvation and death?

> I will recount the gracious deeds of the Lord,
> the praiseworthy acts of the Lord,
> because of all that the Lord has done for us,
> and the great favor to the house of Israel
> that he has shown them according to his mercy,
> according to the abundance of his steadfast love.

> For he said, "Surely they are my people,
> children who will not deal falsely";
> and he became their savior in all their distress.
> It was no messenger or angel
> but his presence that saved them;
> in his love and in his pity he redeemed them;
> he lifted them up and carried them all the days of old.
> But they rebelled and grieved his holy spirit;
> therefore he became their enemy;
> he himself fought against them.

Now the author recalls the memories of Moses. In a situation where people were puzzled about their life and their future, the Lord delivered them at the Red Sea and led them to a new future.

> Then they remembered the days of old,
> of Moses his servant.
> Where is the one who brought them up out of the sea
> with the shepherds of his flock?
> Where is the one who put within them his holy spirit,
> who caused his glorious arm to march
> at the right hand of Moses,
> who divided the waters before them
> to make for himself an everlasting name,

who led them through the depths?
Like a horse in the desert, they did not stumble.
Like cattle that go down into a valley,
the spirit of the Lord gave them rest.

Thus you led your people,
to make for yourself a glorious name.
Look down from heaven and see,
from your holy and glorious habitation.
Where are your zeal and your might?
The yearning of your heart and your compassion?
They are withheld from me.
For you are our father,
though Abraham does not know us
and Israel does not acknowledge us;
you, O Lord, are our father;
our Redeemer from of old is your name.

In an earlier era, people were described with the illness of hardness of heart (see Isa 6). Now the same concern is posed as a question addressed to God: "*Why do you make us stray from your ways and harden our heart, so that we do not fear you?*" What is the nature of human freedom that allows humans to "play God" so quickly in the midst of the struggles of life? And why has God given such freedom to humans? How is it that people can so quickly lose the sense of awe and wonder that comes at the birth of a child or at other momentous times? Such moments do not seem to last. The poet suggests that hardness of heart is a disease that can come in any age.

Why, O Lord, do you make us stray from your ways
and harden our hearts, so that we do not fear you?
Turn back for the sake of your servants,
for the sake of the tribes that are your heritage.
Your holy people took possession for a little while
but now our adversaries have trampled down your sanctuary.
We have long been like those
whom you do not rule,

like those not called by your name.
(Isa 63:7–19)

Tear Open the Heavens and Come Down, O Lord—Isaiah 64:1–12

Again, we sense a time when people knew repeated frustrations and
discouragement. Both external threats and internal strife threatened the
community. Here the hopes of rebuilding the temple seem to be only a
distant dream. Some chose to believe that Yahweh must be once again
punishing the community.

> O that *you would tear open the heavens*
> *and come down,*
> *so that the mountains would quake*
> *at your presence—*
> *as when fire kindles brushwood*
> *and the fire causes water to boil—*
> *to make your name known*
> *to your adversaries,*
> *so that the nations might tremble*
> *at your presence!*
>
> *When you did awesome deeds that we did not expect,*
> *you came down,*
> *the mountains quaked at your presence.*
> *From ages past no one has heard,*
> *no ear has perceived,*
> *no eye has seen any God beside you,*
> *who works for those who wait for him.*
> *You meet those who gladly do right,*
> *those who remember you in your ways.*
> *But you were angry, and we sinned;*
> *because you hid yourself we transgressed.*
> *We have all become like one who is unclean,*
> *and all our righteous deeds are like a filthy cloth.*
> *We all fade like a leaf,*

and our iniquities, like the wind,

take us away.

The poet has described the frustrations of the community and now analyzes the situation. People are like clay. It is God who is the potter.[8] How nice it would be if God would simply tear open the heavens, come down and solve the problems of a struggling community!

There is no one who calls on your name,
or attempts to take hold of you;
for you have hidden your face from us,
and have delivered us into the hand
of our iniquity.
Yet, O Lord, you are our Father;
we are the clay, and you are our potter;
we are all the work of your hand.
Do not be exceedingly angry, O Lord,
and do not remember iniquity forever.
Now consider, we are all your people.
Your holy cities have become a wilderness,
Zion has become a wilderness,
Jerusalem a desolation.
Our holy and beautiful house,
where our ancestors praised you,
has been burned by fire,
and all our pleasant places have become ruins.
After all this, will you restrain yourself, O Lord?
Will you keep silent and punish us so severely?
(Isa 64:1–12)

The Righteous Rule of Yahweh—Isaiah 65:1–25

The poet once again focuses on internal divisions within the community and the complaints of the community. Those complaints continue in the

8. See further, the imagery of God forming Adam from the dust of the ground in Gen 2:7. It is interesting to contrast the imagery of God as the "potter" in this text with the references in Psalm 139:13–18, where God is understood to be a weaver *"knitting us together in a mother's womb."*

first part of this poem and then a divine response follows. Words both of judgment and salvation are declared for the community: those who are evil are told that they will face a new time of judgment; faithful servants of the Lord are promised gladness of heart and physical prosperity.[9]

Promises for the Servants of the Lord—Isaiah 65:1–16

Seven times in this poem we hear reference to servants. All of the references come in the latter part of the poem. Yahweh speaks to the faithful community. Amid the weariness of the world, they are told that servants will eat, drink, and find joy in good things in life. They are assured that former troubles will be forgotten and hidden.

> *I was ready to be sought out*
> *by those who did not ask,*
> *to be found by those who did not seek me.*
> *I said, "Here I am, here I am,"*
> *to a nation that did not call on my name.*
> *I held out my hands all day long*
> *to a rebellious people, who walk in a way that is not good,*
> *following their own devices;*
> *a people who provoke me to my face continually,*
> *sacrificing in gardens and offering incense on bricks;*
> *who sit inside tombs,*
> *and spend the night in secret places;*
> *who eat swine's flesh,*
> *with broth of abominable things in their vessels;*
> *who say, "Keep to yourself, do not come near me,*
> *for I am too holy for you."*
> *These are a smoke in my nostrils,*
> *a fire that burns all day long.*
> *See, it is written before me;*
> *I will not keep silent, but I will repay;*
> *I will indeed repay into their laps*
> *their iniquities and their ancestors' iniquities together,*
> *says the Lord;*

9. Note how this pattern of thinking is echoed in the text of Matthew 25:31–46 and the separation of peoples like sheep and goats at the final judgment.

because they offered incense on the mountains
and reviled me on the hills,
I will measure into their laps
full payment for their actions.

The poetry has been directed at those who forsake the Lord. But at the same time, promises are extended to those who are servants of the Lord, who now receive specific attention in the concluding part of this poem. Those who forsake the Lord will discover judgment and death; faithful servants will settle in the land, eat, drink, and rejoice. They will discover new blessings and sing with gladness in their hearts.

Thus says the Lord:
As the wine is found in the cluster,
and they say, "Do not destroy it,
for there is a blessing in it,"
so I will do for my servants' sake,
and not destroy them all.
I will bring forth descendants from Jacob,
and from Judah inheritors of my mountains;
my chosen shall inherit it, and my servants shall settle there.
Sharon shall become a pasture for flocks,
and the Valley of Achor a place for herds to lie down,
for my people who have sought me.
But you who forsake the Lord, who forget my holy mountain,
who set a table for Fortune and fill cups of mixed wine for Destiny;
I will destine you to the sword,
and all of you shall bow down to the slaughter;
because, when I called, you did not answer,
when I spoke, you did not listen,
but you did what was evil in my sight,
and chose what I did not delight in.
Therefore thus says the Lord God:
My servants shall eat, but you shall be hungry;
my servants shall drink, but you shall be thirsty;
my servants shall rejoice, but you shall be put to shame;
my servants shall sing for gladness of heart,
but you shall cry out for pain of heart,

and shall wail for anguish of spirit.
You shall leave your name to my chosen to use as a curse,
and the Lord will put you to death;
but to his servants he will give a different name.

Then, whoever invokes a blessing in the land
shall bless by the God of faithfulness,
and whoever takes an oath in the land
shall swear by the God of faithfulness;
because the former troubles are forgotten
and are hidden from my sight.
(Isa 65:1–16)

The Creation of a New Jerusalem—Isaiah 65:17–25

The poem now becomes doxology. It is a concluding word of hope for this section of the scroll. A vision for Jerusalem is set forth. Jerusalem will be a new community where life will be pleasing for people and for the Creator of heaven and earth. Like the vision of a peaceful city set forth in Isaiah 2:1–4, the dream is renewed that the human family might find a way to live in peace with justice and integrity as God's people on earth. God is portrayed moving against the forces of rebellion and chaos to restore order in the world and to create a new Jerusalem. But even in this new realm, humans remain mortal. They are born and they will die. According to the author of Psalm 90, seventy years of age (three score and ten) was envisioned as long and full human life. Eighty years of life (four score) was seen to be a special gift by reason of strength.[10] But in this text, in what might have seemed the height of prophetic imagination, the ancient author dreams that one day people might actually live to be one hundred years of age! The poet still speaks of simple joys that bring meaning to life: people build and inhabit homes, and plant and eat from the fruits of a garden. As in the portrait in Isaiah 11:6–9, the vision of peace extends even to the realm of the animal world. God's intention is that the earth should be a peaceful kingdom for humans and for all creatures.

For I am about to create new heavens and a new earth;

10. See Ps 90:10.

the former things shall not be remembered or come to mind.
But be glad and rejoice forever in what I am creating;
for I am about to create Jerusalem as a joy,
and its people as a delight.
I will rejoice in Jerusalem, and delight in my people;
no more shall the sound of weeping be heard in it,
or the cry of distress.
No more shall there be in it an infant that lives but a few days,
or an old person who does not live out a lifetime;
for one who dies at a hundred years will be considered a youth,
and one who falls short of a hundred will be considered accursed.
They shall build houses and inhabit them;
They shall plant vineyards and eat their fruit.
They shall not build and another inhabit;
they shall not plant and another eat;
for like the days of a tree shall the days of my people be,
and my chosen shall long enjoy the work of their hands.
They shall not labor in vain, or bear children for calamity;
for they shall be offspring blessed by the Lord—
and their descendants as well.
Before they call I will answer, while they are yet speaking
I will hear.

The wolf and the lamb shall feed together,
the lion shall eat straw like the ox;
but the serpent—its food shall be dust!
They shall not hurt or destroy on my holy mountain,
says the Lord.
(Isa 65:17–25)

7.

A Concluding Word of Caution
Isaiah 66:1–24

THE FINAL CHAPTER OF the Isaiah scroll echoes themes from the opening chapter. In Isaiah 1:2, heaven and earth were summoned as witnesses to the vision that Isaiah was setting forth. Now heaven and earth are again cited as the realm of Yahweh as creator; heaven is his throne and earth his footstool. Yahweh is affirmed as the source of creative energy in the world for all living things.

PRAISE FOR THE HUMBLE AND CONTRITE —ISAIAH 66:1–2

As in Isaiah 1, acts of arrogance and rebellion are understood to be the ongoing root cause of trouble for the human family. In contrast, those who live with humility and with a contrite spirit are the ones who can live with confidence in the presence of Yahweh. Those people have the proper fear of the Lord. They live with a sense of wonder and awe, even with occasional trembling, keeping a sense of the sacred character of life, awe, and an openness concerning the mysteries of life.

> *Thus says the Lord:*
> *Heaven is my throne and earth is my footstool;*
> *what is the house that you would build for me,*
> *and what is my resting place?*

All these things my hand has made,

and so all these things are mine,

says the Lord.

But this is the one to whom I will look,

to the humble and contrite in spirit,

who trembles at my word.[1]

(Isa 66:1–2)

A WORD ABOUT OFFERING SACRIFICES
—ISAIAH 66:3-4

The author thinks about Jerusalem and the temple, reflecting on appropriate sacrifices which were connected with the rebuilding of the temple and the re-establishment of temple worship practices. As in the opening chapter, the efficacy of sacrifice is once again questioned. The author reflects on sacrifices offered in hollow or inappropriate ways.

Whoever slaughters an ox is like one who kills a human being;

whoever sacrifices a lamb, like one who breaks a dog's neck;

whoever presents a grain offering, like one who offers swine's blood;

whoever makes a memorial offering of frankincense,

like one who blesses an idol.

These have chosen their own ways, and in their abominations

they take delight;

I also will choose to mock them,

and bring upon them what they fear;

because when I called, no one answered,

when I spoke, they did not listen;

but they did what was evil in my sight,

and chose what did not please me.

(Isa 66:3-4)

---

1. It is possible that the reference here to "trembling" refers to a religious party or faction within post-exilic Judaism known as the *heredim.* the term appears four times: Isa 66:2, Isa 66:5, Ezra 9:4, and Ezra 10.3. See further, Blenkinsopp, *Isaiah 56–66,* 51–54.

THE POSTURE OF REVERENCE: "TREMBLING AT HIS WORD"—ISAIAH 66:5-6

Another word of reassurance is given for the righteous. Those who show proper reverence and respect are encouraged to endure taunts from some around them. Evidently the words "*Let the Lord be glorified, so that we may see your joy*" had been used as a taunt song by some who attempted to mock or ridicule the righteous. The author declares that it will be precisely those who taunt the righteous who will be put to shame.

> *Hear the word of the Lord, you who tremble at his word:*
> *Your own people who hate you and reject you for my name's sake*
> *have said, "Let the Lord be glorified, so that we may see your joy"*
> *but it is they who shall be put to shame.*
> *Listen, an uproar from the city!*
> *A voice from the temple!*
> *The voice of the Lord, dealing retribution to his enemies!*
> *(Isa 66:5–6)*

MOTHER ZION IN LABOR—ISAIAH 66:7-9

Zion was left barren when Jerusalem was destroyed. In Isaiah 54, Zion was described as a barren woman or mother who pondered whether God had abandoned her. The poetry of chapters 54 and 62 declares to her that this is not the case. Yahweh has not forgotten her. In Isaiah 49:8–13, Zion's children are envisioned coming home from exile. Now in celebration of that new era, the poet describes Zion giving birth to new children, delivering them even before she has labor pains! Yahweh will serve as the midwife.

> *Before she was in labor she gave birth;*
> *before her pain came upon her she delivered a son.*
> *Who has heard of such a thing? Who has seen such things?*
> *Shall a land be born in one day?*
> *Shall a nation be delivered in one moment?*
> *Yet as soon as Zion was in labor she delivered her children.*
> *Shall I open the womb and not deliver?*
> *says the Lord;*

shall I, the one who delivers, shut the womb?
says your God.
(Isa 66:7–9)

REJOICE WITH JERUSALEM—ISAIAH 66:10-11

Yahweh is creating something new. A new community is being established in Judah. We have before us a tender new vision of peace: Jerusalem, the mother who has given birth, sustains her young at her breast. The vision is of a mother who has an abundance of milk with which she can feed and provide for her children.[2]

> *Rejoice with Jerusalem, and be glad for her,*
> *all you who love her;*
> *rejoice with her in joy, all you mourn over her—*
> *that you may nurse and be satisfied*
> *from her consoling breast;*
> *that you may drink deeply with delight from her glorious bosom.*
> *(Isa 66:10–11)*

PROSPERITY LIKE A RIVER—ISAIAH 66:12-16

The imagery now shifts to a river and the dream that Zion can be a center for righteousness and justice, not just for Judah, but for all nations. And with strong feminine images, Yahweh's love for faithful people is compared to the comfort that a mother gives to her child. Then, the author returns to a word of warning for the unrighteous: they will learn of God's indignation and suffer a judgment by fire.

> *For thus says the Lord:*
> *I will extend prosperity to her like a river,*
> *and the wealth of the nations*

2. See C. Franke, *"Like a Mother I Have Comforted You": The Function of Figurative Language in Isaiah 1:7-26 and 66:7-14"* in Everson and Kim, *Desert Will Bloom*, 35–55. The imagery in this passage is clearly set forth as a contrast to the tragic situations of mothers in poverty-stricken regions of our world, past and present, where they are not able to provide milk for their young. Here, a new mother with an abundance of breast milk is the image set forth for understanding Yahweh's gracious love for people.

like an overflowing stream;
and you shall nurse and be carried on her arm,
and dandled on her knees.
As a mother comforts her child, so I will comfort you;
you shall be comforted in Jerusalem.

You shall see, and your heart shall rejoice;
your bodies shall flourish like the grass;
and it shall be known that the hand of the Lord is with his servants,
and his indignation is against his enemies.
For the Lord will come in fire, and his chariots like the whirlwind,
to pay back his anger in fury, and his rebuke in flames of fire.
For by fire will the Lord execute judgment,
and by his sword, on all flesh;
and those slain by the Lord shall be many.
(Isa 66:12–16)

WARNINGS FOR THOSE WHO SANCTIFY THEMSELVES—ISAIAH 66:17

A word of warning is sounded. It is God who sanctifies; we do not sanctify ourselves!

Those who sanctify and purify themselves to go into the gardens,
following the one in the center,
eating the flesh of pigs, vermin, and rodents,
shall come to an end together,
says the Lord.
(Isa 66:17)

TRIBUTE COMING TO JERUSALEM—ISAIAH 66:18–23

Once again, the author uses the poetic practice of dramatic reversal. Instead of being subservient to other nations, Jerusalem will one day see a reversal of fortunes. The time is envisioned when nations will recognize the glory of Jerusalem and will come with gifts and tribute for Jerusalem.[3]

> For I know their works and their thoughts,
> and I am coming to gather all nations and tongues;
> and they shall come and see my glory,
> and I will set a sign among them.
> From them I will send survivors to the nations,
> to Tarshish, Put, and Lud—which draw the bow—
> to Tubal and Javan, to the coastlands far away
> that have not heard of my fame or seen my glory;
> and they shall declare my glory among the nations.
> They shall bring all your kindred from all the nations
> as an offering to the Lord, on horses, and in chariots,
> and in litters, and on mules, and on dromedaries,
> to my holy mountain Jerusalem, says the Lord,
> just as the Israelites bring a grain offering
> in a clean vessel to the house of the Lord.
> And I will also take some of them as priests and as Levites,
> says the Lord.
> For as the new heavens and the new earth,
> which I will make,
> shall remain before me, says the Lord;
> so shall your descendants and your name remain.
> From new moon to new moon,
> and from sabbath to sabbath,
> all flesh shall come to worship before me,
> says the Lord.
> (Isa 66:18–23)

A CONCLUDING WORD OF WARNING—ISAIAH 66:24

The opening chapter of Isaiah ended with a strong word of warning for rebels and sinners (Isa 1:27–31). Now the final chapter also ends with a serious prose word of warning. Life is a precious gift. Life is to be lived

---

3. See further, Gary Stansell, *"The Nations' Journey to Zion: Pilgrimage and Tribute as Metaphor in the Book of Isaiah"* in Everson and Kim, *Desert Will Bloom*, 233–55.

with care; far too soon it is gone. How parents choose to live will directly influence their children. How communities choose to live will bring blessings or other consequences for all future generations. But times of judgment have come; they will certainly come again.

> And they shall go out and look at the dead bodies of the people
> who have rebelled against me; for their worm shall not die,
> their fire shall not be quenched, and they shall be an abhorrence
> to all flesh.
> (Isa 66:24)

In keeping with Jewish rabbinic tradition, we close this commentary by repeating verse 23 again after verse 24, hearing it as a final word from the scroll. The Isaiah scroll is, after all, intended primarily for reading by those who seek to be righteous, and not for the wicked. Especially for people who live in a war-weary world, this is a concluding and trustworthy word of hope.

> For as the new heavens and the new earth,
> which I will make,
> shall remain before me, says the Lord;
> so shall your descendants and your name remain.
> From new moon to new moon,
> and from sabbath to sabbath,
> all flesh shall come to worship before me,
> says the Lord.
> (Isa 66:23)

Bibliography

Berges, Ulrich. *Das Buch Jesaja. Komposition und Endgestalt.* Freiburg, NY: Herder, 1998.

Blenkinsopp, Joseph. *Isaiah 1-39.* The Anchor Bible 19. New York: Doubleday, 2000.

———. *Isaiah 40-55.* The Anchor Bible 19A. New York: Doubleday, 2000.

———. *Isaiah 56-66.* The Anchor Bible 19A. New York: Doubleday, 2003.

———. *Ezra-Nehemiah.* The Old Testament Library. Philadelphia: Westminster, 1988.

Brady, C.M.M. "Lilith." In *Eerdmans Dictionary of the Bible*, edited by David Noel Freedman, 810. Grand Rapids: Eerdmans, 2000.

Bright, John. *A History of Israel.* Philadelphia: Westminster, 1981.

Brooke, George J. "On Isaiah at Qumran" in Claire Matthews McGinnis and Patricia Tull, *As Those Who Are Taught: The Interpretation of Isaiah from LXX to the SBL.* Boston: Brill, 2006. 69-85.

Brueggemann, Walter. *Theology of the Old Testament.* Minneapolis: Fortress, 1997.

———. *Isaiah.* 2 vol. Louisville: Westminster John Knox, 1998.

Camara, Dom Helder. *The Desert is Fertile.* Maryknoll, NY: Orbis, 1974.

Childs, Brevard S. *Introduction to the Old Testament as Scripture.* Philadelphia: Fortress, 1979.

———. *Isaiah and the Assyrian Crisis.* London: SCM Press, 1967.

———. *Isaiah.* Louisville: Westminster John Knox, 2001.

———. *The Struggle to Understand Isaiah as Christian Scripture.* Grand Rapids: Eerdmans, 2004.

Duhm, Bernhard. *Das Buch Jesaia.* Gottingen: Vandenhoeck & Ruprecht, 1968.

Everson, A. Joseph. "Book of Isaiah." In *Eerdmans Dictionary of the Bible,* edited by David Noel Freedman, 648-52. Grand Rapids: Eerdmans, 2000.

Everson, A. Joseph, and Hyun Chul Paul Kim. *The Desert Will Bloom: Poetic Visions in Isaiah.* Atlanta: Society of Biblical Literature, 2009.

———. "The Days of Yahweh." *Journal of Biblical Literature* 93 (1974) 329-37.

———. "Redemption and the 'New Exodus' in Isaiah: Reflections on Mikhail Gorbachev and Cyrus of Persia." *Word and World* 33 (2013) 147-56.

Franke, Chris. *Isaiah 46,47 and 48: A New Literary-Critical Reading.* Biblical and Judaic Studies 3. Winona Lake, IN: Eisenbrauns, 1994.

———. "Like a Mother I Have Comforted You: The Function of Figurative Language in Isaiah 1:26 and 66:7-14" in Everson and Kim, *The Desert Will Bloom.* Atlanta: Society of Biblical Literature, 2009. 35-55.

Gitay, Yehoshua. "The Book of Isaiah." In *HarperCollins Bible Dictionary,* edited by Paul Achtemeier, 458–64. New York: HarperCollins, 1996.

Goldingay, John. *Isaiah 56–66.* London: Bloomsbury, 2014.

Gottwald, Norman K. *The Politics of Ancient Israel.* Louisville: Westminster John Knox, 2001.

Hanson, Paul D. *Isaiah 40–66.* Louisville: John Knox, 1995.

Heschel, Abraham J. *The Prophets.* New York: Harper & Row, 1955.

Hibbard, J. Todd, and Hyun Chul Paul Kim. *Formation and Intertextuality in Isaiah 24–27.* Ancient Israel and Its Literature 17. Atlanta: Society of Biblical Literature, 2013.

Kaiser, Otto. *Isaiah 1–12.* The Old Testament Library. Philadelphia: Westminster, 1983.

Kim, Hyun Chul Paul. *Ambiguity, Tension, and Multiplicity in Deutero-Isaiah.* Studies in Biblical Literature 52. New York: Peter Lang, 2003.

Kugel, James. *The Idea of Biblical Poetry. Parallelism and Its History.* New Haven: Yale University Press, 1981.

———. "Poetry." In *The HarperCollins Bible Dictionary.* San Francisco: HarperSanFrancisco, 1996.

Matthew McGinnis, Claire, and Patricia K. Tull. *As Those Who are Taught: The Interpretation of Isaiah from the LXX to the SBL.* Society of Biblical Literature Symposium Series 27. Atlanta: Society of Biblical Literature, 2006.

Melugin, Roy F. *The Formation of Isaiah 40–55.* New York: Walter de Gruyter, 1976.

Melugin, Roy F., and Marvin A. Sweeney. *New Visions of Isaiah.* Journal for the Study of the Old Testament Supplement Series 214. Sheffield: Sheffield,1996.

Miller, Patrick D. *They Cried to the Lord: The Form and Theology of Biblical Prayer.* Minneapolis: Fortress, 1994.

Parker, Simon B., ed. *Ugaritic Narrative Poetry.* Writings From the Ancient World 9. Atlanta: Society of Biblical Literature, 1997.

Pritchard, J.B. *Ancient Near Eastern Texts Relating to the Bible.* Princeton: Princeton University Press, 1969.

Rendtorff, Rolf. *Canon and Theology: Overtures to an Old Testament Commentary.* Translated and edited by Margaret Kohl. Minneapolis: Fortress, 1993.

———. *The Canonical Hebrew Bible: A Theology of the Old Testament. Tools for Biblical Study* 7. Leiden: Deo, 2005.

Roberts, J.J.M. *First Isaiah.* Minneapolis: Fortress, 2015.

Sack, R.H. "Nebuchadnezzar." In *The Anchor Bible Dictionary, Volume IV,* edited by David Noel Freedman, 1058–1059. New York: Doubleday, 1992.

Sanders, James A. *Torah and Canon.* Minneapolis: Fortress, 1972.

———. *Canon and Community: A Guide to Canonical Criticism.* Minneapolis: Fortress, 1984.

Seitz, Christopher R. *Zion's Final Destiny: The Development of the Book of Isaiah. A Reassessment of Isaiah 36–39.* Minneapolis: Fortress, 1991.

Smart, James D. *History and Theology in Second Isaiah.* Philadelphia: Westminster, 1965.

Sweeney, Marvin. *Isaiah 1–4 and the Post-Exilic Understanding of the Isaianic Tradition.* Berlin: de Gruyter, 1988.

———. *Isaiah 1–39.* The Forms of the Old Testament Literature 16. Grand Rapids: Eerdmans, 1996.

————. *King Josiah of Judah: The Lost Messiah of Israel.* Oxford: Oxford University Press, 2001.

Tucker, Gene. "The Book of Isaiah 1–39" In *The New Interpreter's Bible, Volume VI,* 27–305. Nashville: Abingdon, 2001.

Tull, Patricia. "Persistent Vegetative States: People as Plants and Plants as People in Isaiah" in Everson and Kim, *The Desert Will Bloom.* Atlanta: Society of Biblical Literature, 2009. 17-34.

Von Rad, Gerhard. *Old Testament Theology, Vol. II. The Theology of Israel's Prophetic Traditions.* Translated by D.M.G. Stalker. New York: Harper & Row, 1965.

Watts, John D. W. *Isaiah 1–33.* Word Biblical Commentary 24. Nashville: Thomas Nelson, 2005.

————. *Isaiah 34–66.* Word Biblical Commentary 25. Nashville: Thomas Nelson, 2005.

Westermann, Claus. *Isaiah 40–66.* The Old Testament Library. Philadelphia: Westminster, 1969.

Willey, Patricia Tull. *Remember the Former Things: The Recollection of Previous Texts in Second Isaiah.* SBL Dissertation Series 161. Atlanta: Scholars Press, 1997.

Williamson, H.G.M. *The Book Called Isaiah.* Oxford: Oxford University Press, 1994.

Young, T. Cuyler. "Cyrus." *Anchor Bible Dictionary, Vol. I,* edited by David Noel Freedman, 1231-33. New York: Doubleday, 1992.